Andee

A Special Gift

God Bless You! Thank you for attending the retreat.

*Love,
Danielle*

A Special Gift

My Inspirational Journey to Healing

2nd edition

Wanda L. Brown

TATE PUBLISHING
AND ENTERPRISES, LLC

A Special Gift: My Inspirational Journey to Healing, second edition
Copyright © 2014 by Wanda L. Brown. All rights reserved.

No part of this publication may be reproduced, stored in a retrieval system or transmitted in any way by any means, electronic, mechanical, photocopy, recording or otherwise without the prior permission of the author except as provided by USA copyright law.

The opinions expressed by the author are not necessarily those of Tate Publishing, LLC.

Published by Tate Publishing & Enterprises, LLC
127 E. Trade Center Terrace | Mustang, Oklahoma 73064 USA
1.888.361.9473 | www.tatepublishing.com

Tate Publishing is committed to excellence in the publishing industry. The company reflects the philosophy established by the founders, based on Psalm 68:11,
"The Lord gave the word and great was the company of those who published it."

Book design copyright © 2014 by Tate Publishing, LLC. All rights reserved.
Cover design by Joseph Emnace
Interior design by James Mensidor
Dedication illustration by Joshua Wayne-Anthony Brown

Published in the United States of America

ISBN: 978-1-63122-214-6
1. Self Help/Abuse
2. Self Help/Personal Growth/Self-Esteem
14.07.10

Dedication page

**To my family:
Shandale, LaToya, Earl, Chauncy, Anthony,
Aliya, Ayden, Chyler, and Chloe.**

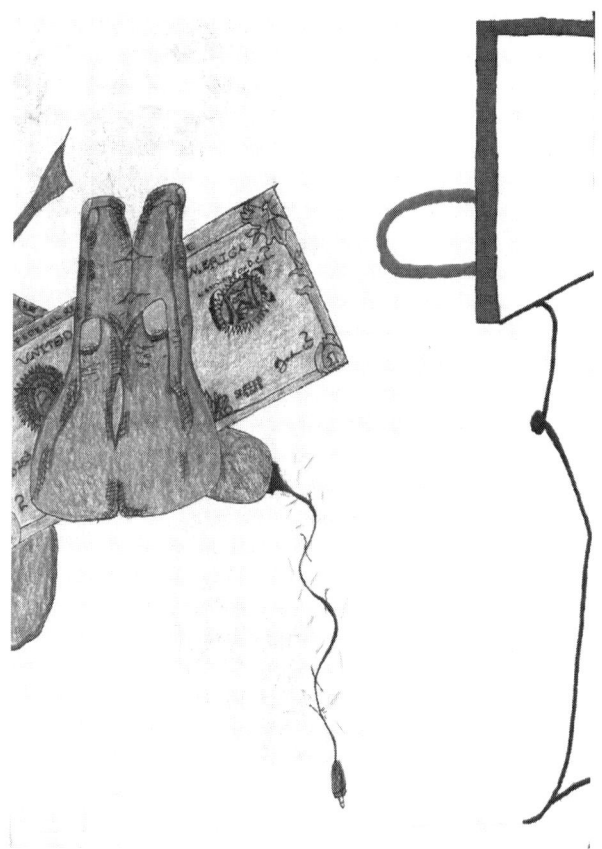

**In loving memory of
Joshua Wayne-Anthony Brown,
Robert Wayne King,
and Thelma Martin.**

Introduction

My one and only birthed son, Joshua Wayne-Anthony Brown, was pronounced dead on March 15, 2008 at 5:04PM at a local hospital. Joshua collapsed on a blacktop basketball court around 2:30PM, while he was playing a pickup game of basketball in our hometown. The grief of my son's death is enormous; later, you will read how his death is personally affecting me. Meanwhile, so that I may continue the testimony of the birthing process of A Special Gift, please be patient with me as I share.

I always believed that God had planted a seed that would grow into writing a book, but my life had so many emotionally tempest experiences that I resisted my own desires to push until God said to do just so. After completion of writing this book, God impressed upon my heart that I used the words "my book," and that the usage of these words is not totally accurate. I was humbled by the fact that everything belongs to God including this book. I am merely a tool that God chose to use to share a portion of my story with you and His words to me.

As God unveiled the examination process, He provided me with the essential gardening tools necessary to uproot the negatively planted seeds which grew into twisted vinegary vine roots. As God offered me footprints, I accepted and He is carrying me through the death of my one and only son, Joshua Wayne-Anthony Brown. God is allowing me to empty the unnecessary issues that necessitated weeding, because there is no more accessible space for the feeblest pains of my life that once penetrated my heart, body, mind and spirit. God is affording me the wonderful challenge to become authentic.

Certainly, I can agree with David in Psalm 38:8 when he states, "**I am feeble and severely broken; I groan because of the turmoil of my heart**;" *now*, I must deal with the greatest pain of my life; losing the son whom I desperately needed and wanted for such a long time. Also, I will share with you some exchanges with my counselor, Dr. Johnson, who so wisely mentored me while I was deeply in grief.

I will allow the spirit of God to lead and guide me as I share with you within these writings entitled, ***A Special Gift***. Wherein, I pray that you will find many different special gifts and that you too may be able to begin your healing.

The scriptures that you will find throughout these writings are not quoted as God opened His words to me, as I wrote. You will find these scripture bolded throughout the writing. God provided many scriptures to share with you. **To Him all the praise, honor, and glory belong.**

I expose some of my repulsive wilderness experiences that you may or may not have the capability of relating, but my prayer is that you, the reader, will find comfort, strength, and a purpose for your life, just as I am finding for my life. I pray that you will realize that God has a plan and a purpose for all of our lives.

As you read along and journey with my writings, feel free to associate some of my experiences with yours. Perhaps, you will no longer keep your secrets and you too will find the strength to expose the abuses that you have faced, or are facing. My counselor, Dr. Johnson explored the topic of secrets. I agree that secrets poison our lives. I pray that you will be able to expose your secrets, (at least with me as you read this book), and recognize that God is in Control, and that **all things really do work together for the good of those who Love the Lord and are called for His purpose, as stated at Romans 8:28.**

While residing in Pennsylvania, I regularly visited the same basketball courts that my son recurrently practiced to improve his game. Often, I sat quietly while admiring the "blue cardinals" that appeared commonly, as I attentively listened for the small *still* voice of God, which is extremely powerful. An unshakeable scripture, **"For I know the plans that I have for you, plans to prosper you and to do you no harm…."** came into my spirit, and I could not think of the chapter and verse.

Upon returning home, I searched the words of this scripture in the concordance, which included plans, prosper, future, harm, and desire, but I could not locate the scripture which was placed in my heart. I telephoned Pastor Grace, because I knew that she would know where this scripture could be found, but she did not answer her phone, which is not abnormal.

So, I prayed, "Okay God, if this scripture is meant for me, you really are going to have to confirm it." I assumed that if this scripture was meant for me it would be confirmed at church the next day. The Bible states that **God uses the foolish things to confound the wise.**

I received several invitations to attend graduation parties. In all honesty, I did not have any intentions of attending graduation parties because this was an incredibly sensitive issue for me. My son, Joshua, was to have graduated this same year, 2009. I did not properly respond by RSVP to any of the parties. On this particular Saturday, I got dressed, and without much thought, I attended my godson, Desmond's graduation party. By the time I left, I became dazed by the experiences at Desmond's graduation party.

Admittedly, my expectation was to receive confirmation of the above mentioned scripture from Pastor, or at least hear it quoted during church services on a Sunday, not at a graduation party. I did not have any design of the agenda for the graduation party or any knowledge that my godson's pastor would be present. After all, it was a party, but God always makes His presence known. **Wherever two or three touch in agreement, He will be in the midst.**

The party began as Desmond's pastor held the microphone to offer an opening prayer and remarks, and he stated these words,

"For I know the plans that I have for you, to prosper you, not to harm you and to give you the future that you desire." As his mouth shaped to form the words of the scripture which were placed in my spirit earlier that morning, my eyes opened wide and my mouth flung open. Next, a preselected woman rose to the platform to read a scripture. It was then that I learned exactly where this scripture is found in the Bible. She said, "God gave me the exact scripture, Jeremiah 29:11 and it reads as thus: **"For I know the plans…"** Not only did my mouth hang open, my lower lip fell to the floor, as my eyes became wider opened, as the confirmation came twice within minutes!

Still, I was not fully aware of the hand of God on my life or that He was speaking directly to me. So, I spoke to God again saying, "Okay God, perhaps you gave me this scripture to confirm your plans for Desmond." In awe of what I experienced, with excitement in my heart for Desmond, and discounting my own blessings to come, I ate, socialized a bit, joined in on the electric slide, and exited the party to return to my solemn state. The next day, I went to my church and Jeremiah 29:11 went unmentioned.

A few weeks later, without expectation or sharing the above testimony with her, I received a manila postmarked package from my ex-high school counselor, Mrs. B. Enclosed in this medium sized envelope was a beautiful journal and on the front of the journal were inscribed words which stated at **Jer. 29:11, "For I know the plans that I have for you."**

Literally, I screamed, which caught my oldest daughter, Maria, totally off guard. With my breath taken away, and words barely spoken, I pointed to the journal while I only repeated the word look. Previously, I had shared my testimony of this scripture with both of my daughters. Maria questioned, "Do you think that God is trying to tell you something?"

People continued to pray for me, and some people probably thought that I had absolutely and positively lost my mind. In my spirit, I knew that God was telling me something that

He wanted me to clearly hear and understand; so, my testimony continues.

About a year later, I heard a sermon by Pastor Paul entitled, Fill Your Horn with Oil and Go. After hearing, digesting, and absorbing this message, I recognized that God **ordered my footsteps** to Texas, but I did not understand all of the reasons, as God did not reveal all of His plans for me at this time. *Still*, I do not know all of them, but I am okay with that fact.

Two weeks prior to my departure, my good friends ushered me off with great lunches, dinners, labyrinth experiences, and other various fun filled events. My calendar filled quickly with many appointments to say "until we meet again." My spiritual grandmother, Theresa, gifted me with an awesome book. On the first page of the book the same exact scripture appears again, Jeremiah 29:11. Needless to say, confirmation upon confirmation continued coming, and has not stopped coming, but this is how my story begins:

Chapter 1

For I know the plans that I have for you, plans to prosper you and do you no harm, and to give you the future that you desire, is recorded in the Bible at Jeremiah 29:11.

By the age of twenty five, perhaps for many, I should have been graduating from graduate school. Rather, my life was in such disarray that I faithfully knelt on my knees each and every night; literally, I was begging God for a son. Be not dismayed, already, I was granted the blessing of two beautiful daughters, Maria and Corrinna. Also, I had been "married" twice; yet and *still*, I continued to only exist. My life was exceptionally unfulfilled. What I did not recognize during this time was that I was stuck in grief from the death of Daddy and the aftermath of horrific occurrences thereafter, which began at the tender age of eleven.

Prior to these occurrences, my world was "perfect." Our family consisted of four members: Mom, Daddy, my sister Debra, and me. We lived in a perfectly made brick home. The foundation of our home was simple, as each red brick was perfectly cemented by hand. Our home was securely surrounded by a bright and sturdy white fence. The heavy, well nurtured, and green grapevines hung downwardly as they produced huge, juicy, purple grapes, and we would neither hunger or thirst.

Many different sounds of life were present, as I could hear our dog bark and the rabbit nibbling on his carrot. Although our cat was blind, I heard her meow, while my only sister, Debra, and I safely played inside of our fenced in yard. In second grade, I shined like the star that I was born to be, as I made straight A's.

My daddy will always be the tallest man in my world, even though his height did not measure more than 6'2". There was not an apparent reason that my childhood would be labeled imperfect or that it would ever be different. My parents worked hard to provide each necessary material and non-essential item that my sister and I needed and/or wanted. Mom toiled as a factory machinist from 4PM until 12AM, while Daddy labored as a welder at a steel factory. Daddy's working hours were from 7AM until 3PM, which resulted in one parent being at home with Debra and me. Everyone recognizes Debra as my mom's angel, but *I* was Daddy's little girl, also known as "Sweetie." The wind beneath my wings, my insides, my joy, my smile, and my hope for tomorrow turned upside down at a very fragile age.

At the delicate age of eleven, the major cornerstone of my life, which was the largest red brick of the place that I once called home, buckled from the foundation. My whole life completely fell apart. My daddy suffered from a headache that morning. By that evening, I had my first encounter with death. In just one instant my human anchor was gone, and I could not see, hear, or understand my spiritual pilot who would eventually take me soaring above the turbulence.

The commanding force behind my father's death was so strapping that it quickly tore down the white fence, enthused whirlwinds, vanished security, and quieted all concerned. This is the day that I began running in a maze of confusion. It was here that I was given the impression that there would never be a way out of the pain that had completely engulfed me.

The grapevines that hung from the vines of our house no longer produced the huge purple grapes. The animals died, and Debra and I no longer played in a secure environment. Although Debra remained mom's angel, things changed for me on the evening of April 7, 1972. There was no expectation that evening that my father would not return home; therefore, home was just an abode. Eventually, it would take a major player of my life to convince me that Sweetie would ever have a chance at any type of victory.

Neither Debra nor I were there when Daddy collapsed on my mom's shoulder in the car while mom drove him to our family physician's office. My sister was attending a convention in Philadelphia, and I was visiting at my favorite aunt's home. My Uncle David and Aunt Louise alerted me that my daddy died.

At that unmoving moment in time, I felt as though Uncle David tackled me in the forest as I began running. I am sure that Uncle David was only trying to tightly hold me, while I tried to continually break free. The stronghold that Uncle David had on me did not release the fact that none of us were equipped with the essential tools to dig through the terrifying forest without bumping into the trees of life.

Tears covered our faces. Obviously, Aunt Louise, Uncle David, my cousins, (Karen and Cher) and I were all saddened, and we began to walk through the valley of the shadow of death, but there was no safe shelter insight in the midst of this unpredictable hurricane.

An even more distressing component was that none of us knew how to begin to mend our broken hearts and stand in the midst of the unannounced earthquake that entirely shook our lives completely. Even with a license to drive, it is difficult to see the signs along the highways during any type of storm. Just imagine an unlicensed and inexperienced driver in the midst of a storm with no directions! It is virtually impossible to see and get to a safe destination due to fear and cloudy judgment. Oh, but **God is able to do anything except fail.**

Actually, I neither saw my mother's face nor did I speak with mom as of yet, but late that night I returned to the place that I had once truly loved living life to the fullest. When I laid eyes on my mother that evening, my eyes overflowed with tears. Although, I am not completely convinced that I actually saw my mom on that first night, as I was blindly being led through the darkness of death, I am reminded of a scripture that asks this question, ***"Can the blind lead the blind, except they fall into a ditch?"***

While constantly crying or when rain is pouring during the storm, a difficulty arises which distorts one's perspective about things and more importantly about people. Each of my senses: hearing, tasting, smelling, touching, and seeing were in a diluted state, and my thoughts went out of bounds beyond your imagination which were awfully foul.

That evening, as well as the next several days, empty faces, both familiar and unfamiliar people overcrowded the space where we once rested. Everywhere that I seemed to turn within our empty house, I noticed strangers. Even those whom I previously recognized looked different. People were sitting and standing. Nonetheless, bodies crowded everywhere, and the telephone rang non-stop.

Food filled the kitchen and the aroma made me ill, as it overflowed into the other rooms of our house. When my nostrils did not sense food, they smelled flowers, but flowers did not smell as a sweet fragrance. Certainly, they did not appear beautiful on that date. As a matter of fact, the scent reminded me that death, rather than life was in the air.

Busily, my mom handled all of the funeral arrangements, but there I was extremely bare, even though I was unofficially introduced to shame or guilt. It is at this moment that I recognized myself as totally isolated. Words cannot describe the feelings of sadness, anger, anxiety, abandonment, and emptiness that attached to me, but I did not have any reason to carry guilt, embarrassment, or shame at this point of my journey.

My daddy accomplished the rewarding task of protecting me from a formal introduction to the awful awareness of guilt, embarrassment, and shame, but the actuality existed that there was not anything to replace those feelings that were extremely personal on this date. Other feelings, such as anger, sadness, anxiety, I had met their acquaintances, but they formally befriended me and dared to let me go as the abandonment and emptiness forced their way into my world on April 7, 1972. Prior to the death of my father, I attended the church next door to our home.

Upon setting one foot in this house known as a church, my first informal introduction to fear, anxiety, and confusion was present. The reality is that as a family, we did not have a "religious" foundation. I recall that my father strongly disliked preachers/pastors. As a child, I did not understand this notion, but as I became an adult the picture became more defined. Surely, Daddy congregated with some of the same types of pastors that I encountered along my journey.

Daddy's funeral process was awfully long. However lengthy forever is; that is the how long it appeared to take for Daddy's body to be buried, and that was just the beginning of the grief period. From the day of dad's death to the time that he was buried was about eleven days, which I calculate as an extraordinarily long day for each year that I had lived.

While traveling to and from Daddy's final resting place in Virginia, we covered many miles. We did not have much rest in between literal and figurative states. Today, it saddens me to think that my mom was responsible for the total burden of burying my father at her tender age of thirty.

My daddy was named Robert Wayne King, but everyone that knew and loved him called him Wayne. There are many people included in that number! Daddy's nieces and nephews either called him Uncle Bunkie or Uncle Wayne. I never heard anyone refer to Daddy as Robert, not even my mother. The enormous amount of people who loved my father complicated the arrangement process.

My mother was very considerate of family, Daddy's friends, and co-workers in Pennsylvania. As a result, she planned two viewings; one viewing was in our home town. Then, Daddy's body was shipped to Virginia for the additionally scheduled wake, funeral, and burial.

During the viewing in our hometown, I unsuccessfully attempted to enter into the casket. I was attempting to get in my daddy's clinched arms. As a substitute, my uncles' arms prepared a stretcher to carry me out of the funeral home. My strong uncles released me into the arms of Aunt Deanna who held me softly; yet, she tightly embraced me, while she intensely kissed my entire face. *Still,* I can feel the warm effects from the way that she held and rocked me while we cried uncontrollably together. Crying did not release the load of anger that death instilled.

For a long time, I robustly disliked the funeral directors, especially the first man who took my daddy's body. Even though I did not truly meet his acquaintances, my childish brain "hated" this male because he took my daddy from me. As I am sure that you can clearly identify, I had no prior experiences or explanations of death. Today, I am much stronger and wiser, and I understand that the funeral director was only earning his family's living.

Thirty six years later, my mother shared that the undertaker was very kind to her and that he acted with total professionalism as he assisted my mother throughout the process of laying Daddy's outer shell to rest. This day, I have a much better understanding about death and church. Attending church yesterday is not the same as today.

As a child, attending worship services terrified me because of the things that I observed behind the closed doors of the church. Sunday services were extremely frightening for me as a small child; yet, I yearned to know God. Some Sunday services included the pastor's daughter foaming at the mouth, squirming on the floor, and screaming all manner of evil against her father. At times, the ambulance came to take the woman away, which frightened me tremendously, but I loved Jesus.

Also, I did not understand when people spoke in unknown languages and screamed as if they had countless fears, but it terrified me. I just did not understand, and I wondered what they were saying. Perhaps this is why the Bible reminds us at

I Corinthians 14:28, **that if there is not an interpreter, let him keep silent.**

In addition, the way that people shouted and "praised God," frightened me. In my childish mind, something seemed to be hurting them, not helping them in any way, as it did not appear that they **Leaped for joy** either, but then too, everyone's joy is very different. *I do know that the* **joy of the Lord is our strength,** *but* **God is a God of order,** He does not operate in confusion, but **as a child, I thought like a child.**

At times, I was fearful of being attacked in the midst of confusion. I just could not fathom what was going on. The thing that tormented me the most was that I really did not want to go to Hell, which is what the pastor preached about most often. Desperately, I yearned for God's favor on my life. I was trying to earn it by several unsuccessful attempts at being "perfect." You see, I was taught and wanted to be just like Jesus.

Now, I can assume that the pastor was "whipping us into shape," but as a child, I did not have an adult who explained these things to me, because my parents rarely attended church with me as a youngster. Now, I was going to experience my biggest, most impressionable moments of church while deeply in mourning.

Although Daddy's first viewing was held in Pennsylvania and the second wake occurred in Virginia, they both were held at funeral parlors. The actual funeral service was held at Daddy's home church in Virginia, where he had accepted Jesus Christ as his personal savior at a young age. During the funeral, many preachers said many horrifying words to my virgin ears, while my body and mind suffered from vertigo imbalance. Many statements were made on that unforgettable day which I was not able to wrap my brain around, and these ghosts haunted me. Until, eventually, I became set free, and **whom the Son sets free is free indeed.**

Please allow me to share some of these most memorable statements. The first set of words that spiraled confusion totally out of control is "God loved him best." Another statement that daily troubled me is "God needed an angel." I understand, as an adult, the *intentions* of these words, but as a child, I simply could not grasp what these people were saying about God. Later, Pastor Grace gently guided me to the knowledge that God puts angels in people, but does not make angels out of men.

As a child, mentally, I compiled a list of questions such as: Did that mean that God loved me less? Did that mean that God hated me? Why would God need Daddy more than me? After all, I was Daddy's little girl. My childish mind became warped with confusion; thus, many more sufferings were induced. Also, I heard a lot more about Hell on this day which was already completely dreadful and draining. It took several decades to unravel the answers to these distressing childlike questions.

I questioned Uncle David, who became a preacher/pastor, and he expressed to me that because my Daddy did not attend church that meant that Daddy was in Hell! My truest desire was to be with my earthly father and my heavenly Father, but the conflict came by people's judgment that my daddy was sent to Hell, which is the exact place that I did not want to go. As you may be able to identify, I did not know how I was going to live without my Daddy, but the fact of the matter is that I did. If my next sentence is possible; although, it is highly probable, I became more frightened, confused, and angry.

Today, I realize that Uncle David's statement is inaccurate. I learned that my daddy gave his life to God and was baptized at a very tender age. I know that I will see Daddy again! This error may have been Uncle David's inexperience with preaching at that time.

Meanwhile, please journey back to the graveyard with me. Daddy's casket was lowered into the ground at Daddy's final resting place; surely, I assumed that the spirit of "Sweetie," (my nickname as a child), snuck in there with Daddy, because I became a lost child with a lack of knowledge. According to Hosea 4:6, **it is because of a lack of knowledge that my people shall perish.**

Dad's spirit was not in that coffin, so how could mine have gone with him?

After the death of Daddy, many negative experiences seeped through the seams of my shredded life. I did not realize that I began fighting life at such a tender age. No one is victorious when fighting against life, as life wins each time. Life continues whether you kick, fight, or scream. In order to accept life, we *must* be able to accept death, as the reality is that death is a part of life.

Grief is very difficult for adults; certainly, it is even more challenging for children. In my eleven year old mind, no one could ever take the place of Daddy. At that time, I did not care if it was the President of the United States. Today, I refute that statement. I really would welcome President Barack Obama!

In all sincerity, I desperately wanted to keep Daddy's memory alive. For me, this meant that no one could take Daddy's place. That statement is *still* true, even as an adult! No one can ever replace Daddy. Now, I realize that this does not mean that I should veto the possibility of allowing others into my heart. At first I typed the word life, but this correction comes because of the realization that it is actually possible to let someone into our lives without inviting them into our hearts. Dealing with Daddy's death was not my only hidden problem.

The walls of security and protection forcefully collided after Daddy died. I was raped prior to becoming a teenager. Destruction does not describe the fears, guilt, shame, embarrassment, dirty, and mixed emotions that emerge with rape. To add rape with the death of a father, the equation is very unattractive. Now a secret was poisoning our family's lives.

Internally, I was shipwrecked; I felt abandoned, I was indecently exposed to a very frightening world, and I took on a tremendous amount of liabilities that were not mine. It was not until after the death of my son, which almost calculates the age of my father at his death, thirty six years later, that I finally confessed the horrific act to my mother.

Prior to the death of my son, I did not know how to covenant these feelings. The outcome of keeping this buried was the casualty of any remote chance of a relationship with my mother. Some days, I blamed my mother for this rape, and other days, I blamed myself.

Another matter that I dealt with was being constantly told, "You think that you are so cute." The ones who made these statements must have believed this, because this false allegation was so far from my truth of the substance. As a matter of fact, I rarely looked into the mirror because I was ashamed, and I did not like what it was that I saw. Rape did not make me feel attractive, regardless as to how beautiful I am on the outside. It was a trap. Please do not fall into the pit. Escape by knowing that people have no control over you! God is in full control.

Once I really began looking into the mirror, God showed me my inward beauty, which is much more important than how I appear on the outside. Also, God confirmed the internal damages that were done by a variety of people and me, but He is releasing me daily. There were many times that I openly expressed my anger and lack of understanding to God for allowing some things to occur in my life, and I do know that God expects us to be honest with Him.

I believe that God is big enough, powerful enough, wise enough, and understanding enough to accept when we admit our anger and fears to Him. More importantly, I know that He forgives us for our lack of understanding. Just read the **Psalms** and you will understand too. I am so glad that **God winks at our ignorance**.

While I beat myself and blamed others for circumstances outside of my/their control, I was trying to figure out how my being born caused such calamities and disasters to befall. Truly, I believed that something was wrong with me. A portion of my thinking was correct, as I suffered horribly from low self-esteem due to various episodes as my life tossed and turned inside a raging sea. Please allow me to disclose my backwards thinking of how my thoughts were programmed.

First, God chooses Daddy because He loved him more than me. Then, I am allowed to be raped, more than once, before I was "ready" to have sex. I began life without knowing my biological father. My mother was the only parent that Debra and I had to become affiliated, while we dealt with our grief individually.

My daddy was the buffer between my mother and me. Our "relationship" only worsened upon his death, and my secrets began to torment my heart. One huge problem for me was that my mom and I grieved totally different. I had the audacity to question if she ever really loved my daddy because *I could not see her cry.* At that time, my anger only related to her anger.

My normal state was sad, angry, confused, turbulent, and a huge part of my world literally died. The fact of the matter is that I was angry that Daddy died, and I did not know how to deal with these newly founded feelings that were unwelcomed. Pushing these feelings away was unfruitful. As I attempted not to deal with them, they were stuffed down further. Thus, I began running from life and for my life. This sprint organization actually enabled me to avoid dealing with my true feelings.

I used school as a "healthy" outlet for my grief. In some aspects, it really was a healthy outlet. It was much healthier than illegal drugs or booze, which I was afraid of too. Thank God for the escape of those hidden dangers! Later, what I learned is that my over involvement in school activities consumed me enough to avoid dealing with my true feelings concerning Daddy's death. I believe that many people busy their lives to avoid dealing with the grief, but I strongly believe that you must give room to grief.

Truly, school became a positive manner by which I could keep busy and attempt to become absorbed. This outlet afforded me the opportunity to continually stuff feelings farther down than I realized possible. Although I was gaining information at school, I lacked knowledge in areas of importance as well as acknowledgement of these feelings which kept me at a distance from properly dealing with or allowance for understanding the method that was desperately needed to deal with these feelings/"new friends" that I did not want to entertain. I believe that the further one stuffs their feelings down, the shorter the fuse becomes that ignites rage.

My feelings did not vanish as I actively participated in many extracurricular school activities and sports. I earned some fancy titles and awards. However, those stuffed down feelings did not grant me the permission to feel proud of my achievements, because there was such a colossal void in my life. I had no designs of how to fill this void, and my image was damaged due to being raped and abused.

Although I partook of many school activities, this kept me around people, but I remained silent, secluded, and remotely afraid of totally trusting and/or loving anyone; perhaps, even my own mother. I met Victor, who magically appeared after the death of my daddy. He walked me to and from Middle school every day, until he departed to the Army. Additionally, after my daddy's death other reasons caused trust to exit from my front window. Suspiciously, I watched those who took advantage of mom's vulnerability. Believe it or not, your children are watching and learning so much from you as well as your experiences.

My answered prayer is that my children will learn from my mistakes, and make new and fewer mistakes. We are all going to make mistakes, as it is a part of our human nature, but I suggest that we learn from others' mistakes as well as our own and continue to make progress in the right direction. **We should look to the hills from whence cometh our help,** even while in the midst of grief.

Recall that my mother worked from 4PM-12AM. Seeing my mom, with the exception of weekends, was a rarity. Around the age of thirteen, mom changed her shift to be home with us in the evenings. Completely, I understand that she had worked this evening shift for the betterment of Debra and me while my daddy lived. My childish mind could neither comprehend the void that I felt from the absence of my father nor my mother's absence. Also, I believe this became a portion of the reason that I did not give respect to her personal method of grieving. I did not fully know or understand my mother. Mom's labor hours of love caused a huge hole in my heart as a child. Admittedly, I was afraid of losing my mother, despite our differences.

Mom and I grieved very differently, which I learned is not abnormal. I became numb, or should I admit that I was totally broken, and I could not feel her pain or mine. I did not have any possibility of recognizable formulated glue to piece my life back together. I had no vision that I could recognize, if a vision was a possibility. I only existed, while anxiously desiring but waiting to feel something/anything again. I was too bothered about many things, including the fact that mom, Debra, and my grieving processes were entirely different. It did not appear to me that mom or Debra missed my daddy the way that I did.

I never recalled seeing my mother cry about Daddy's death. I was too busy watching my mother to even notice Debra's pain or tears. Besides, I sat under the jealousy spell of my sister because she continued with the status of mom's angel. I could not articulate all that I dealt with at that time, but **love is not jealous.** In my bewildered mind, I could no longer contend as a component in the ring of competition because the elimination process as Daddy's little girl seemed to hastily disappear. I was angered. At that time, that was the only thing that mattered. Today, I know that I will always be Daddy's little girl.

I believe that being spoiled is what taught me to attempt to hold onto efforts of controlling things. Maybe I was angry that I knew that I could not control anything. Since Daddy could not be with me, I decided to do whatever I could to be where he was. The only problem was that my greatest conflict was that I did not want to go to Hell, which is where others tried to make me believe that Daddy was not resting.

As a child, my underlying issue that stood out became simple; although, at that time, it was extremely complex. My anger boldly asked, "How dare my mother not shed one tear at the funeral or in my presence?" The fear of loving overwhelmed my mind and this included loving my own mother; despite our differences. I love my mom more than she may ever know, but I hated the idea of loving anyone after the death of my daddy.

So, I found myself trapped in my anger of losing my father. My ill and childlike mind believed tears needed to be visible to my eyes. This was the only true representation that my daddy was missed and loved; perhaps, my mom's waterlogged pillow could tell you a very different story. I am reminded of the scripture that warns us to **judge not that we may not be judged.**

Much later, I figured that since my life became clogged mom's life should have stopped too. During my teenage years, I could not understand how mom could go on. At present, I realize that Daddy would expect nothing less from my mother. Besides, God knows that she is the only woman on this earth that would be able to handle her child's damaged image.

When the school session ended, my focus went, and I tried different things while attempting to escape my deadness. I began smoking at the age of thirteen. One puff of a peer's cigarette, and I became addicted. It felt so good to breathe in toxins and to exhale all of the pains; yet, this created just another vicious cycle of pain. It feels strange to write these words but it really was one method for me to seek relief. By the age of 12, I entered an abusive relationship.

I cannot officially say that this boyfriend, Doug, was my first. That right was stolen from me; eventually, we tried sex, which somewhat released the notice of pain. There was an exchange of release and additional pain. Yet and *still*; sin, pain, guilt, anxiety, depression and shame of being raped *still* went unaddressed.

In an attempt to become free, I tried different churches, and I seemed to be drawn to the churches that had strict pastors who taught the wrath of God, rather than the love of God. Perhaps it was only my anger, anxiety, and fears that were yearning to be fed. As a child, many pastors frightened me as much as the television show called Dark Night, which is an insane amount, because my Aunt Elaine can tell you that my body trembled with horror as I ran out of her house to hide because of that TV show! My trepidation of some pastors was very similar, if not more terrifying.

At this time of my life, I believed that these pastors had these "special connections" with God or with someone/something powerful, and that they got their words directly from God to tell me how to live my life and to avoid Hell. What they actually established in my life was constant torment while I lived in a shell, and I was afraid to stick my head out. Some preachers may *still* be learning who they are, and they may tell you things to boost their own self-esteem.

Unquestionably, even after the age of twenty one, I was afraid of the club scenes; although, I undertook that short lived route too. I was so fearful of the soon coming rapture that many taught. With my history, while Jesus was on His way back for those to be caught up in the air or the rapture was coming, it would be me who was caught doing that which I was taught to be ungodly. At times, I would go into the restroom to pray that the rapture would be delayed.

Some call this conviction, but I call this fear.

A few times, I attempted what I was taught as the "ultimate sin;" although, I do not believe that suicide is the "ultimate sin." **Blasphemy of the Holy Spirit is the one sin that cannot be forgiven.** Many preach that when one commits suicide that their final judgment is a burning Hell, but God has the final say. I have not studied this question thoroughly but I have a question for you. Who in their right mind wants to die?

Personally, I was exploring ways that I might escape and/or ease the pain or allow me to feel again. I can tell you that I had no desire of dying. Since I thought that I was the problem, if I was eliminated the drama may have stopped for my family. However, I never thought about the pain that it may have caused my family. In addition, I desired to stop trying to survive and just live.

Attempting the avoidance of Hell in my condition did not seem to be an alternative. Unknowing how to live, God's detailed answers to the suicide attempts only included one word, "No." During this time, I felt as though God was punishing me again because He would not allow me to die. He did not allow me to do what *I* thought was best for everyone included.

Today, I realize His gracious and merciful answer of no. I assure you that He has the proper answer in every situation. You see, I do not believe that I was ready to meet God. Certainly, I had not begun to smile, laugh, or live; this I am fully assured. Meanwhile, I continued to learn survival methods as I was taught. Survival is not the same as living.

Rape and some other factors during my teenage years taught me that I really was worthless. Feelings that I was of no value actually helped me to find others who really were no good for me. I believe that I began projecting my feelings onto them or they were reflecting that which I was projecting. In general, I believe that my abusers had a sick scent which comes from their own illness that lets these ill ones know that I was absolutely vulnerable, which is when the target is attacked. If you are stable, as opposed to vulnerable, then you are not an easy target because you recognize the signs before you get too involved.

For many years, I wanted to give someone, anyone, love, even if that meant that I had to have children. You see, I assumed that children were safe and would not hurt me. That is not always the case. We are all human and hurt each other whether it is intentional or unintentional. Nonetheless, I needed to give what I believed was missing from within me, which was a lot of love.

As a child, the love and encouragement I received from my daddy refreshed the idea that I could do and be anything that I set my heart and mind to accomplish. I was a really good student before my dad's death and other vicious attacks, but as my life changed, so did my attitude and grades. Parents, your child's report card can teach you a lot.

After Daddy's death, I was an okay student, but I could have done much better after my father died. This, I have been assured. However, being as active as I was in the junior and high school left little time for studying, as I attempted to escape the pains of life. At the same time, I was trying to prove myself worthy, but to whom? Was it to myself or that anyone that mattered?

Academically, I did more than enough to survive. I graduated as a National Honor Society student at the age of seventeen. While in Junior and Senior High school, I was involved in many activities. I was the captain of the cheerleaders since Junior High school, and then again in my Junior Year. Additionally, for all of these years I changed my uniform to play basketball too, while trying to play superwoman, but nothing except God could fill my emptiness. Today, **my cup runs over.**

In addition, I became the president of Student Government in my Junior and Senior Years of High School, attempting to busy up my life to avoid the grief that was necessary to deal with. I did not know how to just be *still* and listen for the voice of God because at this time, I did not understand God at all. This busyness did not fill the voids in my own life. Today, I realize that was and *still* is God's job, not mine, and he was faithful to do just that!

The funny part is that I was graciously accepted by my teachers, guidance counselors, cheerleading coaches, twirling squad mentor, basketball coaches, and many more, but one of the main problems was that I was not taught to accept myself or my life. Then, I met Doug.

Chapter 2

As mentioned, I was the captain of cheerleaders. From ninth grade, Doug was the star of the basketball team. Doug had what I wanted, which was my own smile and "protection." Doug appeared to be really tough, and no one dared to intimidate him. However, ***every knee shall bow and every tongue shall confess that Jesus is Lord.***

Doug's smile and the build of his body, i.e. protection, was all that it took for me to want to be around him every day. My bodyguard/boyfriend, Doug, began walking me to and from school. Upon his return to his house, he and I talked on the phone after school until it was time to go to bed. I met him in the morning for the same routine. Eventually, I became even more isolated as his girlfriend. Beware teens!

After dating him throughout Junior and Senior High School, in my senior year, Doug's coach recruited me to tutor Doug because the school was attempting to mainstream him during his junior year so that he might have an opportunity to use his basketball skills at college. Certainly, Doug was naturally talented in basketball, but I am unsure what the coach was thinking; perhaps he was looking for a miracle, but that is a different subject matter. What was I thinking?

I was so afraid of everything, that I did not take the time to really think. Instead, I retorted without paying attention to the red lights, which tell us to stop, look, and listen. I was charged as guilty, because I did not properly take these precautions. While operating under the fears' confinements, most of us do not handle tasks well. This is a tactic of Satan, as **God has not given us the**

spirit of fear, but of love and a sound mind. I am not being hard on myself. Who really does stop and think during teenage years without listening to accurate guidance? In addition, I believe that rape interferes with judgment and transports massive amounts of confusion that distort love, trust, and feelings. My best advice is to get some help to sort out these issues.

Almost immediately, Doug began physically, mentally, emotionally, and verbally abusing me. I could not tell anyone that he bruised my legs before I was to be his cheerleader. The main reason that he stated that he beat me was because I smoked, which neither he nor my mother ever succeeded in forcing me to stop. If anyone was paying attention to me, certainly, they would have noticed that he was beating me. Perhaps, I was running too fast. I was not the only person or thing that Doug beat.

After my light blue Camaro was kicked in, the police were called. The officer interviewed me in front of my mother. He asked me if Doug was beating on me. Of course, I was afraid to lie to the law. Yet, nothing was done to rectify this situation, and I was too afraid to leave him alone. Doug always warned me that I was his and his alone. No one else would have me. No one witnessed who kicked my car in, and no charges were filed, but the police report was necessary for the insurance claim that needed to be filed because of the immense amount of expenses of the damage. However, I heard Doug outside yelling and cursing, which meant that he was in the area. Since no one witnessed the actual kicking in of the car, charges were eliminated.

In my damaged mind, I needed Doug, because he would protect me from being raped. So, we continued dating. Besides, I became deathly afraid of him. With all hopes gone of ever being loved or freed from Doug's anger, I decided that my only hope for love would come from a child, but before I figured out what I really wanted, I needed to go through the motions. Doug also beat me while I was pregnant.

By the age of 18, I began sitting under a female pastor, Miss Andrews, who was dreadfully strict. We were not allowed to wear pants or makeup. We could not swim, dance, or listen to worldly music. In addition, we could not dress in modern attire or have our hair done as "the world," which interprets to mean fancy hair styles.

Doug's mother, whom I loved dearly, took me to a revival where Pastor Andrews preached in a different city. Once she opened her church doors locally, I joined. When the doors of the church were opened, without question or any excuses; all members were to be in attendance. Yes, I was in bondage. Today, I thank God that the shackles are off of me!

Prior to sitting under this particular pastor, I was a member of another church. In order to have Maria dedicated to God at this particular church, I stood before the church and apologized for the sin of fornication. I was humiliated, but even at the age of eighteen, I understood that it was not up to man to forgive me for my sins, and this is what I stated prior to the dedication of my daughter. "I am standing here because I was told to do so, but I have already asked God to forgive me." My reply was accepted, and Maria was dedicated to God on that date.

I selected certain godparents, but mom strongly suggested that my sister be Maria's godmother, and that is how it went, as I was living under her roof at that time. **Children be obedient to your parents for it is right in the eyes of God.** It seemed that my sins just followed me everywhere I went, even **though God promises to cast our sins into the sea of forgetfulness and remember them no more.** Man is so unlike God.

By the age of eighteen, Pastor Andrews gave me instructions that *God said* that I had to marry Doug, who was my abusive boyfriend and the father of my daughter, whom I birthed out of wedlock. Even with all that I went through, I agreed to honor her words and marry Doug. Admittedly, I was angry at Pastor Andrews for speaking those words. No longer do I believe that

God would give a revelation to tell any member/sister/child of His or hers to marry an abusive male. By this period of my life, I *strongly* disliked Doug, but I listened to her words.

For the first three months of our "marriage," Doug and I resided at separate residences, as Doug did not have means to provide for us, and he *still* needed to graduate. Meanwhile, we resided at our respective mothers' homes. I was blessed with a job at a major insurance company, but I did not make enough money to provide for all three of us, nor should I have had to do so. I Timothy 5:8 expresses that **if anyone fails to provide for his family is an infidel and had lost the faith.** Sometime after Maria was born, Doug graduated and got a job at a factory. Sometimes, my punishment was that he would not go to work, but I continued working.

Doug and I were scheduled to marry on February 20th, 1980. While he was high, Doug got his finger sliced off by a machine, and he needed emergency surgery. The wedding was called off due to this situation, but my fears allowed it to be rescheduled. Perhaps, I should have paused for the cause and really examined the situation, but who does that at the age of eighteen, especially while working under the spell of fear?

On ***March 15,*** **1980**, the worst day of my life **twice**, Pastor Andrews pronounced her judgment, as Doug and I exchanged meaningless words. Others refer to these words as vows. This exchange took place under my mother's roof while Pastor Andrews had her way with my life. When the pastor asked the question, "Is there anyone here who knows any reason why these two should not be joined together?" She continued, "Speak now or forever hold your peace." Our six month old daughter, Maria, began to cry as she saturated her gorgeous yellow dress. Please note that it was very unusual for Maria to cry, unless something was terribly distressing. **A child shall lead them**. May I add that a child can teach you so much, if you are humble enough to learn from them?

Somewhere between March 15, and June 1980, Doug and I conceived another daughter. Either Corrinna was conceived on the evening of our "honeymoon," which was spent in a local hotel room at my expense, or shortly thereafter while my mother went to Poughkeepsie, New York to visit Debra at Vassar College. By the young age of nineteen, I became the mother of two children. After many difficult hours of laboring, with necessary forceps and induced labor, my second blessed gift from God entered this world. Notice how I was suffering while being pregnant, which might explain the difficult labor I underwent.

The next day, I turned twenty. Realistically, I was *still* a baby myself, but I had two innocent little girls who became dependent on me, regardless as to my age. These wonderful inheritances came from the **Most High God**, aka **El Elyon.**

Giving the benefit of the doubt, perhaps, Pastor Andrews was attempting to cover herself as a pastor/church concerning my sin of fornication. However, this I will never know for sure. You may ask, as I have, did Pastor Andrews have any other possible motives when she stated that God said that I had to marry Doug? Perhaps it was about control, despite my bewildered and simple motives. One thing that I know for sure is that God discerns our motives.

I believed that if I served God (or the pastor/god), with obedience and did things His way or the way that she said, that God would bless my efforts. I believe that God did bless my efforts as two beautiful gifts came from this union, known as Maria and Corrinna. Definitely, I was afraid of this woman, but the reality is that I needed to see Jesus for myself.

Another motive of mine was simple. Yet, it was so complex. Other than Doug hurting me repeatedly, *still,* I no longer feared that any other males would rape me. I did not worry about males ever bothering me, because Doug would knock out anyone who attempted to look at my battered and bruised face or legs. I chose to contend with many types of ill events for this measure of "protection" which included but was not limited to Doug beating the mess out of me or "hockers" being spit in my face. Likewise, whether or not my head could take any more contusions and/or concussions became a chief concern.

Finally, I had an excuse to depart from my mother's house and look for my place to call my home and enter into the insecure world that I feared; although, safety was universally absent. As always, my mother continually confirmed that I went from the furnace to the frying pan. At that time, I did not understand this cliché but I now realize the truth of her concerns.

Doug's beatings were so blatant that on our one and only Mother's Day under the same roof, I received no less than ten knots in my head, which were the only "presents" that I received on this blessed holiday. Then, I went to church to play the piano without saying one word. Oh, please allow me to add that after the beatings, my reward was to accept his apology by allowing him to express more of his "love" through sexual engagement. While this occurred, I remained silent and motionless which happened more frequently than not.

Another time, Doug's force behind the blow to my head became so solid that my eyeglasses burst in half. Immediately, I lost consciousness. Please note that Doug punched me on the side of my head, not in the middle of my face. A friend named Pat, who witnessed the whole affair, drove me to the Emergency Room. The triage nurse who took the initial report questioned which instrument Doug used to knock me out. I replied, "His fist," but I refused to press any charges.

Visualize that Doug is a huge and buffed male. He weighed in around 230 lbs., which is gigantic compared to my 120 lbs. Additionally, he measures in height approximately 6 feet 2 inches. Compare his construct to my stature of 5 feet 3 ½ inches, and you will see that there was no match in this ring. He remained the heavy weight champion in this fight at all times, until God opened my eyes and shut that door forever! Oh, but

GOD! The above beatings are the only two that I shared with you, but you can trust they happened at least once a week, if not more frequently.

Finally, the day came that I officially alerted Pastor Andrews about the abuses that I suffered at Doug's hand, as she could not see my bruised body and knots. She made sure that I hid behind clothing. We were practically covered from head to toe, without any ornaments. I wore a lot of moo-moos, as my girls call them. The above mentioned abuse, rather than playing the piano and my giving of my tithe offerings, seemed to be less of a concern to her than the huge non-monetary costs of me being continually abused.

Perhaps Pastor Andrews had these same experiences and someone lied to her, but I am exposing that when someone flips out on you, it is not because of whom you are or your mouth. It is because you are there! Please get out of the situation. If you find out that you *really* do love God and you think that you love the person and yourself, wait and see if they really get the help that they need. Meanwhile, get some help for yourself too. Love neither hurts nor is it abusive.

Pastor Andrews' response included scolding me in reference to my tongue, which she blamed that I caused the injuries. Her accusation was that it was my mouth that the problems resulted, and this piloted a greater method of silencing, but nothing lasts forever. I thank God for deliverance! Today, I know that it was not my mouth which caused Doug's violent reactions. In my heart of hearts, I knew then that it was not my words that caused Doug to beat on me. At times, I got beat because I attended church. I was unable to vocalize the truth at that time, but it is **the truth that will set you free**!

Boxed in beyond fear and not only due to Doug's rage, I was too afraid to rebuttal the pastor. Speaking openly to my mother was out of the question at that time. Mom warned me that someone was going to get killed in this thing called a marriage, as she carefully collected and removed all of the knives from our apartment.

Much later, rather than accept most responsibility of Doug being totally out of control, I realized that the poundings of Doug's fists on everyone were a direct result of Doug's deep seeded anger issues that others were aware of as early as while he was attending elementary school. I am unsure if he graduated from his anger issues or not. I remain unsure of his deliverance or status. Today, Doug is not my concern. Just as my life and issues, Doug's life and issues are in God's hands, and I know that He is dealing accordingly. However, I accepted total understanding of why we are forewarned at Proverbs 22:22-24, **not to make any friendship with an angry man, lest you learn his ways and set a snare for your soul.**

Doug's beatings were not my only hidden problems. There were other major concerns that uninvited guests were in our bedroom which I contended with, while attempting to care for a family of four. Another worry that I silently kept hidden were the embarrassing, humiliating, degrading, unfamiliar, alarming, and disrespectful results of sex outside of the "marriage" which included unimaginable types of sexually transmitted diseases, which I was oblivious concerning.

It was not until the birth our second child, Corrinna that the doctors discovered that Doug infected me with gonorrhea. I was so embarrassed, but I did recognize that it was not my fault. Today, I will not declare that I am a victim, but I am the victor in every situation, no matter how dreary it appears, because of whose child I am.

Upon realization of the dangerously poisoned position that Doug placed on our daughter while I was with child, I telephoned Pastor John, a local minister, who asked Doug which partner was responsible for this disease. Doug acknowledged that he did not believe that I did this, but he never totally owned up to the fact that he did.

Although my family physician previously informed me of other sexually transmitted diseases which silently remain in my medical records, I did not formerly disclose the embarrassing discoveries of the black bugs that lived and sucked my blood from my body, and the other sexually transmitted diseases that I suffered from being in what I considered a monogamous relationship with the man who was portrayed as my husband.

Oh yes, I failed to mention to you that Doug was treated for the sexually transmitted disease at the emergency room. Doug obtained medication and specified medical instructions. After my physician's diagnosis, I realized that Doug left his medication and instructions on top of the refrigerator. He even lacked the decency, respect, care, or concern to tell me, but my main concern was for our unborn child who could have been blinded. Thank God for protection of unseen dangers.

After Doug and I spoke with this Pastor John, who advised me of my Biblical rights to divorce Doug, I separated from Doug for a short period of time. Knowledge of his dishonest actions gave me a Biblical device to avoid what *I* referred to as the wrath of God. Staying in the tight spot at my mother's house had not worked well before.

The evidence of Doug's disease was on top of the refrigerator, but as you can see, my own circles of confusing fears were prevalent in more ways than just one. About a year later, reality set in and I believe that what happened was a direct result of Doug's dirty demises. My right fallopian tube exploded, which almost cost my life, but once again, God said, "No."

The last physical infection came while I was carrying our second child; meanwhile, I waited for my discharge papers after laboring for many hours, and I was *still* in pain. I recognized and spoke with a woman who travailed and birthed a son. She confessed to me that she was unsure if Doug, yes; my husband at this time may have been the father of her son. What is one supposed to do with that type of information?

Devastation, depression, oppression, and disgust ingested my filthy body, (which just delivered a baby), heart, and soul. Daily, doctors diagnose people with postpartum depression. I did not even schedule that appointment because I had so many other things to be depressed about.

Even after bringing two of Doug's children into this world, he continually beat on me without caring what happened to his children or his children's mother. Doug's final punch that finally physically knocked out the "marriage" occurred on a night while I had both of our daughters in my arms. Upon this last strike from his fists, it became a no brainer this was the final TKO of the house and "marriage."

The time came to leave home base forever and never run this course again. Neither Pastor Andrews nor Doug gave me any other recourse, except to be under their control twenty-four/seven, but I felt absolutely compelled to run again. Returning to tag an unsecured base was not a workable alternative, as the fouls continually came. I began to crawl away from this lifestyle forever.

Although, I *still* feared Pastor Andrews, the next and final bout with Pastor Andrews occurred when I secretly placed an envelope in the mail slot of the locked church, which included the following: my key to the church, my tithe offering, and a letter that basically alerted her that she should marry Doug.

Then, I exchanged my bogus marriage certificate for a real divorce to both Doug and the church, but I did not know what the future held for me and my children. I did know that the truth always prevails. Maria was only 18 months and Corrinna only 3 months old when God offered us footprints. Then, my arms carried them out of this dangerous zone.

I only had the clothes on our backs, my girls, and their formula filled bottles in my hands. We did not even have a change of diapers, which meant starting all over again from scratch. Actually, I did have all that I needed when I decided never to return again. Was this a moment that I totally trusted God without realizing it?

I did not know how we would make it on our own. Certainly, I believed that we were subjected to more harm than good in that infested environment of anger, disease, and disaster. I can surely testify to the words of David when he states in Psalms 37:25 that **I have been young and I have been old, but I have never seen the righteous forsaken, nor his seed beg for bread.**

My two baby girls and I moved back into my small bedroom at my mother's house, which is the size of some of your walk-in closets, but I knew that the space was a bit too tight. So, I came up with a long term plan rather than a temporary situation which did not last too long. Debra was away at college, but our rooms remained our bedrooms. It was not until recently that my diminutive bedroom was turned into a small office for my step-father.

About a year and a half later, after becoming a little bit more balanced and back on my feet, I fell into an unplanned relationship. I met a wonderfully made, kind, and handsome gentleman, a friend, named Wayne, who I know continues to love me and the girls without a doubt. This platonic love is reciprocated. Wherever or whenever anyone saw me and the girls, they also saw Wayne.

Although Doug was cohabitating with a female and living in a different city, he was allotted that right because he and I were divorced. Doug chose to terminate my rights to date, because he was not fond of the notion that I was dating Wayne. Learning of this love, Doug turned the tables to threatening my life. In the interim, Doug gave us double trouble as he blackened both of Wayne's eyes, but that never mired Wayne from walking miles to our home to see us again, until he left for the Air Force. Love really does go the distance.

Admittedly, knowing Doug's alter ego too well, I feared his capabilities. Doug had forewarned me long ago that as long as I carried his last name, I *belonged* to him. As you can see, he considered me his property; today, I am known as God's property! I am reminded of another scripture which tells us, ***touch not my anointed and do him no harm***. If only I knew who I was in Him!

Still, I was on the run, perhaps from my call; nonetheless, during this period of my life, the time came to change my last name. About a year expired, and I continued to survive through life, which was no life of my own but a life through my children's lives.

I do not believe that I have seen many movies on Lifetime that have shocked me. It's just that my finale and their endings are often different. Recall that I never filed for these aggravated assaults or terroristic threats, which is why they probably continued. Although I was encouraged and filed for a Protection from Abuse (PFA), which is generally granted if abuse is proven or the defendant fails to appear in court.

However, this court ordered document did not ultimately protect me from being beat, and it appeared to make Doug more out of control because it materialized a bigger power struggle for him. During the 1980's the police needed to witness Doug's punches. Even though I had lumps, bumps, or bruises, the assault was classified as domestic abuse the police limited their involvement.

The most buried secret that kept me silent was that shortly after my father died, I was raped! However, I am sure that Carrie, whom I met at Pastor Andrews' church, exposed Doug's attempt of murder which ultimately could have ended her, my daughters, and my life, but I did not telephone the police. I did take my daughters to counseling but I am unsure if I told my mother, but I am sure that Carrie told her mother.

Nonetheless, I consider the attempted murder an event that eventually ran me directly into Ray's restless arms. While Wayne was away at boot camp, Doug discovered that I was driving a friend's car. The vehicle was filled with laughter, Carrie, and my daughters. Within moments the laughter turned into fear almost instantaneously. Upon Doug's detectable red rage of radar, he spotted us and became irate. He attempted to kill all of us. Fear set in all of our hearts.

During this timid time of our lives, Maria and Corrinna were four and three years old respectively, but they were not too young to meet fear; although, they should have been. For years, I blamed myself as being a bad mother because horrific things occurred, which I was not totally responsible for but they were charged only to my own account by me.

Never did I find the courage to press charges against Doug for reckless endangerment of our lives or aggravated assault for any of his abusive behaviors. I did not give thought about beating on him while he was asleep or causing him any harm at any time of his life, as Carrie suggested. However, this offense subjected him to strict supervised visitation rights when my girls' psychologist turned this mandatory information over to Child Protective Services. Perhaps, my fear was that I would be held liable for somehow creating a monstrous monster by having Doug locked up, if that was possible.

Another fear was that many times the police did absolutely nothing. If I told, it only worsened matters for me. Another fear; perhaps, not reality, was that Doug's family and others would be mad at me, rather than have compassion for my injuries. Besides, I had an extremely guilty conscience that hurt really badly and easily, which probably resulted from keeping secrets and not exposing darkness to light.

Actually, despite what others did to me, my issues of guilt continually went unattended. To wrong anyone meant that I had to stand up for myself. All praise to God, I am growing! A problem never came to surface while standing up for my children, without even thinking about the consequences of my actions. For me, I admit that much difficulty arose.

One time, Doug threatened to keep the girls after a visitation, as he adamantly refused to bring the girls back.

Until the policemen safely returned my girls, I was determined to get my daughters back. Neither Doug nor I filed for custody, but after that event, I headed straight to the courts and filed for and received primary custody for both of my daughters.

The wise thing to do would be to create boundaries, let go of the fears, and not keep silent on issues. I believe that you must have the resources to establish boundaries. For most of my years, I did not have an inclination of the definition of this word called boundaries. I did not have any idea of how to set them, and this is another chapter in silence. I believe that rape and other ill abusive treatments tore down the possibilities of boundaries and nailed my walls in place. When the storms of life were raging, I had no shelter, and I continued to run.

Chapter 3

On July 14, 1984, my girls and I returned home from the circus. Aunt Louise's daughters, Karen and Cher invited me out to a club in a large city, where "famous" radio announcers broadcasted live. After going to my closet, I dressed in clothing which probably were purchased from a local inexpensive store; although, Wal-Mart was my preference.

Even though, I worked three jobs we were labeled as financially "poor." My daughters' needs, wants, and how they were dressed were much more important than my needs or what clothing I wore. My children's safety, happiness, needs, and wants were my only heart's desire at this time. God provided the desires of my heart because my children never lacked for anything.

In an effort to get dressed and add some flavor of the my outfit that consisted of a white pair of Capri's and a pink top, I tied a multicolored scarf around my head and cautiously proceeded to go out with my cousins to the club; although, I would have rather stayed at home with my children. Finding good babysitters was a hard task. Besides, clubs never did a thing for me.

I was not enthusiastic about going to this major city. In all actuality, I was definitely afraid. For a long time, what appeared to be hours after our arrival, alone and lonely, I sat by the phone booth with a few dimes in my hand.

Finally, the male of the hour was present. He was the number one announcer of the nighttime airways. A brief introduction warranted some women pushing me out of the way. To my surprise, in the midst of about one thousand or more women, Ray found and invited me downstairs to another floor of this vast club for conversation and drinks. The club was huge, as it had at least four floors. Ray offered to drive me home that evening, but I refused that approach. I came with my cousins, and my only plans were to return home safely with Karen behind the wheel, but I did go to the first floor to talk with Ray.

I shared that I came out of an abusive marriage, that I had two beautiful daughters whom I love dearly, and that I was supposed to play the piano at the church, which was music to Ray's ears! In my eyes, he found a church girl! Ray and I talked until the wee hours of the morning, and we exchanged phone numbers. At the last song, Ray requested that the DJ play a song that included the words slow dance, and "we slow danced." After that last dance of our lives, my cousins and I headed back home with silence in the car. I think that Karen was a bit upset with me.

Today, she may very well thank me.

The fact remains that I never really knew this man they called Ray, which is not his first name. For some unknown reasons he has several alias. Why does Ray refer to himself as his middle name and have about seven different aliases? You don't suppose that his name changed each time that he got married, or did it? Certainly, my last name changed each time that I married.

Ray wore a wedding band, and this mystified me. As a result, I asked him, "Are you married?" Ray denied being married. Rather, he stated that he wore his ring on his left fourth finger as a detour; you know, as a method to keep women away from him because of his popularity. Personally, I only heard different bits and pieces of information concerning Ray which my cousins, especially Karen, briefly mentioned during our hour drive to the club. This was the only previous information that they heard from others, because they did not personally know Ray.

Karen and Cher had the dial tuned to the radio station and they were at the club prior to inviting me; as the third wheel, I was totally imbalanced once again. My cousin, Karen found Ray extremely attractive, but I did not see him through her rose colored eye glasses, but his confession to me was that he did not know Karen.

I had very limited knowledge of this "celebrity/legend."

Upon meeting Ray, I did not know where to set the dial on the station, what time his show was on the air, or much else about this popular and number one radio show host of the midnight airways, called the Thunder Storm. As you may recall, worldly music was not an option for church folks who sat under Pastor Andrews. My continual belief is that it impressed Ray that I was unaware of him or his on air status, and I know he was happy that I attended church. I chuckle now, but I wonder if he thought that his secrets were safe from me?

I believe that he was floored by the fact that I refused to allow him to take me home the first night that we met. Most women at this club gave me the impression that they would welcome a one night stand with the master of the Thunder Storm. I believe that one of the reasons for the packed club was an effort for single women to meet him or other air personalities after hearing their "sexy" voices on the radio.

At some point during the night, Ray gave me the phone number to the "warm line" at the radio station, and by the end of the night, I was upgraded to the "hot line." I do recall thinking that it was odd that he did not give me his home number. Additionally, the iced tea did not totally intoxicate me. I did not trust that Ray was unmarried, but that truthful answer did come that following Monday.

My cousins and I closed down the club because Ray and I talked all night. Then, Ray and I danced on the last song of the night. I think it was between 2 and 3 AM by the time that we left the city. Upon my return home, I called one of male cousins named James. I informed him that I met Ray. In response, James called me a fool and told me to go back to sleep because it was only a dream. Then, he reminded me of our routinely scheduled Sunday morning coffee meeting within hours. I was insulted, as

I was a tad bit naïve. I am not a fool, at Psalms 14:1 the Bible states that **the fool states in his heart that there is no God**. From early childhood I always believed that God existed, and that He sent His only begotten son into the world to die for our sins. Now, I realize that is the testimony that saved me. I just did not understand the things that others taught me about God.

Furthermore, concerning James's comments, I was not dreaming, and the evidence is in the fact that a thunderstorm really did pour into my life at another delicate time. Around five that morning, my telephone rang, and Ray identified himself as such, stating that he called to verify that I did not trick him by giving him the number to a phone booth. That statement bothered me, because I would never think to do anything like that, even if I should. I was confident that my phone would ring, but I was uncertain that it would be that soon.

Ray telephoned me many times, and within two days he called to ask permission to visit. I attempted to persuade him otherwise, but he was insistent. Rather quickly, Ray advised me that he was praying and that he asked God if he would see me again, and that he received a clear answer of yes. I think that there was a mark on my forehead that read, this scared little girl really does love God, but does not know who she is in Him, or perhaps he was hallucinating. It could have been either or both, but obviously, Ray followed the sign on my forehead and the directions that I described in detail.

Prior to Ray's arrival, I threw some hamburger in the oven and named it a meatloaf, and I heated up a can of peas for my girls' dinner. Shortly thereafter, Ray arrived at our home. With prudence, I asked Ray if he wanted some dinner, and he replied, "Yes, these are my favorite foods." Later, I learned that Ray's favorite foods are actually chicken and rice. It did not take long to become familiar with the music or games that Ray was playing, or his works. Nightly, I became hipped to the popular R & B station, as Ray and I talked every night; while he played, I listened.

Routinely, each Saturday night, Ray would drive over an hour to pick me up, and we would travel back to the largely populated city to the club where it all began. The reality is that we did not do many other things together other than drive to the club on Saturday evenings, as I watched him work his magic. Notice, it awed me that Ray would drive that far to pick me up to be in his company while he made money. Ray is somebody to everyone who listened, and I wanted to know myself.

Although he never took me on a real date, often he asked me, a single mother of two young daughters, for gas money and loans for his insurance premiums. What was I thinking? Oh, I guess that I was a Good Samaritan, which seemed to be my normal character. Regardless, being with Ray temporarily filled the emptiness that I longed for. My fantasy was to feel as though I was somebody and that I could be someone special to Ray. What I learned is I became someone that Ray was using! Wow, if I only knew who I was in Christ.

Within two weeks, Ray professed his love to me, and I met his oldest daughter, Renee on this same day. *Still*, I recall the alarming feeling that I felt due to his confession of what he thought was love. I was honest with Ray when I told him that I did not fall in love with him.

I did not want to hurt his feelings but I added that I believed that I could grow to love him. I think this is when Ray became silently angry with me. Did I just interfere with his original motives? Upon sharing the above with an old associate of mine, Richard, he replied, "A man can grow a beard," and we laughed. The truth is that I was not in love with Ray. I was probably looking for a father, rather than a mate. Clearly, I was running! Ray is sixteen years my senior, and he is only four years younger than my mother. I was Ray's trophy on his arm during many outings, but I became other things to him during the day and night.

Ray had the audacity to tell me if I ever got fat that it was over. Technically, I became fat in 2001, but I lost the weight within months and returned to my normal size. I am sure that I gained weight as a barrier to men, but some men like "healthy" women too. However, before this "marriage" ended I lost weight rather than gained an ounce because I was starving for affection and love from a male.

Conceivably, I was so shallow that he recognized my youthfulness. In some ways, I was displaying a very naïve little girl. This should have been a crime, but we were considered adults according to the law of the land. I have my concerns about some of the laws of the land, but I do know that the Bible teaches us to respect the laws of the land, as long as it does not go against the Word of God.

Although I was frightened, lonely, and missed Wayne terribly, I did not have any interest in any other relationship; rather, I continued to run through the maze of confusion. One thing that I learned concerning my life is that the thing that I strive to run from the fastest with fear in forefront is the exact thing that I run right into, but in a different form.

Today, I have a better understanding that this is what my mother meant by the phrase that I go from the frying pan into the furnace….it just gets hotter and hotter; at least until God led me to the core of the coals and then He put the fires out, HALLELUJAH!

Additionally, I learned why I became such an analytical person. Generally, my mother gave me clichés. I did not have a choice except to go deep to figure things out. Today, I can say that I thank God for that ability, and the teachings of my mother. If I was not her child, I am unconvinced that I would be who I am today!

The man whom I truly loved, Wayne, joined the Air force and was away training at boot camp, which tore my spirit apart further. Doug attempted to kill us in the car, and I did not know which way to turn. I fell out of fellowship with the church. Basically, I was on my own with two daughters to raise. I thought that I had a better understanding of God during this time of my life, but the truth of the matter is that I *still* had not been brought into the fullness of God. I did not comprehend God's love for me. Now, I realize that I was *still* suffering deeply with unresolved issues of grief, as well as being broken from old man life.

I believe that people who know me discern that I have a heart after God's heart. Also, I believe that it caused many to consider me naïve, but I feel sorry that they do not know **that believing in God is the beginning of wisdom.** Ray assured me that he prayed and received a word from God that I was to be his wife. Does that remind you of what Pastor Andrews did? Certainly, it reminds me of her words.

Is there a pattern here in my life?

I used to challenge these words that Ray swore that he received from God. Today, I realize *that all things really do work for the good of those that love God and are called for his purpose.* I am grateful for that scripture, regardless at to what Ray's god's name was or is. After all, Ray told me that he believed that everything God made was good, but his version included weed, which I begged of him not to smoke around my daughters. Despite all that I went through, I praise my God, because without this union, Joshua Wayne-Anthony Brown would have not been who he was.

Now, I question, was God hiding me during this storm to give me what He knew that I would need and the desires of my heart? Doug no longer physically abused me, and I ended up having good relationships with my daughters throughout their childhood. After all, the Bible clearly tells us that **our heavenly Father knows exactly what we need even before we ask.** Certainly, it was not God who instructed Ray to treat me in the fashion that he did. Another recent entertainment is that Ray's third or fourth set of divorce papers were timely, because he only received them the Monday after we met; hence, the wedding ring that he wore on his finger.

Within three months, Ray proposed to me with the most gorgeous ring that I ever saw. The shining tri tone ring was only sized as a half carat diamond; undoubtedly, it was the biggest "rock" that ever went on my hand or any hand that I knew. Literally, I did not have the ultimate *encounter* with the **real Rock**. Suspiciously, I accepted Ray's proposal. That same evening, Ray's first wife, Darla, who is the biological mother of his oldest daughter, Renee, telephoned Ray's home, and I answered the phone. Ray had pneumonia, which is why I was there to take care of him.

Credulously, I spoke with Darla. I did not have any reason for instinctual distrust. Renee is only seven years younger than me. Ray and Darla were divorced for numerous years. Therefore, I never considered that Darla would have any reason to fill my head with ill intended information about Ray. At times, I questioned, did she?

Upon hearing my voice, explosively, Darla disclosed many of Ray's past secrets. Additionally, she disclosed that his mother and sister were not fond of me at all. I was unaware of any incident that caused the last statement to be true. I only met Ray's mother and sister one time, and I could not think of what I did to receive mal treatment. I did not have boundaries. Therefore, I carefully examined their reasoning. This was their issue not mine.

Along life's journey, I heard someone say it is none of your business what others think about you. I believe this is a very true statement. I learned and offer this advice back to you; you do not have to wrong anyone for people to dislike you. Sometimes all you have to do is to walk in people's presence, but that is not your issue, it is theirs!

Darla's wild accusations about Ray sounded like something one may hear on a Jerry Springer Show. Frankly, I did not have a clue as to whom I should believe or whom I should trust. The information that Darla shared turned out to be rather accurate. Certainly, Darla gave me very excellent reasons to pause for the cause, but I laced up my track shoes, ready to run again. After Ray completed his conversation with Darla, I entertained the gossip with Ray, and he gave me his rebuttal. He made a few comments about Darla, and we kept an even pace, while we jogged around the real issues at hand.

The engagement ring was packaged in white wrapping with a white bow, but boxed inside were many of my unsettled fears. The purity was ripped off, and the sparkling engagement ring was placed on my finger. However, no ring was ever placed around my heart. One of my fears was wearing such a "big diamond." Fear will drive you nuts if you allow it to control you. Know that **fear is from Satan!**

There is a fact that this ring was real gold and the diamond was of perfect clarity, but everything that glitters is not gold, even though it was properly insured. While I ensured that my diamond was secured, I sniveled all the way home. I was making an attempt to escape the madness in my life. Somehow, I was thinking that God would/could just fix it.

My rights were relinquished the moment that I failed to consider the fact that I had choices and serious decisions to make in this situation to prayer. Instead of being *still*, I attempted to escape one portion of madness in my life by introducing another chapter of insanity into my life. Nonetheless, God is *still* in full control. **What Satan means for our bad, God can turn it into our good.**

Even though Ray stated that God said that I was to be his wife, God did not tell Ray to treat me as he did. God's word tells men how they should treat their wives; **husbands love your wives as Christ loved the church.** This is not a suggestion that you put anyone before GOD; but if you put God first you will respect, honor, and love the man that God has called to be your husband.

I've witnessed too many women who have what appear to be God fearing husbands who get very little, if any respect, and time. Please read and meditate on ***Proverbs 31*** and know who God has called you to be as your husband's wife. Men, please read

Proverbs 31, and pay *careful attention to verse 18, which states that* **he that finds a wife findeth a good thing and favor with God**, which is the key. **Husbands LOVE your wives!**

Although I knew that **God could do anything except fail,** God did not fix my situation with Ray. Maybe that was a result of my reckless behavior and no longer having a desire for God to fix the situation, but God did answer many of my most sincerely requested prayers. Also, God answered many questions which include, is it possible to love anyone, yourself or God if you do not know Him?

Oh, I failed to give props to my mother who told me these exact words, "Don't you listen to everyone who tells you what God said." My mother is a wise woman, and she became much wiser when she accepted Jesus Christ as her personal savior, but at that time in my life, her voice was extremely muffled.

At the very least, from the day that Ray and I met, I can tell you that Ray and I had a *rocky* relationship, which included bumping hard heads together. It seemed that we produced more rocks along the way. We had many failed mountain climbing experiences. Denial would say that we did not know each other long or well enough to get married. Ray and I met shortly after midnight on July 15, 1984 and we were engaged by October 12, 1984, despite the fact that the referee of life had thrown several enormous red and yellow flags, which spoke volumes. Perhaps, if my ears were uncluttered, the ability to listen and get the accurate directions for my life may have been heard. All that I could hear was that I was unworthy. Here is the real question; did I really hear the directions for my life without knowing it? That following May 3, which was less than a ten month time frame, Ray and I got married. We could/should have talked and prayed about our problems, but we failed miserably at communication with each other and God.

I was talking to God, but I was not listening for God's quiet and *still* voice, as my ears were clogged by the rain of tears that fell inside of my eardrums. Speaking of communication, my thinking is that if there is a lack of communication, everything else is mute. How can you physically communicate with someone that you cannot verbally communicate?

Realistically, Ray and I did not date or spend much time alone; just him and me, with the exception of our phone talks, but that was mostly during his working hours; yet and *still*, we were not alone. Many of those hours of chit chat involved many untruths and so much vital missing information, but I never hid the fact that I had two daughters whom I love dearly.

On May 3, 1985, I stood under my mother's roof wearing a white jumpsuit, as I exchanged meaningless words once again. Lawfully, Ray and I became husband and wife. I will admit to you that I am not one who generally drinks alcohol. I am not a fan of it. However, prior to this appointment, I asked a neighbor for a pint of vodka.

After the vodka, it did not matter that the wedding had been called off countless times for several different reasons. Perhaps the real deal is that we knew each other, but did not want to see the red flags for the red rages of absences in our own lives. Let us ponder this…Ray and I did not even talk about where we would live before or after we were introduced as husband and wife. Did Ray already plan to tell me the next morning that he really did not want to be married to me? Was I ready to accept that answer?

Strange, is it not? Needless to say, we were not one. In my opinion, Ray did not strive to become one at any other time.

The Bible questions us, **how can two walk together unless they agree?** The Bible also states **that a double minded man is unstable in all of his ways.** However, I do believe that one has the right to change their mind or opinion. There were several times that I called off the engagement, but I did not give back the rock than was only worn by my finger. Many years later, I pawned that rock for less than $100.00, and I had an authentic encounter with the ROCK of ages which is free. This is becoming a freeing experience for me, despite my challenges. Certainly, there was no ring placed around my heart or his, with the exception of a ring of pain. Our hearts never beat as one. As a matter of fact, I cannot tell you that I ever heard Ray's heart beat!

A valid reason for one of the terminations of our engagement was that Ray expressed his confusions of whom he truly loved. Was it me or his most recent ex-wife, wife number three? What number was she? Is it not strange that I never mentioned Wayne? How many wives were there? According to Darla there were more wives than Ray openly admitted. Who was this mysterious male with a sexy disguised voice hiding behind a microphone, that I should soon be his wife? Could this man be the Wizard of Oz?

Was I about to pull his curtain, as he attempted to tear me down? These answers, I do not know; regardless, all of these unanswered questions and hidden messages should have been a bright red flag that would literally call my true name, which is not Dorothy. Was I on the yellow brick road that leads to a fantasy? Admittedly, I lived in a type of a fantasy world, as I believed that I had something to prove to everyone who ran across my path. What is that you ask? The answer to that question is that I had an irrational need to prove that I was worthy of being loved by a human. The fact of the matter is that I could not believe that God loved me.

Although I admitted to Ray that I was not in love with him, I silently suffered by keeping it a secret that I really loved Wayne. I kept Doug's crimes of attempted murder, battery, and aggravated assault very quiet, as well as the massive amount of diseases that Doug exposed me to, and being raped, which was called a train. This wrecked my life for a long time, but God put me on the right tracks.

Another question that I should have asked a long time ago concerning relationships is **except a house be built by God, how can it be built?** There was no way that Ray and my "marriage" had much of a chance of survival, just as I was barely surviving. How can anything survive that never existed? Even though Ray and I repeated some charming words you can clearly identify that we were nowhere near close to being one. Ray was not at total fault for all of the problems that existed in our marriage; although, most times, I do skew things to my side. This, I am confident that you may understand shortly.

Early the next morning, after our short lived honeymoon night, which was spent at the club where it all surmounted, an announcement went over the airways that we officially became husband and wife. After consecrating the marriage, that next morning back at my place, Ray made an urgent announcement to me that he had made a mistake in marrying me, and he walked out the door.

Putting it mildly, I am unsure that I was devastated, but I do know that I became dumbfounded to say the least. There was not anything that I could do to transform Ray's thinking, and I am unsure that I had any desire to change his mind, but I wanted to know why I was unworthy of anyone's love. The real answer is this is not love.

Surely, my self-esteem took another beating, which did not stop me. I had two little girls depending on me, whose self-esteem I wanted to preserve, just as my lovingly father did for me. A week later, I telephoned my attorney to begin the process of an annulment. Another four weeks passed before I received a long awaited return phone call from my attorney who stated, without reason or advice, that Ray inadvertently changed his mind. However, my belief is that the song's lyrics, it's cheaper to keep her, were playing over and over again in Ray's mind or on the radio. Firmly, I believe this song had some strong influences on Ray's decision. In other words, I believe that his wallet spoke volumes because it was already hurting, as he was earning under $20,000/per year at this time period.

Eventually, Ray and I discussed where we would live. Either it is hilarious or ridiculous that we were silent about this issue until he admitted that he no longer wanted to be married. Something is seriously wrong with that picture! As we made attempts to compromise, I adamantly refused to move my daughters to the large city due to my own fears and the desire to have my girls in a decent school district. Ray refused to travel the distance from my place of residence to his job on a daily basis. Love really does go the distance.

After three months of living separated, finally, we agreed to meet somewhere in the middle and reside on the Main Line. I can shout now and share with you that I can sing with praise and thanksgiving that *Jesus is on the Main Line*, and we can ask him for anything that we want. If what **we ask for that which is within His will, He will listen** *and hear us*. God's word promises us **that if we seek the kingdom of God and His righteousness that everything else will be added unto us** at Matthew 33:3. Without a question, I now know that God was at work in my life, even though this marriage was not made in heaven.

Below, my life demonstrates yet another pattern, but I am so relieved that God has the final outcome of the total design. After being separated from Doug for three months; again, *after three months of being separated* from Ray, we finally moved in together. Moving in with Doug and Ray was worse than living separately for ninety days. Each experience was horrific, but I was able to find added joy in the lives of my two daughters, Maria and Corrinna, who were added supplements.

Although we eventually moved under one roof, Ray and I practically survived by living separate lives, but we added confusion being in the same territory. While we often escaped the weight of being at the house, the girls and I had loads of fun shopping, skating, bowling, and so many more discoveries were founded. I became their and others' Brownie leader, Service Unit Director, Choir Director, and Youth Leader. Pretty much, if you can name it, concerning my children's involvement, it is possible that I did it. In addition, I took vacation days to chaperone on my girls' field trips.

I involved my daughters in many activities. Whatever they were committed to, I became an active participant. Doing things outside of the house was a great distraction for all of us. Besides all of these fun things, we shopped until we dropped. This was an outlet for the massive amounts of frustration, which only swept my real problems under the rug; ultimately, it created more problems, which eventually exploded. The hidden dust consumed all of us.

Not one day passed without Ray's verbally abusive words. He constantly reminded me that he did not, under any uncertain terms, want to be married to me. Without reservations, bold females would ring our telephone and bluntly request to speak to my husband. I assume that Ray communicated to these females that I really did not matter. While playing the role of his maidservant, I would politely pass the phone. I just played the role that I learned to play very well.

Until these writings, I did not once consider the enormous amounts of disrespect. All that I knew was that while these things were happening, my pain became unreachable and extremely intense. Silently, I cried rivers or maybe even bodies of oceans, but the howl was much louder whenever I was not in my daughters' company. I believe that God does see and feel saddened because of our tears, and I am confident that He will wipe away each one, if we just allow Him to do just so.

The feeling of endured aloneness with Ray was not one that became familiar to me. To be with someone and continually feel lonely is one of the most prevalent abandonments that I have ever encountered, even though my father had been dead for thirteen years. I have never felt so alone, and you can trust that I was one lonely young lady. I packed everything and moved away from my family. During this time period, I sought professional advice. This counselor's first and last question to me was. "Have you found someone else too?" Needless to say, that was the last appointment with him. My mother always taught me that two wrongs do not make a right. I did not always listen. In this case, I attempted to do everything that I could think of to be accepted by Ray and any organization.

My efforts to keep the house immaculately included but were not limited to cleaning, cooking, doing laundry, purchasing, and picking out his clothing, which sometimes that task included his underwear. While the aroma of home filled our house by the fragrances that cooking placed in our house, the clean smell of bleach and other cleaning products consumed our nostrils at other times, but these efforts *still* did not make our house a home.

As I was taught that a good wife should, I made certain that Ray did not have to raise one finger, except to take the fork and put the food in his mouth. This was not totally in vain. My efforts were to prevent him from allowing any other cleanup woman to take his blues away, but I am not the cleanup woman anymore. My rewards from Ray were massive rejection. I was only accepted by Ray as his unpaid servant who was not worthy enough for hire. I have fibroids to prove it.

I planned what I considered fabulous 40th birthday party for Ray. I cooked a full course soul food meal for a selectively invited guest list. The cake was perfectly ordered in the form of a record. I went out of my way all week long, while working and providing at home. I hid things to surprise Ray for his birthday party. However, I was the one surprised. The only comment that Ray made to me was that the collard greens were gritty. This is one time that I openly cried, and I was greatly embarrassed. I was taken for granted in front of guests, as I never recalled hearing him say these two words, thank you. I thank God that Ray is not God. Ray is not the one with the final say. Certainly, it is not over until God says that it is done. It is at this moment that I realize that Ray only gave me exactly what he claims that he was given; WOW! Perhaps that is all that he knows. Have mercy Father!

Not only did Ray remind me daily that he made a major mistake by marrying me, he was extremely strict with my daughters. Ray stated his hypothesis concerning children which is basically, what is the use when all children do is grow up and leave you? My rebuttal to that statement is not true. I believe that when you put in the work the rewards are great and the children always come back home, because home is where the heart is even if they never step one foot in your front door.

Rather than continually debate the issue, I just made sure that the girls and I went out, and especially on weekends. Another one of my requirements was to keep my daughters quiet on Saturday mornings, because he worked *four* long hours the previous night. While I was at work Monday through Friday in the mornings, they were in school. Sundays were not problematic because the girls and I attended church. We left the quieted house to Ray. Until dinner time, Ray was rarely at home, unless he was sleeping. Ray read the newspaper while he ate, as if no one was in his company. After which, he rested prior to working his four hour shifts.

According to Ray's thesis, when he was at home, my children were to be out of his sight and not heard. This did not work well for me at all. When I was not slaving as his maidservant, I felt categorized as the same, it was better for me to be absent. I just needed to leave evidence that I completed his heifer do-list. I believe that children should be seen and heard, and that they only have one childhood. Ray was not going to ruin it regardless as to the extreme measures that I needed to take! It was no surprise to Ray that I had children, nor how I feel about my children. Often, I found myself reminding Ray that I did not hide my children in the closet while we were "dating."

Something good came out of his attitude, as this is when it was impressed on my heart to take the girls out and do fun things with them to avoid at least one episode of drama at home. Often the girls and I went to the movies instead, or we found something to do. We stayed on the go, as we ripped and ran. After approximately three years passed, Doug finally accepted that I moved on by marrying Ray.

My personal belief is that Doug was intimidated by Ray's alleged status of power of being on the airways, and Doug did not know what Ray looked like, who he knew, or how Ray acted like either. Doug did not know how Ray treated our girls. I am unsure if that mattered, even though Doug allegedly was one of the physically toughest male in my world.

I was hopeful that Doug changed when I recognized the need/value that children have when both parents are in their lives. This awareness and desire to do the right thing was an attempt to have a father in my daughters' lives, as Ray was an uninterested party. I chose to violate the restricted court ordered visitations by contacting Doug to request if he would meet the girls and me at a local McDonalds to spend some time with his daughters. Doug showed up at McDonalds once or twice. Most of the time, Doug was a no show and this began to pull at my girls' heart strings.

Eventually, I stopped tormenting my daughters through these hardships by terminating the request and adhering to the court ordered visitations, which was not a condition that Doug chose to see the girls. At this point, I became more determined that my children would become my entire life. My determination grew to protect them, as best as I could. I recognized that I was the only human they really could depend on.

Although I refused to allow anyone to mistreat my daughters for as much as I could control, I continually mistreated myself by vain measures of attempting to change my situation into a marriage. One cannot blink their eyes and change something into anything that it is not…it is what it is.

Things are things; they do not change unless people convert them into something diverse. The fact that two people purchase a house does not translate to mean that one automatically acquires a home. Buying a home is a business transaction, but having a home requires that love be present. You can have the finest and richest mansion on this earth and *still* not have a home. You can be the most miserable person on this earth with many possessions.

Along Ray's journey, he stumbled upon a beautiful house in a ritzy area, and he made numerous attempts to convince me that if I could outline a way to get this house for him that he would convert his ways. He vowed that our "marriage" would work, which involved excessive toiling. This idea of getting this house for him mimics the word conditions. Remember, real love is unconditional. I am uncertain that I can tell you that I wanted this situation to work, or that I believed Ray's lies.

I just wanted peace which I thought would come with more space, and this house was much bigger than the apartment that we lived on the Main Line, which resulted in much more space. Feeling rather stuck in the mud, while attempting to dig myself out of the hole, I dug a bigger hole to climb into, but God brought me out of the miry clay! I began to literally and figuratively spin my wheels by working overtime. I was trying to make sure that my salary would compensate financing the place, as Ray did not have good credit at this time of our lives. I filled out the paperwork.

Ultimately, we got the house, but the abode did not maintenance for our problems; as a matter of fact, affairs continually worsened. All of our problems were swept under the rug, but the dust of disgust kept us all in a sickened state by hiding our problems while disrespecting their absolute presence. In this spot, I see myself becoming extremely allergic to nonsense. There was no respect given to the truth that charity begins at home.

Most of the time, my heart was worn on my sleeves while wiping my tears with the nearest cloths with hopes that no one noticed, but I know that God sees and knows all things, as He has kindly and completely wiped my tears about this situation. I did not have the essential tissue of life skills. I guess that you could say that I was really homeless, but I always found shelter in my heart for my children, as we moved on in our lives.

Shortly after we moved and got settled into the new place of residence, a new twist turned off more of my utterances when Ray announced to me that he fell in love with another woman. I whispered, "What did he just say?"

Ray was the master of setting off waves. After all, it is a part of his profession as a radio announcer. Finally, the inauguration of being sick and tired began. Without hesitation, shame, guilt, or embarrassment concerning this issue, I telephoned his mistress, Ms. Ashmond, and I brazenly asked her to take Ray as a full time job, not just on weekends after I dressed him, fed him, did his laundry, fixed his ailing credit, got the house, and took care of practically everything, as the list continued.

After this turn of events, I became even more silent, while tears fell, rest was lost, and my hunger pains were unnoticed. No longer do I totally agree that all silence is golden, as sometimes silence can internally kill you. *I* tried to change myself but not my views. I made an effort to be accepted by someone who obviously did not know how to love me. Ray did not choose to love, respect, and appreciate a good woman.

The excessive laboring did not pay off. This tactic does not work either a person likes/loves you for who you are. There is no way that you can make another person accept you. There is no need to make this meaningless effort. I was only wasting my energy when I needed to accept, respect, and love God, and then myself.

Meanwhile, I had multiple unsuccessful attempts at being accepted elsewhere; faithfully, I attended church and shared my abusive history, musical, and talents there, but I did not find a safe haven even at church. I was welcomed, but I put myself in a position of burn out in an effort of being accepted because of my talents, not just for who I was made to be. Pastors have the accountability to allow God to shepherd them as well.

My ex-pastor, Herman, of the church that I poured myself to, attempted to counsel Ray and me, but Ray did not keep it secret from Pastor Herman or anyone else that he made a choice and decision. He did not want to be married to me. It might have been wiser to pour into my alabaster box, but I did not

Chapter 4

Constantly, I was attempting to fill my emptiness with volunteer activities, but to no avail. I tried to be worthy of love. The worthlessness remained, even though I obtained so much from the giving. Actually, I became heavily engaged in burning myself out in the youth ministry and other functions. Consistently, I volunteered at my children's schools doing whatever anyone needed done. I desired to be accepted by any means because I did not know who I was; instead, I became burnt toast. Who likes burnt toast? I do not. Do you?

Certainly, I was unavailable to myself. I was too busy being there for everyone else. Yes, we are to carry one another's burdens, but I believe that God charges us with the responsibility of taking care of ourselves. If we cannot take care of ourselves, how can we take care of anyone else? When you are only a half of a person, how can you expect to have a whole relationship? Only God can make us whole and holy.

As mentioned earlier, with very limited time on my hands I found the time to shop until I dropped the bags and the available credit, but these things were only temporary fixes. However, it did not fix my indigestible pain. Not knowing what I was continually doing wrong vexed my spirit. I could not fathom why these calamities came upon my life. In *my reality*, I was only trying to be good to anyone and everyone who crossed my path. The Bible warns us **not to cast our pearls to swine**.

What I realize is that you cannot force love. If you do not know God, can you know love, even when it looks you directly in your eyes? Was I trying to give what I never had? No, my daddy loved me with all of his being. Did I love myself? No. I was abusing myself by attempting to love those who rejected my love by using and/or abusing me. If I abused myself, what did I expect from everyone else, LOVE?

Understand that a part of my problem was that I felt sorry for Ray, Doug, and others who crossed my path. Feeling sorry for someone is not equivalent to loving someone. It is okay to have sympathy for anyone but about things situations that they have no control over. Ray was thirty nine when I met him and if he desired to heal, he had roughly twenty eight years prior to my introduction to thoroughly deal with that issue. How could I just step in within a year or a few months and fill that void? Did I expect him to fill my void? Please allow me to remind you that neither drugs nor alcohol are a replacement for voids in our lives.

Later, Ray attempted to convince me that he was in a drunken stupor when he made his prior proclamation that he fell in love with Ms. Ashmond. My personal belief is that cowards have a way of telling the truth of their feelings and the alcohol or other substances that they abuse/use masks their craven behavior. It allows people to tell you the truth, but this is only my opinion. I learned that I have the right to change my opinion, and that an opinion is just that an opinion, and only God's word is absolute truth.

And so, the saga continues with the manner by which I learned that Ray was overly involved with another woman. Ms. Ashmond was not one of the women on the other line who I politely passed the phone to Ray. No one directly asked me if Ray knew that I would see and question the bill; certainly, Ray knew and totally disregarded my feelings concerning seeing the phone bill. Ray knew and obviously cared less that I would see the long distance calls on the telephone bill.

Ray was recuperating from a delicate surgery, while I ran home in between shifts to nurse him to get back on his health.

He was not at work, which is where most of the phone calls were probably made. The reason that I assuredly share this with you is because on one particular Sunday, while I was on my way home from church, I decided to surprise Ray with a visit.

I looked beautiful in my red and black sheik dress, but by the time that I left, my anger turned red. The security guard secured me and my daughters' entrance. However, the guard did not warn me that Ray and his third ex-wife were having a pizza party behind door number one.

Fortunately, Ray was on the air, which automatically locked me out when I twisted the handle, but unfortunately for them, there was only one way out of the studio. The third or fourth ex-wife and Ray were about to see my red face. I did not physically attack the female or Ray, but I did allow them both to hear my words, which I repented for the choice words. I thank God that it was not worse. Perhaps my anger would have been lessened, if I did not deal with so many issues regarding Ray.

Prior to my unexpected and unannounced visit to the radio station, a psychiatrist telephoned our house to warn us that a female threatened that she was going to kill Ray. Oh my God, what had he done? The story I cannot detail it all, but I went with Ray to see the psychiatrist who asked Ray if he received a nine to fourteen page letter that was hand delivered to the radio station by a particularly disturbed female. He replied, "Yes, but I just tore it up." This sounded awfully suspicious to the psychiatrist and me.

The psychiatrist informed us to be extremely careful around the holidays because this is a time when mentally disturbed people look for their glory. I feared for my daughters' lives. I did not know what this woman looked like. Ray pretended that he did not know this woman.

Soon thereafter, I learned that this was untrue.

Eventually, a friend agreed to visit this facility and meet this woman. I found out what she looked like. After all, who knew what Ray told her or what she knew about me and my children?

Certainly, other women did not have any respect for us, why would she?

The female was lonely and opened up with her story. This woman knew the hidden secret that Ray's car was purposely set on fire while at the radio station so that he could get out of a lease and have the ability to purchase another car. Another sad fact that this woman did not know is that the radio station co-signed for some of Ray's vehicles. I became livid because I knew that again, Ray repeated his behavioral issues.

Men, please think of the bigger picture before you put your family in harm's way. Eventually, we moved and Ray was contracted with a new radio station. I did not know what happened to this female; although, I do think of her often and pray for her too.

Meanwhile, back to the Ms. Ashmond; if Ray knew anything about me, he knew that I would question the constant calls to this number because another part of my many responsibilities included making sure that all of the bills were paid on time. I telephoned Ms. Ashmond, and she told me that someone did the same thing to her, and this was her excuse for doing this to me. Obviously, she did not heal and the saying that hurt people do hurt people rang truer to my ears. Ray's excuse was that he was drunk.

Ray knew very well that I was not foolish enough to believe that he was in a drunken stupor 24/7, but hung over and drunk or high again; yes, that was a high probability. Ray might have entertained the thought that I was naïve. Many times I acted in densely manners as a measure of distance. So, if you ever see me looking at you as if I am stupid, or if I give you a confusing answer, you know my exposed secret.

Unfortunately or fortunately depending on your view, Ms. Ashmond, who Ray daily and nightly telephoned from our house chose not take care of Ray's full time needs. She did not run to rescue me either. I am unaware of what happened to their "love," which he was saving for her, but it is my belief that his affair with the other woman did not work.

While Ray played the song "Saving All my Love," I rebutted with my favorite record at that time, "I'd Rather Be By Myself", even louder than he played his favored record, but my record never broke. Yes, we both acted childishly with no other method of communications than silly love songs. However, I do believe that the other woman heard and read between the lines of my spoken words. As by this time, I would gladly give her the little rock placed on my left hand.

My best assumption is that Ms. Ashmond had the ability to **calculate the total costs**, which is something that we each should do; then, I placed myself in another precarious position. Silently, I survived, without whispering a word to anyone with the exception of the rental agent at U-Haul Company. Gracefully, I backed that rented U-Haul truck into our garage and began loading it with my daughters' and my things. Meanwhile, Ray fell down on his knees, with tears in his eyes, and he began to beg me to stay, but the last straw weighed in.

I believe that the first straw was broken when he slammed Corrinna into the door and she began outrageously vomiting. The other very touchy situation occurred when Ray drove my vehicle because his top of the line vehicle was in the shop. He agreed to get Maria off of the school bus, and then, pick me up from work. The second straw broke when I received a phone call from Ray stating that Maria was not on the bus. I was frightened for certain. Where was my child? I began telephoning the school, crying, and praying. The sad part was that all Ray needed to do was to ask the bus driver where was Maria.

By the time Ray got to my job with my car, thank God the bus driver had competently done his job. As he swept through the bus to look for things that children left behind, the bus driver found my child, Maria, asleep on the bus. Thank God that bus driver checked the means of transportation on that day.

My cousin, James always reminded me to always go out like a lady. I did not have any spoken hopes of ever becoming happy.

I convinced myself that I was the basis of the problems; after all, these were some of the things that I was taught…even after all that I contended with.

During a prior counseling session while working through the demises of Ray a different counselor yelled at me, "You are not Jesus," but I *still* do have a burning desire to love Him with all of my heart! If this truly was Ray's problems that stemmed from his childhood, it was just that, Ray's problem, but I took on the responsibility of compensating for what I believed he needed. I was supposed to be his spouse.

Eventually, God gave me another special gift named Joshua, and I believe that I became an even better mother. However, my love for each child is equivalent. Love is what it is. According to I John 4:8, **God is love**, and according to John 3:16, **God so loved the world that he gave His only begotten son;** now, that is LOVE! God is a gentleman. **He stands at the door and knocks.** He never forces Himself on anyone, and where there is love you will surely find God. Later, and still without any hope of life, happiness, or being loved, I agreed to surviving in a ruined "marriage". I repeated until death do we part, although I was killed internally. S*till*, I could faintly breathe. I did have some life left, but I ventured for more than I could ever imagine. Rather, I convinced myself that *Ray's life* would be forever changed, and that our "marriage" could be rescued, if we could have a child together.

In the midst of all of our confusions, and without a plan as to how to figure this situation out, I thought that perhaps a child would change Ray. After all, my daughters' births had begun to change me. In addition, I believed that a child would rectify our situation; perhaps, I thought that a baby would link us together. What a responsibility to attempt to place onto an unborn child?

Ray agreed to accommodate my desire to seek help from a fertility specialist who informed us that we would never conceive a child without surgical implantation of sperm to fertilize the eggs. He diagnosed me with endometriosis, but there were other complications. In April 1982, I had emergency surgery due to an ectopic pregnancy, which only gave me a fifty percent chance of ever getting pregnant.

After my right fallopian tube burst, I almost lost my life. I did lose the baby.

Prior to this episode, I went to work at the bank every day. I did not have any other source of income during this time of my life. This bloodcurdling situation caused me to hemorrhage for eighteen days. I am reminded of the woman in the Bible, who had an **issue of blood, but she touched the hem of His garment and Jesus asked, "Who touched me?" Then He states, "Woman, thy faith has made thee whole."**

The ectopic pregnancy complicated conceiving, but it also created problems for Doug as well. Looking back, I never cried during Doug's severe beatings or while my tube burst. The doctors mentioned that I had a high tolerance for pain. I wondered if they knew my abusive history without my confiding in them. My mother had toughened me up pretty well before Doug came onto the scene.

At this time, I may have thought that my primary problem was Ray, but what I came to realize is that the chief problem was that I did not love myself. I did not know my valuation by God. My decrepit unworthiness assumed that I needed an indecent human to validate me. Whether you grew up in a carnal or dysfunctional family where God is not operating as the head, males are in bodies of men, and mothers are just that in title, or if you had some unforeseen occurrences befall you, make sure that you heal prior to rebounding into any relationship. I call this rebounding experience allowing a human to lick one's wounds. This friend is not love, as it is actually sick and can cause you death in the natural and or spiritual!

Something called self-esteem was as foreign as Chinese, which is a dialect that my mind could not properly translate, tolerate, or comprehend. It remained undeveloped much longer than it should have. My newly founded belief is that secrets create guilt, which creates despair, which creates neediness, and it continues to snowball until either an avalanche occurs or the **Son** begins to shine in your life and melts the hurts away by allowing you to see where it all began. My weakened state did not afford me the opportunity to correctly stand. I wobbled, and I failed to see because of the tears that clouded my distorted view!

At this point in my life, I did not choose to believe in myself, as this was not something that I was taught along life's journey. *Still,* I do not totally believe in myself, but I rather believe and trust God implicitly. I mess up somewhere along many minutes of each day. There is beauty in the fact that **God's thoughts are not like our thoughts, neither are His ways like our ways,** as stated at Isaiah 55:8-9. This scripture really speaks directly to my spirit. You see, God does not see me as I saw myself. Instead, He recognizes how He made me, and He recognizes the best in you too, even if you do not! **Everything that God made is good.** That includes you and me.

In all actuality, before my tube burst, I would have never asked Doug for a penny to support my daughters, but I forfeited my jobs when I was unable to work after my fallopian tube burst. With desperation, embarrassment, humiliation, and without any other options; silently, I applied for public assistance. I only received $1,000 worth of emergency food stamps, which is where child support giant grew.

Within four weeks, I forced myself back on my feet after taking a secretarial class, and I was rewarded with a job at a Power Plant. Also, I worked part-time taking care of a doctor's wife who was disabled. Pride allowed me to find myself newly employed before the doctors gave me permission to return to work.

I was too embarrassed to be on Welfare, even though I did not properly heal. In addition, I developed ulcerative colitis due to the amounts of stress that I underwent. I had two daughters who needed to be cared for, and my bills were adding up. Although

Welfare only awarded us a onetime emergency assistance, they insisted that Doug did not have an option except to pay child support. Rightfully, they wanted what was paid out on his children's behalf because he was a responsible party in making the decision to have the children.

The arrearages continually tallied as Doug ran to Bermuda. More importantly, if my boss did not insist that I close my teller window and immediately telephone the gynecologist, I may have lost my life. Once again, God said, "No!" Upon telephoning my physician's office, the receptionist notified the doctors of my condition. The directives were: do not pass go, do not collect two hundred dollars, do not receive a paycheck from the bank, and get into the doctor's office immediately. Later that evening, a minister from the church which I attended in my early youth prepped me for emergency surgery, as she worked in the operating room.

While Ray and I were attempting to learn if we could get pregnant, the fertility specialist ran tests and shared several of his educated opinions as to why he believed that I would never conceive again due to endometriosis and the prior ectopic pregnancy. Once he gave me his educated opinion, we did not return. Obviously, he did not know who I knew, someone much bigger than him, you, or I.

Instead, I decided to go through to the spiritual realm for a son rather than to go through the fertility processes of man. I am so glad that I made that decision. It was one of the best decisions that I ever made. The fertility specialist is not the hearer of my prayer. The doctor did not know why I needed and wanted the son that *I thought* would perhaps change Ray's life or "our marriage", but the reality is that God had an even greater plan for my life.

Maria and Corrinna grew up too fast. Perhaps, I was in denial that it was I who was in desperate need of love, but I did not know that my life was about to be changed forever. Nonetheless, I continually prayed for a son. In 1986, I began begging God for a son. With this petition, I made God some faithful promises, which included naming my son Joshua. I probably looked like a drunken woman just like Hannah, who was barren. Faithfully, each night, I kneeled down by my bedside while tears came streaming down my face, and I prayed unlike I ever prayed before. In essence, I unconsciously continued in the center of my grief. I bargained with God for a son. God is so faithful! He states in His words that **we can ask for anything that is in accordance with His will and He will listen and hear our prayer. If he hears our prayers then we will know that we have prayed according to His will.**

Specialists, doctors, and other professionals are only human, and they really do not have the last word. This is because God made them, and He designed their brains too! Ultimately, the last word belongs only to God and God alone. He is God all by Himself, aka **Elohim**, and for this I am so grateful

At times, Ray knelt down beside me, and for that I will always be grateful. I know for a fact that Ray recognized that God is real, powerful, and faithful too, because he witnessed the fertility specialist's testimony, my passionate tears and pain combined with prayers. Also, Ray witnessed the evidence of sufferings, more grief, and then he witnessed the answered prayer. God is so faithful! The Bible declares at Luke 11:9, **that if we ask and it shall be given; seek and ye shall find.** However, the Bible does not state how or when we will receive that which we ask or seek, nor does it state how long we will have it, but **love never dies.**

About two years later, on 8-8-1988, my life altered drastically. At this difficult time of my life, no one could have persuaded me that this was another worse day of my life, despite all that I already endured. While Ray was at house either sleeping or relaxing while playing the same old songs and games, I was on my way to the house while on a break from work. It was my plan to prepare dinner, as I thought that I would be working late that evening.

During this period of my life, I was employed by a world known courier service, which I considered the best monetary occupation in the world for the finest courier service company in the world. Great hours, salary, benefits, isolation in my truck, great co-workers, supervisors, management, customer satisfaction, and a fun job that I loved were just a few reasons this was my most favored paid career path. You can ask my children, I had many, way too many, employment opportunities! Attempting to meet their needs and wants meant that my feet needed to hit the floor and get paid.

While on my way home to prepare dinner, my most favored employment opportunity began its closing stages within one instant, but it did not crash my attempt to fight the inevitable. With my right foot securely locked on the brakes; slowly, I recall slightly applying my lusciously red lipstick, as I patiently awaited the flagger to prompt the stopped traffic. The traffic congestion was due to construction. As my car sat on an incline, within an instant, one second in time, a woman sped over the hill.

Obviously, she was not paying attention to the pattern of the trapped traffic, as I recall she fiercely cursed at her son. Rather than press her own brakes, her method of stopping resulted once she slammed into the back of my one and only brand new vehicle. A chain reaction of collisions occurred. My vehicle slammed into a van in front of me. As I recall every detail and each second in this moment of time, I recollect screaming "Are my children okay?" My children were not in my car, and I thank God for that every day. The rear end of the car was knocked pretty far into the front of the car, and there I was desperately waiting for someone to remove me from the vehicular accident and from my life.

Sirens were all around, but the most prevalent sound that I recall hearing came from a meek woman's voice which softly, yet firmly stated, *"Don't move."* On that day, her words did not affect me as much as hearing the alarms of sirens. From this day forward when I heard an alarm, I went into a state of panic, but eventually, God delivered me from that as well.

My head cracked the windshield. Later, I was reminded that if I did not have a seatbelt on that I would have died for sure, but once again, God said, "NO!" Perhaps this is the peaked point that my confusion began unraveling! Next, the EMT carefully removed me from my totaled car, as they added all types of body braces. Meanwhile, someone notified Ray as well. Ray's body arrived at the scene, and he followed the ambulance to the hospital; afterwards, he drove me to the house that I was attempting to get to in the first place. My vehicle was impounded, but I was sorry that I disrupted his schedule.

The next day, Ray drove me to a specialist, but it only took about twenty minutes before the physician politely requested for Ray to step outside. I was already undressed, which made this request extremely odd. With absolute polite bedside manners, the annoyed specialist calmly asked me why I accepted this type of mal treatment from Ray. This physician perplexed me, as I did not say one word except ouch, but I was waiting on the doctor's findings. He obviously was examining more that my physical injuries.

This doctor was a stranger. Neither Ray nor I ever met him, and we were only in his presence for twenty minutes. It was obvious to a professional stranger that love did not fill his patient's room or her husband's heart. This doctor was neither a psychiatrist nor a psychologist, as he is an orthopedic specialist.

Obviously, this physician had my best interests at heart, even though he was not my cardiologist. The only thing that I had the ability to do was allow the tears of sadness from my *silent* injuries to drip quietly, but I never said a word. God knows that I was internally and externally wounded. God understands the language of tears, but He also **knows just how much we can bear.**

Upon Ray and my return to the house, I pleaded with Ray to retrieve my prescriptions, which were filled at the local pharmacy. Within seconds, Ray adamantly refused. Reacting immediately, I telephoned my mother; although, she barely recognized the words that I spoke, as the pain did not allow me the ability to articulate my words. My sobbing stemmed from unbearable sufferings.

The distraught tone of my voice interrupted the lines of communications. Just as a mother does, my mom found the ability to decode my words and pain. There is no doubt that my mother is a tough woman, and she recommended some of the best therapy available at that moment. Although I was afraid, exhausted physically and mentally, and wounded, I took her prescription in its proper dosages. Mom did not offer to pick up my medications, but she did order her own prescriptions. She told me to get behind the steering wheel of the car, drive to the pharmacy, and pick up my own medications, while immediately facing my fears. I did just so.

Physical, mental, emotional, and financial pains overtook my body, mind, and spirit. I cannot guarantee which was worse during this time period. Often, I think that emotional abuse can be the hardest to recover from *if* the physical blows do not kill you. Unfortunately, they generally go hand in hand. Although I am a firm believer that no abuse should ever be tolerated, I believe that if recovery is an option, the physical abuse is easier to recover from than emotional abuse.

When the bruises disappear, the discolorations of the skin change back to the skin's normal color and the swelling from the knots do eventually go down, but when the color of one's heart is changed from red to blue from the verbal/emotional abuse, there are no visible signs that healing is taking place without resuscitation. Internally, I stuffed my feelings deep down inside of my guts, and they became attached to my heart, which resulted in a surgically removal of the pain by the best physician possible, whose name is Jesus! Did you know that **He is a rewarder of those who diligently seek Him,** and a restorer? He is also the Physician of all physicians, **Jehovah Rapha** and such **a wonderful Counselor?**

My best advice is to not tolerate abuse. If you have tolerated abuse, once you opt for healing it does and will eventually come from **Jehovah Rapha**, but you must trust that He is very capable. One must rely on His strength because our strength alone is not enough. Remember that *the joy of the Lord is our strength.*

I was exhausted from the extraordinary stresses of life, and I became even more desperate than previously. When my head hit the windshield I realized that surely, as an isolated injured party, I lost the minuet salvage value that I had to Ray. Once again, the pain is a beggaring description, but I can tell you that each breath that I somehow managed included tenderness. Please, do not do as I did, if you ever have these feelings; rather, ask God to breathe on you, and He will!

None of the above factors removed the verity that Maria and Corrinna continually depended on me for many things, as they did not have another alternative. *Still,* I continued to do all of the things that I thought that a good wife/mother should do. I attempted to keep the house immaculate, grocery shopped, cooked, sorted, washed, dried, folded, put away laundry, assisted with homework, took total care of my children, ironed, and paid the bills on time. I was ordered to bed rest. While I "rested" in the bed, I chose to allow Ray to use my body, as I thought that a good wife should. I related to Celie, in the Color Purple 1,000 times over.

Still desiring to be needed, I continued to offer music selections or "hook ups," for Ray's evening show. How could I possibly heal when there was no rest for my body, heart, or mind? Surely, I was waiting to exhale. Nightly, Ray mentioned to his listeners to lay their troubles on the radio because it was healing time. I was never able to feel those vibes. Yet, and *still*, life continued, days became nights, and holidays continued to come and go.

Mother's Day was always a very special holiday to me, as my supreme joy in life was being mommy. I love the job God gave to me as a mother. This is an awesome gig; although, it is not always easy. It provides super rewards while on earth. However, on this holiday, the gifts that I received from Doug or Ray lacked assessments to the value I had as a mother.

My ex-husband and Ray seemed to have no respect for this holiday, or should I confess that this statement reflects the lack of respect that they had for me? I have to acknowledge responsibility of my part, which is that I did not know who I was, and lacked self-respect. All things really do come to an end, with the exception of the Word of God. **Heaven and earth may pass away, but His Word will always stand.** In part, I agree with the statement that you cannot give that which you never received; however, I also learned that giving more than you received can support the healing process of one's own void(s). Which do you think?

I believe that we all can learn. Learning is merely a matter of choice. As a matter of fact, I believe that you and I can do or be anything that we choose to be because the sky is the limit. I witnessed God open up the windows of Heaven and rain down blessings on my life! Even beyond the Heaven belongs to God! Today, I chose to soar, how about you? I respect the fact that journeying beyond our comfort zones can be extremely painful. As Corrinna states, one of the Marines' sayings is that pain is a matter of the mind, and if you don't mind; then, it really does not matter.

As mentioned earlier, my first ex-husband beat me on for Mother's Day 1980. Approximately seven years later, I received another painful present on Mother's Day. I do not recall if or what material gifts that I received in between from these two males. For me, without giving respect, material gifts were immaterial. Regardless as to how small or big the ticket, the item was not valuable.

Ray's memorable special Mother's Day was presented over the airways, while he wished his mistress, Ms. Ashmond, and his mother a Happy Mother's Day. He knew that I, his relatives, and the tri-county area, were listening as he read a poem to his mistress from a book of poetry that I gifted to him. Another relative and I were flabbergasted, while not wanting to believe what our ears had just heard. The radio waves captured each moment in time, and there I was once again in pieces. The torment did not only consume my body, but it intertwined throughout my mind, heart, and soul. My depression set in deeper as I pressed towards full physical recovery. During this time, it was probably highly unlikely! My experience is that the mind weighs on the body, which hinders healing in the physical. I had several counseling attempts, but I was discouraged by clueless others, and/or the lack of progress at times. Some counselors just looked dumbfounded as I shared my stories. I believe that professional feedback is vital.

Many excessive amounts of weeds wildly matured which required a combing process. I was not sick and tired enough to toughen it out. My roots became so deeply kinky, and I had enough of my own negativity, but others continually attempted to project their fears and negativity onto me. I did not learn to reject their issues, which added to my own burdens.

Repeatedly, I went before the throne of God in prayer, but my biggest question of the second, minute, day, year, and even century was simply, WHY God? What did I do to bring these calamities upon my life? I really did not understand. Today, if I had to do it all over again in order to get this message to you that you might begin to heal, would I go through it again? I believe all of the things that I went through got me to the place that I will always know as home, Exeter, PA.

I would go through it without hesitation, but with an entirely different attitude, because if I did not experience these things, someone else would in order to allow you to learn from their mistakes. I find such reward finally understanding that **God never**

changes because you see, He is **Jehovah Shammah**-*The Lord is there, and He will never forsake you.* You see, He is **El Olam**-*The Everlasting God!*

Clearly, I see it was not even about me! The leading problem with this question was that I was looking for a reply from God that I would never receive, and a vicious cycle resulted until God said, "No more!" I was in so much pain that I really did not totally recognize what it was that God wanted from me. Somehow, I tried to believe that I did the right thing by marrying Ray. My heart's desire is to do the right thing before God and in front of my children. I am so glad that man looks on the outward appearance, but God sees our hearts!

Daily, it haunted me that Ray and I experienced sex outside of marriage. **The spirit is willing, but the flesh is weak.** I think that this doubly tormented because I knew that I did not fall in love with Ray. Did I have a fear of being rejected if I did not cave into his desires? That was bogus because I became rejected anyway. Perhaps, if I appropriately dealt with the particular rapes, then the result may have been different, but I was raped and continually raped, even in the church, again, and again! Also, I thought that being married or rather carrying that status would keep me safe from other men, but that opinion changed drastically.

In addition, I believe that I was trying to figure out a way to forgive myself for my sins. Perhaps this stemmed from my teachings of Pastor Andrews, as well as from sins of other and sins of my own, while attempting to eradicate them myself, but now I realize that task is impossible, as only God can forgive our sins. He is **Jehovah Mekoddishkem**-*The Lord who sanctifies you.* Meanwhile, my saga with Ray continues. I had a plan, but God had greater plan for me.

As I calculated the monetary costs of leaving Ray, I had several unsuccessful work attempts; then, I became successful at one attempt to return to work, despite my doctor's recommendations.

Also, I began college studies. In addition, I continued physical therapy, but *my plan* was to remain employed in an effort to get out of this thing aka "a marriage."

While I was returning to our house from a physical therapy appointment, I was involved in another accident. As you may have already considered, I did not properly heal from the previous accident. Immediately, my injuries were compounded and became more complicated, as I sustained more injuries.

Believe it or not, within two weeks, I was rear ended by a different car and hit a third time. At this point of my life, I thought for sure that I was doomed for failure, but what I later learned is that God really was working things out for my betterment. Please notice this, if I had succeeded at *my plans*, I would have returned to work. I would have left Ray forever without having the will of God carried out in my life.

You see, in the midst of these storms, I jumped ship without Ray; perhaps I was not listening to the captain of my ship, but I returned ashore because of the injuries I sustained in other car accidents. Was that woman's *still* voice that stated, "Don't move" telling me that I just needed to be *still*?

The initial recommendation of the doctor was that I should not to return to work; finally, this recommendation became an official order. Do you see any resemblance of the story of **Jonah, who ended up exactly where God had wanted him to be and doing exactly what God said that Jonah would do?**

Now, I had a new challenge. I became unable to maintain my apartment, which meant that my girls and I needed a place to live. There were only two options. I could return to the house that Ray occupied or return to my walk in sized closet at mom's house. With the quickness, I seized the first selection, moving back into the house with Ray. There were stipulated conditions which were not honored, as Ray agreed to sleep on the couch. The girls and I arranged to sleep upstairs. However, these stipulations were unmet.

Around February 1990, I realized that something strange occurred. I did not recall the torment of sufferings while having sexual intercourse. No longer did I continually pray for a son. I was not making any attempts to have a child. I did not believe that I was in any my physical or mental state that was either functional or stable enough to have the blessing reward of a child. I lost hope that my health would allow me to do this job well.

Eventually, I became a better mother, and I was not that bad of a mother with my daughters. Our thinking can be so wrong; truly, God knows best! Yes, I made mistakes, but I did my best to ensure that my children were full and fulfilled. They had self-esteem, were as healthy as possible, and they looked nice. Also, they were taught morals and values of God. Certainly, I ran after them in everything that they did, despite my illnesses. Most importantly I love my children as a mother should, and I did not fail to let them know this. Although, one of my daughters admitted that I may have shown them too much love. My counselor, Dr. Johnson, whom you will read about later, stated that he did not believe this was possible. Today, I am unsure that is possible!

Upon missing my very regular menstrual cycle, I went to the pharmacy to purchase a pregnancy test and the strip turned true blue. Beyond any reasonable doubt, I was blessed with being impregnated with a wonderful seed. As soon as the strip turned blue, I knew that I conceived a boy. Appearing to be out of my mind; immediately, I went to the doctor's office with the strip in hand.

Initially, I am sure that they thought that I was crazy, but my physician agreed to do a blood pregnancy test. Sure enough, it became factual that I was with child. Albeit, I did not anticipate that my prayer would be answered for a son during this laboring period. Somehow, I knew the instant that the stick turned blue that I conceived a son, and that his name would be called Joshua. **Our heavenly Father knows what we need before we ask**, this I am a witness!

Ray and I discussed my pregnancy in details. It was at this point when he decided that *he* would do better. Eventually, Ray changed his attitude towards our "marital arrangement;" eventually, he stopped abusing drugs and alcohol, but he continued to be absent in my mind. So, to say that Joshua only impacted my life would be an understatement. Based on the facts that I learned upon Joshua's life and death, many people's lives were impacted. However, Ray's attitude was not the only attitude that changed. My attitude radically changed. I kept silent while my mind was at work.

Ray went to my mother's home to offer an apology to my mother and step-father for being such a horrible son in-law, but they did not directly suffer from the anguish of his abusive ways. Of course, my mother heard my distraught voice time after time, but she continued with her life. I did not have a life, besides the lives of my children. This is another hidden mistake. My mother and my step-father readily forgave Ray, but in my heart, body, spirit, and mind, I was fatigued beyond exhaustion. I no longer wanted this thing we labeled as a marriage.

Even during the renewal of our vows, May 3, 1990 at the same time, 11PM we exchanged the first set of lies with a different preacher, who had counseled us and told us that we needed to renew our wedding vows. The pastor asked me if I would take this male to be my husband, my accurate response was "I will try," as I wept. This should have been a caveat to every person who was present; although, I was totally absent.

Neither an ounce of trust for Ray nor his motives were available. Certainly, I did not trust that all of a sudden Ray really loved me; *still*, I did not love him, this I knew for sure. I was naïve, but he skilled me about himself. I was learning who I was in Christ. An unresolved issue of mine snowballed during this time, and it added fuel to my fire of anger. It distorted my lack of distrust for the male species.

I do not find any reason to confess that I regret the eventual fall of this thing known as matrimony, but I apologized to Ray and God for my part in the final destruction of this totally dysfunctional state of affairs. However, for Joshua's sake I regret and possibly resent that Ray was not more proactive in his life. Regardless as to whether we remained together was the unimportant issue. Joshua was the most important result of this "union." I neither have power or any desire to charge anything to Ray's account, only God can do that, and He can remove the charges too; prayerfully, Ray has repented, if he understands the damage that his absences created.

Prior to Joshua's birth, between 1988 and 1990, a normal day for me consisted of continual laminating and questioning God about all of these accidents, incidents, and horrible relationships. I reiterate that Romans 8:28 is so true and we know that **all things really do work together for the good of those who love the Lord.**

For as much as I knew/understood about God, I loved Him and hindsight is always twenty-twenty, but if I had to go through the accidents again would I? The answer to that question is absolutely, but my attitude would be so different. I do agree with the statement that one's altitude can be projected by an attitude. Although I do not believe that God put me through those accidents, I do comprehend that He allowed these occurrences. Although I was desperate to take the blame for just being in the wrong places at the wrong times, I was trying to feel anything, but there are just some things that we do not have any control over!

God is omnipresent, and He has full control, authority, and power; this I do fully acknowledge. The more I learn about Him, the more I love Him and want to know about Him. I want to love Him even more than I do right now. In addition James' words at chapter 1 verse 16-17, **whatever Satan means for us that is bad, God can turn it into our good.** God answered my prayer request for a son with gladness; I can tell you this just by the quantity of joy that Joshua brought into my life.

Embarrassingly, I will confess that I asked God why concerning the timing because of my health issues and inability to steadily work. I know without a doubt that conceiving Joshua at that moment was the exact time of my life that God knew that I needed Joshua the most. I was sightless too, but I thank God for allowing me to notice! God is so good! I was blinded and broken in my mind, body, and spirit. My girls were growing up right in front of my cataract eyes, and my false treaty with Ray was severely broken. The third cord was never properly placed. Recall that **God is love.**

To tell you that my daughters did not need or love me during this time would be very dishonest, but they needed me in a diverse approach. At this time, my daughters' ages were eleven and ten, and they had their own set of friends and interests. They were not as dependent on me as when they were younger. Frankly, at that time of my life, I needed to be needed.

The "relationship or marriage" was destroyed, and I was severely shattered in all ways, but before it was completely defunct, Ray and I both eye witnessed a miracle. We both recognized that Joshua Wayne-Anthony Brown was completely a gift from God.

During my pregnancy, for a millisecond in time, I entertained the inspiration of naming my son Robert Wayne King-Brown, in honor of Daddy. Please note that it was Ray who warily reminded me of my promise to God, and I recognized that God was so faithful. I am so grateful that I did just so. I am so glad that I did listen, as Joshua lived out his name.

Chapter 5

One of the most precious and most blessed gifts of my life; Joshua Wayne-Anthony Brown entered this world on November 13, 1990 at 3:52 AM. Whether or not the sun was shining outside is irrelevant, but this day undoubtedly shined as the brightest Tuesday morning of my life; even though, I entered this world on a Tuesday. November 13, 1990 was the one day and perhaps only day that Ray and I ever walked in total agreement, as we witnessed the birth of this son that only God granted to us. After Joshua was examined by the physicians, Corrinna, Maria, and my mother became the next to welcome him into this world. Joshua is the most adorable and wrinkled little baby boy that I will ever see.

Joshua's original due date was assigned by the ultrasound as October 31, 1990 which was a scary thought, but Joshua arrived thirteen days later. Maria, who was eleven at this time, exclaimed in a childlike voice, "He looks like ET." Of course, I was offended, as from my point of view, Joshua is the most handsome male, baby boy, that I will ever lay eyes upon!

Joshua's forehead with a defined vein on his forehead had, his bottom lip, and teeth definitely are characteristics of Ray. The other parts of Joshua's face are clearly identified as my genes, especially his eyes, nose, and dimple! Joshua's black hair was slicked straight down, and he had the longest fingers and toes that I laid my eyes on and fell in love with. The doctor assured me that Joshua was going to play basketball because of his long fingers, and she stated correctly. From Joshua's ongoing activity in my belly, I already believed that he was playing football.

My heart already joined with his heart lying underneath mine, and he scored several touchdowns in my belly. The extra points that Joshua scored were effortlessly tallied, but the heart attachment became even much stronger than I ever imagined possible as Joshua was laid on my chest moments after birth. Immediately, our hearts become one at the moment I realized that I was with child. Joshua and I had an incredible connection from the very beginning. Often, I wondered if God whispered in Joshua's ear just how many times I asked for him, loved him, and wanted him before the formation of his huge heart. God reminds us that **before we entered our mother's womb that he knew us.**

I know that God knew even before I asked that I needed Joshua Wayne-Anthony Brown. God did not promise how long my borrowed gift would be on this earth. As long as Joshua's flesh was here, I kept him very closely tied to my hip. While in the hospital, I kept Joshua in my room. More than likely, I violated hospital policy. The nurses seemed to understand that I wanted to watch every breath that he took, because he took my breath away every minute of his life. The nurses or doctors never said a word contrary to my need to keep Joshua in my room.

As a matter of fact, whenever they needed to medically treat Joshua for any occasion, they would willingly return him safely to my room, after I watched them closely. Friday morning, the doctors discharged us to go to the house that we perpetrated as a home.

Joshua, Ray, and I returned to the house in style, as the radio station sent a limousine. The pediatrician released Joshua soon after he was circumcised early Friday morning, but because he did not urinate there was an added stipulation to bring him home at the time the limo arrived. I needed to call the hospital as soon as this christening occurred.

When we arrived at the house, I attempted to check the status of Joshua's diaper; instead, he urinated right away, and it splashed in my face. At least three of us heartily laughed on Joshua's first day out of the hospital. Immediately, Joshua brought many smiles, laughter, and contentment into our house, but it *still* was not completely a home, as the "marriage" continued in a very confusing and disruptive mannerism, just as my health.

While carrying Joshua and after I birthed this precious child, my attire was consistently draped with neck and arm braces, as pain induced my body. It spiraled totally out of control, just as our lives, if not more. As time progressed my prognosis worsened, and my hungry physicians identified several more surgeries that I needed in an effort to mend many of the damaged nerves and soft tissue injuries.

I was diagnosed with bilateral Thoracic Outlet Syndrome, bilateral TMJ, Ulna Nerve damage, Radial Nerve Damage, Carpal Tunnel and Fibromyalgia, for which there is no cure. Other diagnoses that I was labeled with were chronic pain disorder, Degenerative Disc Disease, and other soft tissue defects, and depression.

In an effort to begin the repair process, I had two arthroscopic surgeries on my TMJs, which were deemed unsuccessful. As a result, I needed to have bilateral open surgeries, which involved approximately fifty seven incisions from my head to my ears bilaterally, but none of my injuries kept Joshua from growing and flourishing.

Our welcomed addition to our broken family truly became an instantaneous blessing! Maria seemed to think that Joshua was her baby doll. Often, Maria carried Joshua on her hip, which meant frequently I had to correct Maria's thoughts and actions. Corrinna seemed to suffer from the middle child syndrome. I think that she thought that she no longer was the baby, but she knows that she will always be my baby girl, no matter how old she gets.

Joshua grew quickly. He began walking by the age of 10 months. He was very active and alert. Mine eyes have seen and touched one of the glories of God. I had never seen an answered prayer and a prevalent miracle in my lifetime. I held this miracle very close to my heart. Joshua and my most favored sleep position was his heart on top of my heart as an infant. I was too busy asking God where He was during the difficulties of my life; *still*, desperate for love, which is God!

Joshua grew as quickly as his vocabulary increased.

The teens that came to our opened home used to ask, "Where is Doggie, reading a book? Most people recognized the brilliance of Joshua, including his third grade teacher who recommended Joshua for the gifted program. Joshua loved the gifted program, as it challenged him. Sometimes Joshua's boredom did not persuade him to work to his full potential, and especially in math.

Joshua scored exceptionally well in social skills too, and he took that to another level. Joshua made friends rapidly. He befriended a smelly child. Joshua had all types of friends from a very early age; Caucasians, Blacks, Mexican, Indian, and more, because Joshua was colorblind to skin tones. Although many of Joshua's friends were normal, he had friends that physicians considered psychologically abnormal, but Joshua had a strong compassion for people! Joshua was well loved from the time that he was born, and it became extremely evident by the type of life that he lived! I am reminded of the scripture that tells us that **in order to obtain friends, one must show himself friendly!** Joshua knew that scripture without even reading it, because he lived it from the age that he began to play. You have no idea; unless, you really knew him. Truly, a gift from God.

Although we remained under one roof, our family was already wrecked. Ray remained in the house, but not necessarily in our live. Until Joshua turned four years old. Ray went out with a bang from the pain that I did not know how to manage. My ex-pastor, Saul, whom you will read about later, did not help either. My guilt, depression, exhaustion, and other factors asked Ray to depart, and he did just so.

Although things were happening with Pastor Saul, I believe that Ray had his own thing happening with Shirley at their church. I gave Ray the money for the down payment on his apartment. I prayed that the apartment complex would accept him into their community, and they did. I believe that Ray moved near Shirley, who became his girlfriend at some point. Eventually, she became another wife. Therefore, this was convenient for them. Prior to Ray's move, they were attending the same church.

Previously, while I was in the hospital having a major operation, Ray did not visit the day of the surgery, and he did not answer the phone the next morning; therefore, he did not realize or seem to care that my surgery was completed. He did not know that was I discharged. Needless to say Ray did not come to pick me up. As a result, I telephoned a co-worker/good friend, Matthew, who rushed to my aid and drove me from the hospital to the house. I did not know what was happening beyond the doors of our house.

As I opened the door and walked inside the house, used champagne glasses displayed piercing hints which sat quietly by the fireplace. My husband had partied the previous night, perhaps with another woman, as my children spent the night with my mother. The morning of my surgery, Ray obdurately refused to walk my daughters from the house to the school bus that morning, but a kind neighbor was willing to handle this menial task. She stated, "I just don't understand."

The soreness from the major operation did not compare to the sting inside my aching heart. I recognized the very limited possibility of ever properly healing while operating in this infected environment with Ray. I knew that it was over at this point in time, as this was the final straw, but now, I knew that the time came to get off this road that did not have an outlet. Silently, I remained until I could no longer continue stirring in the wrong direction while circling around the same problems without finding a new avenue. Giving up these living arrangements required many things that I had to bear alone, but I would rather tolerate my burdens alone without having a mate who was present but essentially marked as absent.

Actually, we both left the crime scene, because even though Ray could see, feel, and touch me, I bailed out a long time ago. Certainly, other than the love of my children, there was no love in our house. It is bad enough when one person just exists. It is another book to express what it is like to have two people who coexist, but have no life collectively or independently. Now, my children and I would have to work together as a closely knit family, but I did not recognize the struggles that would come physically, financially, and mentally of single parenting combined with all types of painful ailments.

To put it mildly, single parenting is very difficult for a healthy parent, and complications of single parenting manifested due to several serious surgeries and injuries. More often than not, I came home the same evening of major surgical procedures. I did not have *anyone* to aid me with my children. After the dangerous thoracic outlet surgery, a hospital bed was placed in our living room. Going up and down the steps became a strenuous challenge. Several serious risks were identified with having the thoracic outlet surgery, as the orthopedic and vascular surgeons had the seven hour task of scraping the scared tissue off of my jugular vein.

I was in so much pain, that death seemed to be the easier of the two choices. I believe that the risks of death were as high as fifty percent! One slip of the knife around the jugular vein was all that it would have taken. Again, God said, "No." Although, I was praying that I would not awaken if I had to tolerate the pain and it could not be lessened. My physical condition warranted the need for constant medical attention and assistance around the clock, but I did not have the money or medical insurance available.

My physician prescribed that I have someone to clean, cook, and take care of all four of us, but with limited income and support, this were impracticable. Fortunately, Maria and Corrinna supplied much help with Joshua and the chores, but they needed some type of life. My girls remained active in school sports, extracurricular activities, and they were decent students.

Although our lives were extremely complicated, we overcame the stresses of my illnesses by the grace of God. I used many medications; including but not limited to morphine. That is another book in itself. With massive amounts of pain already, the dangerous Thoracic Outlet Surgery caused me to develop a disease called RSD.

Reflex Sympathetic Dystrophy is a nerve racking disease, which is an irrational burning pain that is endlessly present. It is not only exasperating, but it hurts like Heck! It seems to spark my nervous system with a continual fight or flight message. If the spot is touched, I can and my blood pressure has literally gone off of the charts. As my tear filled eyes look back, I am sure that it was very painful for my children to watch me suffer, both mentally and physically and to witness my fatigue from the pain in my body, and the pains of life had to be extremely taxing.

I apologized to all of my children, but some things were out of my control. Maria and Corrinna had the choice to observe or leave and allow me to deal with Joshua and my pain alone, but their observations did not discount their maturing or growth. My pain did stop life. No one except God knows all that my children bared.

On Christmas Day, 1996, I received a call that my one and only true friend died. I cannot describe to you how I felt on this date. A few months later, in 1997, our lives tumbled totally out of control. These issues were not about men. I did not meet many real men since I knew my daddy, with the exception of Wayne and Victor, who did not cause me any pain or sufferings. Now, the most significant issues occurred with my children. Joshua seemed to be the only one who was stable at this time in our lives.

God shielded Joshua in so many ways, for which I am so grateful. Surely, God provided a hedge of protection around him all the days of his life, which was another answered prayer. Joshua lived a full of life. As a child, he played while he refilled on laughter, food, and liquids which resulted in positive energy; regardless of our circumstances that encompassed us. I consider all of my children a blessing even through the hard times.

Daily, I thank God for my daughters and their assistance with Joshua's livelihood all the days of his life. I do not believe that we would have made it without each other. Certainly, if the Lord was not on our side collectively we would have never made it. You never know what your gifts will do for you when you need them the most! Surely, Jesus did work it out!

Your children may be the only ones available to offer you room, board, shelter, and/or even a drink of water. My mother used to say it this way, be careful what bridges you burn, you may need to cross them later. Some people say do not bite that hand that feeds you, but the flip side of that is that one day your children may have to spoon feed you. My children became my world, and I am unsure that this is the healthiest way for anyone to live, but it is how I survived.

Survival can be a production of being raped or emotionally, financially, spiritually, and physically abuse, if you allow these horrific experiences to silence you. The traps of silence can have the isolation affect, which is very difficult to climb out, but remember that God is a deliverer.

Soon, after Maria's graduation in 1997, Maria made the decision to cut the apron strings quickly and abruptly. The strings were so tight that the sting was unexpected but it ended extremely thorny, which came from one of my most beautiful roses of God's garden. I have taken my portion of responsibility for holding on, as I was unable to let go.

I referred to Maria as my right hand! I did not know what I was going to do without her by my side. Likewise, she did not know of the financial situation or the total picture of all of the stresses that I was enduring. I still had a secret which I tried to keep sealed from everyone including myself, as I continued to suffer in silence.

Maria graduated from high school, and she became college bound. I am very proud to tell you that Maria earned a few full scholarships, and she decided to attend college at a not too distant University. Today, her highest and most favored degree is that of motherhood, which she is graduating summa cum laude! Eventually, Maria earned her Bachelor Degree of Science, and she graduated with honors of cum laude.

When I had very little money God saw fit that she was rewarded for her academic achievements, which was another rewarding time of my life. The Bible tells us to **give thanks and praise to God for all things.** Even though Maria did the hard work, it was God that supplied her with the brain, and for that matter with her life! Hallelujah anyhow, but sometimes things really do get worse before they get better.

A few months later, my baby girl, aka Corrinna was stricken with new challenges during her senior year. While in the senior high school, another student cut my daughter with a box cutter. Corrinna's face and her wrist were literally sliced open. In my opinion, the girl who slit my daughter's wrist and face actually attempted murder. Additionally, I am saddened to report to you that at least one of our extended family members was aware of this attempt and never gave a warning to her blood relatives. I guess that the saying that blood is thicker than water depends on the type of blood that one has.

Although charges were pressed, our goal was not for the female to be put away for life, but rather that Corrinna would heal internally and externally. Corrinna continues to have outward scars, but I give all praise to God that she has healed inwardly. May I tell you that I am so proud of Corrinna and how her life shaped thus far? I am proud of all of my children, just in case you did not identify that fact as of yet.

Both of my daughters graduated their senior year at the age of seventeen with National Society Honors. As an elected School Board Official, I suffered because of my stand on this position. However, I did not keep totally silently on all issues, as I exposed many of the secrets, while protecting my own. The reward was the privileged opportunity to hand Maria her diploma. I was able to lift my head with pride, as both of my daughters marched across the stage to receive their diplomas.

At Corrinna's graduation there was an extra measure of pride which came because her internal and external scars began to heal. Corrinna is a survivor. I believe that the person who cut my daughter and the extended family member are more of the actual victims. Medical insurance does not guarantee healing, but it is a necessity when one is injured or ill.

Ray and my divorce maintained stipulations that he was the responsible party for medical insurance and medical bills. Unbeknown to me, Ray eliminated our insurance benefits and had adamantly refused to purchase the COBRA option upon Ray's remarriage.

However, I am unsure if it mattered whether I knew or not. Corrinna was cut in the high school gymnasium during the beginning of her senior year. When the EMT arrived at the school, Corrinna was rushed to the hospital with her face and wrist slashed wide open. I did not have health insurance. Unfortunately, I was not forewarned of either occurrence.

Many life lessons were established during this episode of our lives. As I entered the high school gymnasium, I bawled unlike I ever wailed in my lifetime, as I kneeled on the hard wooden floor beside her. I was wearing a black and red hooded sweatshirt, a pair of jeans, and sneakers. The picture is as vivid as yesterday.

The shock of seeing Corrinna lying on the gymnasium floor with blood gushing out of her face and wrist is beyond articulation, but the fear of losing her and the dread of the harm that these wounds could potentially cause internally for the rest of her life were most severe. They were only fears, even with the reality that this nightmare experience occurred during broad daylight. At that moment, having no medical insurance and how the bill would be paid were my least concern.

This insurance dilemma did not deter me from demanding immediate precise medical attention for my daughter. I telephoned a friend, Mrs. B., who was my daughters' and my high school guidance counselor. As God would have it, Mrs. B happened to be on the hospital board. With boldness and as if I was the richest woman in this world, I did not have any urges of hesitation while I demanded that the best plastic surgeon in the area be made available. Did I trust God again without recognizing that is what I was doing?

My Father is definitely rich, and He did immediately provide the best plastic surgeon. Eventually, He provided the means to pay the medical bill. Finally, the finest plastic surgeon in the area arrived and several hours later, with several hundred stitches, Corrinna recovered from surgery. It was the most grateful moment to see her face with the exception of the day I first saw her face. Although the bandages blocked Corrinna's view of me, I am positive that prior to her awakening from the anesthesia that Corrinna knew that I would be right there.

Corrinna remains one of the most beautiful females in this world; she is definitely a star survivor. Without inclinations of how I was going to pay these medical bills, these delinquent accounts were not my biggest problems. Eventually, we worked through each ounce of pain which stemmed from the internal wounds that this crime committed. The outward scars represent the amounts of healing and a reminder that we never would have made it without God in our lives.

Actually, I am unsure as to what happened to the little girl who cut my daughter or our relative, but my hope is that they too have made a full recovery from their pains of distress and anger, as this really was a senseless crime over a boy. As the tides continued turning, we lost our home. Many thought that I was afraid because I identified many truths about the deceptions within the school district in the town that we lived in, but the fact remained that Corrinna had the capability of finishing her education in the school district because of the time period that we relocated. Fortunately, some more good came out of serving as a School Board Director despite all of the bad! Carefully, I studied the laws of the Department of Education. Corrinna was able to operate under the benefits of being homebound. Excellent teachers came to our old home before the doors were locked, and Corrinna had one on one contact with her teachers, which became an awesome experience. Corrinna received a private education in a public school district.

Corrinna and her teachers did an outstanding job in completing her education with honors! Some of the courses that I recall her having during this time were Physics, Trigonometry, and Pre-Calculus. She ended her senior year with the honors. The costs were astronomically high, but I did not pay a dime for her education. The school was responsible for this bill because the horrific crime was committed inside of school property and her blood was on their gymnasium floor. The nonmonetary price was extremely hefty, but Corrinna trumped the odds and excelled tremendously. Her education was tenable, while her internal and external sutures slowly healed. Eventually, after much hard work, Corrinna became more secure than I ever witnessed, but our house was unsecured.

Not only did my daughter have massive amounts of medical bills, but my medical bills piled up from the involvement of more car accidents, and not being personally medically insured. I stopped counting at car accident number seven. Once the motor vehicle personal injury coverage was exhausted, I did not have any other medical insurance. My prescriptions were outrageously priced and with no medical coverage at times there was nothing that I could do except to suffer. Eventually, I had a morphine implant installed, but that story is two different books.

There was never a choice that I needed to make concerning whether my children would eat more than peanut butter and jelly, but there were other choices that had to be made verses if I would get a prescription filled, and I continually suffered. Concerning who got what they needed, my children and their wellbeing humanly came first. For that, I do not offer an apology! However, I do see that I was totally imbalanced, but the rewards are great. Funds were unavailable to pay all of my costly medical expenses or all of the bills created by the thieves that entered our lives by night. My children were not the only ones who thought that I had a tree in my back yard where they imagined that I went to pick whatever amount of money they wanted for that day. However, I did not have ATM stamped on my forehead either. *Still I* do not. As of yet, my name remained unchanged because I continued to sob. Through each tear, God gave me the strength to get things done.

The hospital/doctor that treated Corrinna threatened and possibly sued me. Her biological father, Doug was relaxing in Bermuda. God stepped in again, and a not-for-profit agency eventually paid all of my daughters' hospital/doctor bills in full, while Ray was nightly professing his love to his new wife. We continued to struggle. Do not think that God did not see every tear! Oh it is so true that God will wipe every tear!

Filing for bankruptcy was not an option. I had already petitioned the court for bankruptcy under chapter seven in 1996 or 1997; therefore, this was an unavailable alternative. I made several attempts to get my medical bills taken care of, by going to court and attaching them to arrearages. The problem with attaching these paid medical expenses to arrearages was that they were to be paid for first. If I didn't have the money, at times, I went without the medical treatment.

At times, doctors performed the services. Then, they billed me, and I had no clue how they were going to get paid. When I could pay, it took a lot of time to have the money returned. After appealing to the court for restitution, I would only receive a small monetary amount per week. So, I was in a no win situation with man anyway.

I did not abruptly drop the ball which went into the gutter aimlessly. I did put forth the effort to make a strike. While I was supposedly healing from surgeries, I continued unsuccessful work attempts. I petitioned the courts without legal representation to have Ray satisfy his obligations, and especially, I continued to pray.

I initiated and attended court hearings because of Ray's contempt of court for discontinuing the health insurance. My hope was that Ray might be merciful. I put cuffs on the judge's hand by pleading with the judge not to incarcerate Ray. Somehow I did not think that it would be advantageous to anyone; besides, I was in the midst of learning that God would make a way. I just did not know how, but God's grace and mercy really are sufficient. He is a great teacher.

I have yet to receive medical coverage from Ray, and I did not get reimbursed for my outstanding bills. However, God is *still* good and in full control, and life continued. During this crucial time of our lives I examined another broken pattern! I praise God for deliverance. I telephoned my pastor at this time, named Saul. I was on heavy amounts of pain medications which did not help with the amount of pain, but manifested my depression.

I confided the ill treatments that I received from Ray, and that I no longer wanted this thing that was called a marriage. I openly admitted to Saul how much I missed the love from my father, which was a HUGE mistake! All of the things that I received in return I will not share the half, but I will share that he stole money from us.

Until I confided in Saul, I had never gone to the casinos, but I quickly learned why people get hooked with the bright lights, ringing bells, and the temporary fix that winning money brings. Also, I learned about the anger, humility, and desperation that comes when one losses all of their money. The bright lights and attention were a distraction from the pain and what was going on, but only temporarily.

Angrily, I witnessed Saul take the manila envelope offerings out to gamble money. However, what I learned is once we give money from our heart, it is not on us what others do with the money that was collected. I am grateful that the burden was released because when you give, God gives back so much more; regardless as to how one's money is spent.

While we were at the casinos he took money out of my ATM account, which was more than I had agreed upon. I used to be naïve too, but preachers are only humans. Then, without any evidence of shame, guilt, or repentance, he rolled the dice and hollered, "The baby needs a new pair of shoes," as if he did not do anything wrong.

Suspiciously, I wondered why he never exposed my receipt from the ATM. but I did know that I would reconcile my bank statement upon its arrival in the mail. I questioned him about the amounts that he pilfered. I offered to accept that he stole the money if he only admitted to doing so. In addition, I agreed to make him an authorized user on my credit card account, because it was my understanding that the church was putting padlock procedures on the doors and stopping payments to him. Ironically, it is my understanding that the church and I experienced the same actions from Saul.

This male audaciously overcharged my credit card that I allowed him to use on behalf of his family. He seemed to think that his behaviors were extremely funny. He made light of the situation while he laughed about the belts, boots, and unnecessary items that he went over the limit with my credit card. He did not stop laughing and joking about the situation until the judge ordered him to pay full restitution.

For Saul's sake and to avoid public humiliation, I made an attempt to halt the hearing, at Saul's request. The Bible tells us **to**

take the accused person in the witness of two people and then before the church, and if he does not repent, then treat him as **a Gentile**. In addition, Saul quietly petitioned me to remain as he was undercover with news reporters. I believe that my only comment was that I was playing the role of a Good Samaritan. At that time, I attempted to keep silent on the issue, but the newspaper already reported the story.

To my knowledge, Saul did not have any income, and I gave him usage of the credit card in the event that he or his family had an emergency; instead, he selfishly purchased items, which were luxury items while I needed medication. Then, he irresponsibly went over the limit on my credit card amount, but I irresponsibly agreed to a portion of this three ring circus.

I am so reminded of the Bible story of where Jesus walks into the temple and gets angry because people were selling doves in his house. Jesus stated that the **place of worship was turned into a den of thieves**. I believe that on that day that God turned that temple upside down.

Just as God forgives all of us, he can forgive Saul if he repented. Some people think that people need to apologize to people, but I believe the most important thing is to ask God for forgiveness. However, the Bible states that **if your brother has any ought against you that you are to take your gifts from the altar and reconcile with your brother**. For all I know, the light may have shinned upon Saul.

Upon appearing before the judge in an effort to stop this madness from spreading and recontamination of the community, the judge stated, "Sorry ma'am that case was already settled because the defendant failed to appear, and this resulted in a judgment against him." Sealing of the deal may have been the only reason that I was eventually paid.

Saul and I met at an attorney's office upon his request. I assume that he wanted to keep this knowledge silent; besides, to my awareness, an attorney cannot enforce a written agreement.

As God would have it, Saul selected the attorney who represented me for the PFA from Doug and he had worked on my behalf during the potential annulment process with Ray. The attorney knew of the abusive ways of the males of my past. Additionally, he knew me too well as Ms. Understood.

My good intentions did not get me very far. The attorney read my well prepared organized and honest statements. He spoke wisely chosen words to address Saul. The attorney notified Saul that he believed that what I said was true. I had a lot of solid evidence. The attorney gave Saul his spiritual and/or legal council that he needed to take a seat from the pulpit, but Saul had his own agenda and refused his attorney's advice; although, allegedly, Saul had agreed to do whatever the attorney suggested.

My girlfriend Carrie was present. She heard the full statement of the accounts that transpired, which included much more than stealing the money and abusing the credit card. Carrie said these words to Saul, **"The blood shall be required at your hands."** That following Sunday morning during their services, her words appeared to be confirmed. I heard through the grapevine that My Aunt Elaine, who continued sitting under this preaching, threw up blood throughout the sanctuary, and she was rushed to the hospital via ambulance services. For many who heard Carrie's remarks, that was the end of fellowshipping with this male known as a pastor, Saul.

When my son died, I reflected on this episode and how it was one of the incidents that stirred me and my family away from churches, as it became painful to crawl through the doors of any church. In addition, I thought about the Saul of the Bible, **who was on the road of Damascus, and a light was shined on him and Saul had an encounter with God and his name was changed.**

I shared my full testimony concerning Saul with a pastor during the tears of these pains. During my tearful testimony, he said these words to me, "It is a wonder that you ever walk through the doors of anyone's church." For a long time, it was extremely painful to walk into a church. I cried every time that I stepped foot into a church, but my motives were simply to heal and to follow God, not man.

I believe that Satan attempted to silence me all of my days, but today I can stand confidently and say that **surely goodness and mercy shall follow me all of the days of my life, and I will dwell in the house of the God forever**. I will only allow God and the husband that God has chosen for me; if He so chooses one, to set the pace.

Please allow me to share this with you that upon attending counseling, my counselor, Dr. Johnson, became a bit annoyed with me because I shared that I had felt the need to apologize to Saul for Saul's crimes and deceptions! That is referred to as acceptance of faulty guilt. Please don't misunderstand, I accepted responsibility for both of our sins in this situation, but I am only accountable to God for what I do wrong.

Perhaps, for the first time in my life, I only stood up for myself without actually attempting to do that. I had the nerve to feel badly about doing it. I guess that you could say that I was out of my comfort zone! However, I felt that this was another sad day for those of *us* who were allegedly representing Jesus Christ. For a long time afterward, I did not want any parts of the church. Notice that I said with the church, as I did not mention God. *Still*, I yearned to know Him.

My best friend, Joyce, and I received letters stating that we were no longer members. The letter was based on the fact that we did not pay our dues, but the fact of the matter is the dues were overpaid! Jesus paid it all! At this time of my life, I did not have any interest in any church. In all honesty, I was uncertain if I ever would. Today, I thank God that we were thrown out! Guess what God did in the interim of this event and while writing these words to you? I never imagined that I would ever receive mercy from this same credit card company.

Once the credit card was over the limit, the bank repossessed my credit card. My credit score was viciously attacked. The balance was to be paid immediately, and the interest rate increased tremendously. Although I could not afford this bill, I paid it in full and sent my card back to the credit card company, as it was frozen anyway. The bank applied all of these rules and charged it all to my account! I am so grateful that God did not charge this to my account!

After reestablishing my credit, one bank merged with another, and another bank had merged with another bank. Today, I have the exact credit card company which took my credit card from me with an increased credit limit. God is so faithful, and all I needed to do was to wait on Him.

Meanwhile, I was learning how aimlessly the school district appeared to be spending money. My anger resulted in a mission to stop what I felt was abuse of money that the taxpayers supplied. Thus, I made up my mind that I was going to do whatever I needed to do to stop this recklessness within this city. I thought that the majority of the money was to be put aside for the children's education. In my opinion, my children were being cheated just like everyone else's child in more ways than one! This is one opinion that has not changed, and I attempted to make a change.

During my second attempt to win a seat of the school board, I won a seat on the school board on both tickets by a landslide. The people spoke in the election, but there were many challenges for me to overcome. Maybe people were ready and willing to see a good fight for a change, and I thought that I was ready to give one. I did the best that I could with what I had to work with.

The school district did not provide many modern text books. The purchase of library books was limited, but school board members were enjoying perks such as free dinners and unnecessary traveling expenses. As a member of this Board, I refused to sup with the administration or other board members on these accounts or unnecessary travel. You can believe that the administration and some other members were as hot as the food that they ate at the taxpayers' expenses.

In addition, prior to getting on the board, I learned that the district was collecting money for a certain program, but they did not offer this course to the students. Where was the money going? Would you believe that was a mistake? I assume that is a possibility. The more I learned, the more frustrated, angered, and disgusted I became. Again, I began spinning my wheels in circles. The district was already financially depressed, even more depressed than I was if that is possible.

I realized that the community members did not have complete understanding of my concerns. Many subjects were talked about in private meetings, which were a violation of the Sunshine Laws. This angered me even more. May I share with you that some entity was charging; and perhaps still is charges students to ride a yellow school bus. I believe; according to what I read, this was strictly against the LAW of the Department of Education! Continually, I voted against the administrations' large salaries. Our children hungered for an education. The money was limited, and is not school supposed to be about children?

The community members may not have understood, but I guarantee you that those other eight school board member, the administration, audit teams, attorneys for the school board, and those reporting the news had an understanding of my one and only purpose in doing the things that I did. One board member constantly told me, we must look at the bigger picture, the children. My concerns were for the sake of our children and taxpayers' money. Everyone may not have understood my presentation, but the end result was that I was fighting for the right things. If people read their packets, they too would have understood. How does one void checks within a treasure's report and still subtract them from the ending balance?

Still, I get frustrated writing about it. However, a vote of one or two out of nine does not go very far on the school board. To change things, there needs to be a majority vote. In this case, a vote of five to four was needed when all members were present. Please explain to me how does a district get away with all of these things? Simply stated, unless taxpayers get together and file a law suit, there is not much anyone one person can do. You must have a majority vote to make change occur. Ultimately, I believe that prayer changes things.

I read every ounce of material that I was able to get my hands on, even material which was not put in our packets. How does anyone make a sound decision on their vote without thoroughly doing their homework? How does anyone expect our children to be successful? One woman, another board member asked me, "Where do you get the time to read all of this stuff?" My question was how could we not afford to read the materials? I assume that they believe that the sky is their limit, but we all must see Jesus for ourselves. The consolation is that **every knee shall bow and tongue shall confess that Jesus Christ is** Lord!

Perhaps many in the community did not know the real truth, as the meetings were practically empty. When I summoned a few taxpayers to come out, one lady yelled out and called me a token while I was working hard on behalf of this community, but God knows all things. I was trying to bring awareness to the taxpayers that charging to ride a yellow school bus was illegal according to the law, but the problem is that the school board is the highest authority. I am of the opinion that if a law suit is not filed, that the district continues to rob the people of their rights. Many people within this district cannot afford to have their children transported, which is the school's responsibility. So, I assume that filing a law suit is impractical thinking unless someone is generous to do this pro bono.

By the end of my journey, I surrendered because someone threatened to have my one and only son, Joshua, taken away from me. Nightly, our security alarm went off while alarmingly my children trembled. I threw my white flag of surrender, but it is not over until God says so. Morning finally came, and the local editor printed a very nice favorable editorial stating that I was always fighting for the taxpayers. I was only the messenger. Today, I realize that this battle totally belongs to the Lord, and I do not believe that it is over. It is never over until God finishes the battle. I believe before it is all said and done that God will clean this town/state up to its full potential, which is one of my prayers in the name of Jesus.

Even after Saul stole my money from my account, borrowed unreturned money, and abused my credit card, Saul spoke these words to me, "You really are a beautiful person. It is sad that more people do not know the true you." Nonetheless, his kind words were spoken well after this incident when I tearfully apologized to him while I expressed my concerns that our actions hurt rather than helped this polluted community. My goal was to counter some of the poison in the community. I have two words to say, good intentions. Recall that the Bible tells us **to put on the whole armor of God, which includes the helmet of faith, the breastplate of righteousness, and the sword is the word of God.** *Remember this scripture too;* **no weapon formed against us shall prosper.**

The three thousand dollar amount of money that Saul was obligated to repay was not the true issue. The money was eventually paid in full by him, as it was court ordered. However, the more important issue became the credit that I was attempting to reestablish. It perished quickly, and the large bill that I had to pay took a lot of money out of my pocket, as it was nearly $2,000. Once again, I waited to be reimbursed. If I had the available credit, it would have been more than enough to save our home, but what Satan means for our bad, God turns it into our good!

At that time, my feeling was that having to pay this debt that I indirectly piled up took food out of my children's mouths without one concern or thought, but our new replenished grapevines grew plentiful. My children have never hungered nor thirsted. At the drop of a hat, I could stand up for the sake of my children, but when it came to me, I did not have any desire to fight, but my episodes with Ray spurred me.

Unfortunately, I only needed less than $1,000.00 to make the mortgage payment, but I never said a word to a soul, not even to my mother. Silently, I continued to cry.

Once again, I was suffering in silence, but God sees every tear that you and I shed.

I was accused of moving because I was afraid for all of noise from rocking the boat on the school board. This reason could not have been more farther from the truth. I assumed that I kept silent due to my pride which resulted due to my guilt, embarrassment, and shame mixing with depression. However, God knows and see all things, and He is so wise! No one, except **God All Mighty, El Shaddai**, knows the troubles that I have seen, and that is fine because **He is the one who will ultimately restore double for everything that has been taken away!**

After the realization came to light that we were in jeopardy of losing our home, I did not see any other way out, except to leave prior to the date that a sheriff may have come and locked us out of the house. Monetarily, I became flatly broken after the medical bills piled up. Money and credit card abuse were also a factor. Nonetheless, I continued to be the lender, not the borrower, especially for Carrie's sake.

The check that I eventually asked Ray to sign was returned from the mortgage company because I filed bankruptcy. They refused to accept anything less than full payment. I was forewarned that the mortgage company was ready to foreclose on the property. At that time, I did not have the money. Before the mortgage company moved further, I began looking for another place to call home.

My apartment search did not extend beyond the area where I became acquainted with the fact that a quality education existed. While serving on the school board, our school educational role model was the district that I desired to move. What I did not know at this time was that more importantly than the education, which was a definite concern of mine, that we would find so much more than a quality education. Eventually, we were found by some very good people of great class.

Although, I must admit that I whined like a slurring drunkard who sang a song full of Ebonics entitled, "Woe is I," until my solo was warped and it could no longer be sung or played. Now, I sing *Grateful by* **Hezekiah Walker,** *Never Could Have Made It by* **Marvin Sapp,** *God Favored Me by* **Hezekiah Walker,** *and my favorite song of all songs is Wipe Your Eyes by my favorite artist,* **Joshua Wayne-Anthony Brown.** Today, I stand firmly and I utter these words, when you cannot see any way out of a way, you must know that God is *still* on the throne. You see, He is **Jehovah Jireh,-The Lord will provide**! Now, I ask why not me?

After filing bankruptcy, losing the right to my credit card, losing the house, and the massive amounts of medical bills for Corrinna and me, the condition of my credit score matched the poor dilapidated neighborhood that we moved into, and I became very unhappy and embarrassed concerning our surroundings. However, I did move into the community that had a great school district.

I had never lived with roaches, bugs, or mice, but there can be a first time for everything. God will work it out, if you allow Him to do just that! I am a witness! We relocated into an apartment building which I actually believe should have been condemned. In my opinion, this apartment complex was worse than the projects, although they collected a decent amount of rent.

There is a high price to pay when you do not have good credit. Even after cleaning with bleach and disinfectants, setting off bombs, the pests *still* were visible during the light of day. I despised living in this type of milieu with a passion. Undoubtedly, there were some very good reasons why we moved into this community. **A good man's footsteps are ordered by God!**

We only tolerated these horrific conditions for about two months, and we were granted the ability to move again due to a different reason. We may never know what God is doing behind the scenes. It is not our job to know everything that He is doing, but it is our task to just trust Him!

Despite the pains, I remained proactive and intertwined in Joshua's life, which included but certainly was not limited to his education. At my whit's end, I sought the advice of Joshua's school guidance counselor concerning a situation that I could not grasp. Joshua was only in first grade when his guidance counselor promptly advised me to move my son away from our surroundings, but these deplorable conditions did not have anything to do with the pests. My embarrassment concerning the rodents did not permit me to express a concern to the guidance counselor about these problems. I was highly concerned about inappropriate behaviors from another child who resided in the same apartment building.

The elementary school guidance counselor became extremely agitated that my son lived in the same vicinity of one particular child, who lived in this same building. The mother was extremely abusive as she dealt with demons from her bipolar disorder and other dysfunctions. I witnessed her chasing someone with a knife in her hand, what a frightening ordeal!

I pray that the child and the family had an encounter with God! Immediately, and with urgency, the guidance counselor urged me to move once again. I became more alarmed by the counselor's reactions than any pests, and I always thought that my greatest phobias were a strong tie between mice and heights/flying.

Without hesitation, I placed my concerns in writing to the landlord, who immediately addressed my concern. To my surprise, on that day, the landlord immediately responded. They notified me of a vacant space for rent, which I believe was less expensive.

Certainly, the conditions were not as deplorable as the apartment. However, due to a lack of credit, the area was not the best neighborhood in this county, but God has a way of moving you up in the world. He really does open doors that no man can close.

Without any reservations, the landlord offered another place to us. My mother taught me early in life about the importance of credit, just as she taught me to always keep my word. Sometimes things are just out of our control, while other times, we make bad choices and decisions and we can pay dearly, even without having funds available.

Although I do not like to move, we happily packed our belongings and moved to higher heights. I smile, as I picture Joshua patiently sitting in the van as we moved, once again. Can you visualize the hand of God in any of our situations?

To describe the trailer at its best, it was very old, and the outside was yellow and white. Eventually, we reconstructed the problematic yellow dingy paint by covering it with a black glossy paint in an effort to mask the deficiency of our new place called home. Toleration of roaches and bugs was no longer a concern at our new place known as home, as we carefully shook and cleaned our belongings.

Field mice, especially during the winter, appeared to be very common in this vicinity. I believe that this was a factor because of the amount of fields, trees, and land. Actually, I was too embarrassed to invite my mother to my home, but we moved back up in the world, as I paid my rent on time. As soon as another much nicer place became available, Joshua, Corrinna, and I were able to move again. One thing is for sure; wherever we moved, we permitted love to open the door first, as everything else was secondary.

An additional benefit included moving rather close in distance, both miles and emotionally, to Aunt Louise's home. I had the wonderful blessing of learning and loving her even more, as she shared much of her insight, wisdom, sweet potato pies, recipes, and love which were all pleasant experiences. Aunt Louise was extra specially made for me, as *she was a major player in my life.*

Chapter 6

Please recall that Corrinna did not return to college in 1999, but after I got back on my feet, she sounded the alarming provoking announcement that she signed on the dotted line with the military. A portion of Corrinna's childhood dream included becoming a Marine, but I refused to allow this dream to manifest by refusing my permission while she was underage which resulted from my fears.

Both of my daughters graduated at the age of seventeen, but once Corrinna turned eighteen, I had no authority when it came to her commitment to servicing our country. The only thing that I could do was to begin to pray and cry once again when she enlisted as a First Class Private Marine.

At times, the only sounds I could make were sighs, moans, and groans, but I believe that God hears and understand all types of sounds. I was fully anxious. Many unsettled fears became the beginning of a new internal war.

Also, I know that He is a heart regulator.

One positive side of this endeavor was that Joshua and I were able to drive to Paris Island, South Carolina for Corrinna's graduation from boot camp. Joshua and I had more bonding opportunities as we traveled to various states to see his sister, Corrinna.

Evidence of Corrinna's maturity manifested after her boot camp training. Corrinna became much more disciplined, and she appeared to have worked out many of our frustrating ordeals. God brought her from a mighty long way! All praise belongs to the Most High!

At times, it was appropriate for Joshua and me to drive to various states, but traveling to some states demanded that we fly the friendly skies. Joshua did not appear to be frightened of flying. It is possible that he acted bravely while busily internally laughing as a result of my past fears of flying. Should I say that I had past fears of heights, which eventually, I became set free from. **God did not give us the spirit of fear, but of love and a sound mind.**

When my girls were younger, they loudly laughed at me in front of my face and the airline stewardess about the phobias that I had concerning heights and flying. I was shaken with fear. I assume they were trying to make me shake the devil off. We laugh now at how ridiculous it was at that time. Then, I did not find anything funny. The sad part was that I flew to take them on vacations.

At times, jet setting became the only available method to voyage within a reasonable time frame pertaining to visiting with Corrinna. If a decision was between fear and my daughter, there was only one choice, my daughter. Truly, love knows no distance. I am living proof that **perfect love really does cast out all fear**, as written in I John 4:18.

I reminded my children all of the time that I was an imperfect mother, but my love for them was perfected. I beat myself up for invalid reasons, as there is no such thing; not even your mother or my mother is perfect, but they were perfectly designed and selected to carry you.

Just as I am making you aware of the fact that I am proud of each of them, be certain that I shared this with them individually and collectively. When Joshua and I had the occasion to drive to visit Corrinna, Joshua would sing and/or talk to me to make sure that I remained in a fully awakened state.

Joshua helped me decipher the signs as we traveled along unfamiliar roads. The days before I knew about GPS units, I had a human GPS named Joshua. God gave him to me to help me get in the right lane on the road called life. At this stage of my life, I was not a veteran with the computer, nor am I currently. However, by the grace of God we always arrived at our destination safely.

As I proudly witnessed Corrinna graduate from Marine Corp boot camp, tears of joy and sorrow fell, but these were the beginning of the tears that I would shed concerning my daughter's decision to join the United States Marine Corp.

Guess what? Yes, my daughters' dad, Doug, attended her graduation from boot camp. This time, he was the one that was running.

Do you recall when my tube burst? This tragic experience resulted in showing my shameful face at the Welfare office. This is how a child support court order was placed in affect. Doug bluntly disobeyed this court order, and this resulted in a warrant for his arrest. It is funny how things go around in circles even if you have nothing to do with their origin. The world says what goes around comes around, but Galatians 6: 7 remind us that **we shall reap what we sow.**

Another change was right around the corner. I believe this event was preparation for that which I eventually faced. In 2003, I received a phone call from Corrinna. Although the conversation began well, it did not end the same. Corrinna's words went something like this…Mommy, I cannot tell you where I am going, or what I will be doing, but soon, I will be unable to communicate with you for a while.

Another devastating period of my life sprung inside of my eardrums. Almost every day, we had spoken via the telephone or email. There was not a declaration of war at the time this call connected us, but we definitely were on the brink of an outbreak. Before the call disconnected, I knew that Corrinna was going overseas.

I neither had any idea of the directions that she was heading nor the directives that she was given. I did not know how or what Corrinna would endure or if I would have the faith to endure.

The Bible states that **the race is not given to the swift, but to him that endures to the end shall be saved.** This definitely was a time for stamina, and full trust in God.

While my daughter was overseas, the dreadful day came when our president declared a war. Fear, despair, depression, and anger gripped the small portion opened in my worn heart. With this intensity level of panic, I did not know how to totally trust God. I terribly worried each second of the day. **God's Holy Spirit is a great teacher and He will teach us all things. He will not keep his children in darkness.**

The pain and fears that I felt are labeled as indescribable. Now, it is only a blur, just as the labor pains of birth comes and goes. At that time, the pain was very real and concentrated on the possibility of losing my daughter in a war that I view as senseless.

The news consumed my every second while Joshua alarmingly and nervously observed my state of panic, but he always reassured me that Corrinna would be okay. Joshua's wrinkled forehead alerted me of his concern for both of us. I turned CNN on one television while MNBC reported the war on another TV.

Vividly, I recall the day that an announcement was made that two prisoners of war were captured. Their names were withheld. It was reported that at least one prisoner was an African American female. With the type of stuff that happened in my life, I could not prevent wondering if one of these prisoners of war was my daughter. Mental stress triggers a response by the name of PAIN.

Without signing in at the front desk, the hospital staff at the emergency room called my name upon seeing my face. The physical condition that I endure triggers from stress and depression, which are signals for intense pain. The emergency room doctor wrote several prescriptions for me; one in particular, was "Do not watch the news!" Who could stop watching the news during a time like this?

I could not hear Corrinna's voice. I did not know where she had journeyed or what her job entailed. Did my spirit become too frantic to hear the quiet and still voice of God? Fear is definitely a distraction, but it is not of God. Fear became a vital signal for me that I am not totally trusting in God. I knew that Corrinna's normal job was an IT administrator, but it was unknown if Corrinna was on the front line, the back line, or behind the scenes. During the wait, your guess is as good as mine, because I did not know! I thought for sure that I would lose my mind during this time. However, I did not lose my mind, and God sent an angel of mercy named Ellis.

Whenever my telephone rang my heart raced, but I would slowly answer the telephone. Whenever an unexpected knock came on the door, my heart pounded with each knock, as I panicked again. It became a vicious cycle. I wanted the phones silenced, but I realized that they needed to be turned on in the event of an emergency.

One particular phone call was made by my daughter's gunnery sergeant, Ellis. He introduced himself. Oh my, at that moment, I thought that death came to me, and he attacked my heart. He was one of the first men that ran across my path in a long time. He acted with such a gentlemanly and mannerly disposition. Certainly, I figured that if he telephoned me that something must have been wrong with my daughter. Yes, I was actually wrong.

My considerate daughter, Corrinna, asked Gunnery Ellis to check on me from time to time because she knew that I would not be in a good mental or physical condition until I knew that she was in a safety zone. How is a safety zone possible when anywhere near a war? ***With God all things are possible.*** I am unsure if I began to cry before or after he explained his reasons for telephoning; eventually, my tears turned into tears of joy. I was happy that my phone was not silenced.

This period was another time of turbulence, to say the least. It became absurd to be grateful that the fallen soldier on the news was not my child, but I became pitifully saddened that someone else's child died. Some describe this as bittersweet, but for me it was a rather confusing time of unexplainable grief and turbulence. I shared with Gunnery Ellis that I was back and forth to the hospital and that my blood pressure and my pain went off the charts. My blood pressure elevates in accordance with my level of pain. Ellis's concerns also escalated and so did the amount of times that he phoned or emailed to check on me. He helped to ease my mind, while he gently massaged my heart at the same time.

Finally, about six or seven months later, my daughter was released from her overseas duties. On her flight home, she had a layover in Baltimore, Maryland. Without hesitation, Maria, Manuel, Tony, Joshua and I traveled to Baltimore to get a glimpse of Corrinna arriving home safely from the war zone. Corrinna is now an official veteran, and she is no longer on active military duty. All thanks and praise belongs to God!

Once Corrinna got settled at her duty station, Joshua and I had the opportunity to visit Corrinna and Joe in San Diego, California. While visiting Corrinna in California, I met Ellis. He drove me over the largest bridge in San Diego. The relevance here is that I was afraid of high bridges, but I took the ride without even a thought.

I believe that God provided Ellis as a tool to bridge me during several times of fear in my life. However, we agreed to stop communications. After my son died, Ellis's heightened concern for our family created many conversations as I journey through the process of grief. I have only seen Ellis twice in my entire life, as he and his son stopped in Texas on their way to Louisiana. He was the male father figure that was absent from Corrinna's life.

Ellis, a real man's entrance into our lives is one of the many benefits of my daughter's choice to enter the Marine Corp, despite the stresses we endured during an awful time of war in the natural and the spirit, as well as inside of myself. Another beauty of Corrinna joining the Marine Corp is that Corrinna, Joshua, and I were able to see many parts of the world that I would have never imagined. The only place that Joshua and I did not drive or fly to was overseas, and I am sure that you understand.

Our family increased in size and in value. Although we are classified as "poor," according to the world's statistics, but we certainly are rich because we are wealthy in love!

Chapter 7

Joshua has a song on the CD which states that it is his time to shine. Thus, the title of this chapter originated. Joshua was a very special individual, and I just want to share some memories of him with you before I share my experiences from his death.

My heart condition shows on my face when it lights up with a smile because of an experience concerning Joshua. It is one that commences the healing processes of my heart from the grief that males have inflicted onto me. Joshua overheard my dilemma concerning having to battle Ray for custody. While speaking with an alleged adult male, I mentioned that I did not have the means to hire an attorney for this custody battle.

In the past, because of affordability dilemmas, I went to court without legal representative, and I actually won against my ex-husband, Ray. He had the wealth to retain attorneys. The staff at the court house smiled as I gave all praise and honor to God for these painless victories. Nonetheless, I was unwilling to take such a risk with one of my most precious gifts from God, Joshua Wayne-Anthony Brown.

Joshua came from his bedroom into the kitchen with his little white piggy bank, and he presented me all that he saved. My heart cried, but this was a very special weep. It was not a hurtful, sorrowful, and salty howl that I experienced since the age of eleven. It was a thank you God moment which included tears of joy, praise, and thanksgiving that said, "I thank you for the love of my son!"

Already, God showed His incredible favor on my life by showering me with this precious gift of the life of Joshua Wayne-

Anthony Brown, who defied all the laws of nature. Healing ones, I should have held on tighter to the fact that twenty one years ago, God's favor was evident on my life by the gifting of Joshua Wayne-Anthony Brown, and that He has an awesome plan for my life, but my tears clouded the vision.

The victory really is in the praise! Satan, and people, get confused when you continue to praise God and smile through your hard times. The internal victory was already mine, and God fought the battle, and my walls slowly began to crumble because of pure, unselfish love of a male and the loving relationship with Aunt Louise. It is so true that the battle belongs to the Lord. Our job is to be a good soldier during the battles and follow **The Mighty Warrior/Prince of Peace** as He leads and guides us.

The day Joshua offered his last pennies marks another day that my life began to change forever. I guess that you could say that I stretched out on faith, but I retained an attorney without breaking Joshua's his piggybank. Retaining of an attorney was not because I lacked trust in God; rather, I recently came home from being on life support and in a coma for 36 days.

Once again, Ray and I took a stand before a judge, and that became the second time that we amicably agreed in the twenty five years. After I denounced the right to be heard, with good reasoning abilities; *still*, I was blessed with the privilege to keep my son at home. If my memory serves me correctly, joint custody resulted as the resolution, but nothing really changed because Ray's limited involvement in Joshua's life remained the same.

In my opinion and according to others, including my son, other than picking Joshua up for scheduled visitation to his house Josh was confined to his bedroom. This appeared to be the extent of Ray's duties; well, he did pay child support. If this is factual, the burden lies on Ray that he and his son do not have many fond memories.

Although the court order stated that we were prohibited from calling each other, Ray granted me the invitation to telephone him at his job. I accepted because of the importance of trying to maintain some type of communication concerning our son.

Continually, I strove to involve Ray during his shift. I shared Joshua's report cards, dilemmas, game schedules, and more. Regardless of his reasoning; clearly, it was Ray's choice not to become more actively engaged in his only son's life. After much thought of getting a life, Joshua and my life became extremely busy, I no longer made a noticeable effort to ensure that Ray was informed on Joshua's life. Instead, again, I welcomed Ray with the opportunity to make the effort to call Joshua either our home or on Joshua's cell phone.

I am not totally convinced that my attorney's presence made a disparity in this "custody battle." Although lawfully, a court battle took place, but the real issue here is that my son belonged to God from the moment of conception. Ray and I made a public declaration by having Joshua publicly dedicated back to God. One of my favorite cousins asked to be Joshua's godmother, and I honored her request. I asked her husband to be Joshua's godfather. My cousin is resting safe in God's arms too.

Another huge difference was made in my life that resulted due to the initial notification that a custody battle was sought with the courts. Joshua imprinted another loud statement on my heart that day by offering his last penny, which surely will last a life time. *I am reminded of the* **Bible story that tells us that a woman gave all that she had, which were two pennies**, but the value of it to God was enormous. **She gave all that she had from her heart**.

Even in the midst of my blessings, things *still* continued to spiral out of control. As mentioned earlier, I did not feel competent enough to attend a hearing without the presence of an attorney because it was only recent that I was able to literally breathe on my own. Actually, the pain continued to labor from the removal of the feeding tube which was removed after I began to overeat. Prior to being summoned to court, I was misdiagnosed with a brain tumor, and this mistake nearly cost me my life. I almost flat lined and I ended up on life support, in a coma for 36 days, but once again, God said, "No."

My daughters were away in college, but they both dropped their books and came home to attend to Joshua and me. Corrinna fainted from the news while she was attending college. Maria broke all records getting to the hospital. Despite the severed apron strings, Maria stayed by my hospital bedside around the clock.

Upon awakening from the coma, Maria was the first person that I saw. *Still* on a respiratory machine, my first request was for a soda, as I wrote it down. Maria attempted to get me a soda, but the nurse told her that was impossible. Instead, they inserted strawberry flavored liquid into my feeding tube, and the smell alerted me that I was starving.

I will never forget the first failed attempt to breathe on my own, and I could not. While awakened, they reinserted the ventilator that I might be able to breathe again. It was a terrifying feeling, as I was not able to breathe on my own; eventually, all tubing was safely removed, and I could breathe again. I thank God for total healing.

All three of my children stayed with my mother, while I recovered in the intensive care unit. It was only the grace of God that my daughters, my mother, and my step-father kept our family together, and help was on the way. My step-father, my mother, or one of the girls drove and picked Joshua to and from school every day. Even though Ray picked Joshua up from my mother's home for his regularly scheduled visitations with Joshua, I am unsure that Ray questioned why.

Joshua was nine years old at this time. I believe that you may be able to see the lack of communication, which is evidence of an unhealthy relationship or no relationship at all, depending on your view. Ray was unaware of the fact that I nearly lost my life His son's mother was on life support for more than one month.

Eight years later, I shared the actual facts to all cases, why we lost the house, that an enemy within threatened to have Joshua taken from me, and the fact that the doctor notified Children and Youth of suspected abuse. Ray's response was, "WHAT!?" Ray was absolutely clueless and speechless. Nonetheless, after this episode, I knew that our lives had to change once again. This time, it would be for the betterment of us all.

Once I was home and somewhat stabilized, Maria returned to college, while Corrinna made the decision not to return to college. Some of Maria's professors did not work with her despite that I was on life support, and she chose to remain by my side; eventually, Maria earned her degree.

I did not know what would be in store next. Immediately, after getting out of the hospital, I returned to the workforce. Once again, our money was stolen while I was sleeping. I worked third shift, so that I could be home with Joshua during the day. While I worked, I paid a neighbor to watch Joshua during the night. *Still*, Joshua continued to blossom more, and his love for me was so amazing. My tolerance for unhealthy relationships became very limited, as Joshua taught me how I was supposed to be loved by any male.

Whenever Joshua recognized that I did not feel well, he would tell his friends that they needed to play outside and/or to quiet down. This is one minor example of Joshua's love and respect for me. Joshua did most things that I asked of him, and he kept his things in excellent condition. I did not believe that any male could ever love me so much and give me as much as "that boy." Joshua was a different type of child; perhaps, it is because I was a different type of mother, this I am still unsure.

While I was raising my daughters, my issues concerning my childhood were being conquered. Slowly, my girls seemed to be conquering their issues of missing their dad. My health issues and the chaos from all of our choices and decisions were wearing. With a son, it was different. Perhaps this difference was because God gave me just what I needed to begin to totally heal. Joshua gave the missing unconditional love from a male. This love will never depart. Joshua loved me unconditionally, and his love for me included my good, bad, and indifference. Through it all, he never turned his back on me. Although there was many times that man, boy, or girl easily could have.

This is not to say that he liked everything that did because I am imperfect. When someone loves you they accept you for you with your flaws. Joshua was such a delight in my life, and he had a natural way of making me feel very special and extremely proud to be his mother. He demonstrated appreciation for my cooking, as he rarely wanted to eat fast foods.

Generally, Joshua was a compassionate, respectable, lovable, and happy young man with a huge heart, literally and figuratively. He was truly a beautiful rose from God's garden that I needed and wanted at God's appointed time! Joshua rarely deviated from his personality, but when he did, it signaled to me that something was immensely bothering him internally.

I stayed as in tune to Joshua as I possibly could. When I was not working, while trying to make up for all that we were robbed, my time and attention focused on Joshua. You see, I did not want my children to needlessly pay for my sins or anyone else's sins, which continues to be one of my prayers. I had two choices, sit and cry about the things that were done or go to work and cry about why things were done. Actually there were more choices, but I chose the latter.

Regardless as to how I felt physically, I volunteered at each of their schools; although, I was disabled due to my massive injuries. I could sit at home and feel the pain more intently or volunteer my time and take my mind off of the pain, even if that meant that I would suffer later. There was so much joy in assisting Joshua's second grade teacher whenever I could.

Joshua and I refused to ask Ray for anything extra or above his regular support ordered amount. No worries and you can rest assured that Joshua did have the best. I took jobs and denied myself to ensure that Joshua would have his heart's desires. It was obvious that he was appreciative.

One compliment that Ray gave me was that he knew where his child support ordered money was spent; actually, the money became mine to do whatever I chose to do with it. I did not have any other desire except for Joshua's heart to be satisfied and happy, and his belly full, (and believe me, the boy could eat one out of house and homeJ)! Whatever I could not do for Joshua, my daughters made up for. Corrinna and Joe purchased Joshua his own personal computer. Maria and Manuel always took Joshua to 76ers' games, and other lavish activities.

Watching Joshua eat was one of the things I loved doing and Joshua really enjoyed eating, which is one of the many reasons that Thanksgiving is so difficult for me. I loved to cook for him too. During Joshua and my girls' lives, I made sure that they had the essentials, nice clothing, and whatever else they needed/wanted even though my credit was still under reconstruction. Not once did we ever have our lights turned off and our cupboard was always full. I am reminded of another testimony that I must share with you! After the ectopic pregnancy, my electric bill grew seriously delinquent, as I had limited income. Perhaps I had short term disability, which I believe is why Welfare only offered us onetime emergency food stamps.

Nonetheless, the electric man came to our home to turn off the electricity. Please know that the entire house was powered by electricity. The kind gentleman came to the door with the tools to turn off the electricity, and my perfume caught his attention. He asked for the name of the perfume that I was wearing and I told him.

We had a nice talk that day, but by the conclusion of that day our lights were not turned off. He did not step foot inside my home or anywhere near the electric box; wherever that was located. The electric man was happier that he found a nice fragrance that his wife might enjoy. Either he forgot to turn off my electricity or I would rather believe that God touched his heart. Oh, God does have all Power! Nonetheless, our electricity was never turned off, as we were never without the light! After all, **Jesus is the light of the world.**

The next day I went to the mailbox. Inside was a check made out in the amount of $150.00, which was exactly what I needed to pay my utility bill. I did not tell any human about my problems. Perhaps, I did not tell my mother. Mom dropped my girls off after I returned from having major surgery, hung a curtain, and returned to the comforts of her home. My stomach was stapled instead of stitched. Literally, I crawled on the floor to get to the kitchen to feed my children. Going upstairs was an even harder task. Maria was about thirty months old and Corrinna was fifteen months, and there we were. Oh, **God does take care of His children.**

God knew my situation, and He touched Sister Barb's heart to send me that check, which was exactly what I needed. Sister Barb was unaware of my situation, until I shared my testimony with her after this kind gesture. **God will supply your every need according to His riches in glory.**

When I telephoned her to say thank you, she said that while she was praying for me that God put it in her heart and she did just so! A male friend went to the store and carried in heavy bags of groceries for us too, as lifting was an impossible task. Oh, I do believe that God puts angels into our lives, and that we should **be careful not to entertain a stranger for they may just be an angel of the Lord!** I also believe that God puts others in our lives to teach us things.

It was obvious to Ray that Joshua had a good life and that I used the money to benefit. Unfortunately, according to Joshua, Shirley did not appear to have the same vision as Ray and I. One Sunday afternoon, Joshua came home really upset. He shared these words with me, "Shirley held my cell phone up to her sons and said, "Look at what child supports gets you."

Again I became furious, but I chose not to say one word to Shirley or Ray about this incident. I knew that my son was to return to this house at least until he was of age. Please allow me to add that I always reminded Joshua to telephone Ray. It was a sore subject matter for Joshua.

I do not ever recall an increase in child support for the thirteen years that Ray paid. There were a few times that I needed to rob Peter to pay Paul, especially when it was stolen from us, but money never stopped me from giving the time that I had, which I believe is the best gift that God gives us to share with those who matter the most.

Joshua always seemed to welcome and appreciate my presence. If for some reason I could not attend, Joshua became quite inquisitive. Many people kindly commented and some unkindly remarked about Joshua and my relationship. Some were amazingly jealous of our relationship and would call him, "that boy" or make sarcastic remarks that I was going to make him a "momma's boy."

I did not waste my energy or time in a rebuttal because the fact remains that no one knew the railroaded experiences that Joshua, I, and my girls went through. No one except God saw "that boy" and my girls witness their mother in intense pain. No one was there when I came home from the hospital on the same evening of major surgeries. Most times, there was limited help with my children.

Still, I continued my responsibility to cook, clean, help with homework, or do whatever needed to do be done so that Joshua could have any type of life. May I add that I love being my children's mother! In fifth grade, Joshua needed to choose someone to write about. He asked me for advice of who he should write about. We talked in length and detail about Ray, being the number one radio announcer in one of the largest cities of the United States; perhaps he is a legend. I explained to Joshua what Ray shared about how he entered the radio business, and I thought that the issue was settled.

Joshua brought home the starred paper in which he wrote about me. He stated that I demonstrated to him the strongest woman in his world. Tears *still* come to my eyes when I read it or think about many of Joshua's writings. He wrote about my struggles with having twenty some surgeries, and the fact that I *still* had to cook, clean, and pay all of the bills. Joshua was around the age of ten at this time, which detailed another part of my healing process. This valuable inscription was placed in Joshua's scrapbook that Corrinna lovingly put together upon Joshua's death but more importantly in my heart.

Upon purchase of this particular scrapbook, my *intentions* were to design it during Joshua's senior year. Please do not make the same mistake that I made and wait to have a scrapbook made upon anyone's death…the person cannot see or enjoy it with you while you reminisce. **Tomorrow is not promised to any of us.**

Still, his writings bring tears and a smile to my face, and now I say, "That Boy!" Joshua was a very good writer. In fact, that is how he became a rapper. He melted his hurts onto pieces of papers and added beats, which I believe somewhat helped his healings just as they helped mine. Also, Joshua did other things that he loved to do.

Joshua loved to play; often, he came home smelling like a horse after playing so hard. He loved to play football with his friends in the neighborhood, and when it was time for football little league registration he faithfully signed up. Please allow me to add, when Joshua was not playing or eating, he was in the shower.

Some days Joshua took two or three showers a day. Eventually, he learned to cut his own hair, and this was a part of his gift too, because Joshua always wore a "mean" haircut once he put clippers in his hands. As recorded in another song, "I don't know about you," but Joshua was fresh! Joshua enjoyed football, but he did not continue in that sport until later in his life.

Each summer, Joshua faithfully asked to register to play football. It was a bit pricy to play little league football, but I did not mind that Joshua would quit. Actually, I looked forward to him practicing for about a week or two, having some fun, and turning in his equipment! People had the gall to shake their head at me because they believed that I wasted at least $100.00, which did not have anything to do with their money. The fact remains that I never really wanted Joshua to play football for the fear that he may be injured. I did not know that it was unhealthy for him.

Long ago, I learned that money is not a device designed to make anyone happy. Neither I nor any doctors, who Joshua regularly visited, many times even due to a sneeze, knew that Joshua had a condition which intense exercise exasperates. Today, I am so grateful that money was not my number one concern. Please do not allow money be your main focus. There are more important *THINGS* in life, as written on Maria and Manuel's walls at home.

After gaining wealth for my ex-husband, Ray, I exited the arrangement. It became a done deal. My developing self-respect and my children's self-esteem were of much more value than any dollar amount. Prior to my divorce from my ex-husband, I also acted as his unpaid agent and negotiated his contact with a new radio station.

This deal afforded him the opportunity to make an excessive amount of $100,000.00 per year. I did not worry about leaving that paycheck Ray earned, as long as Joshua was taken care of was my main concern. I was extremely miserable, and I needed to breathe so that I could learn how to live without an oxygen mask from all of the hidden dusts! I view my ability to negotiate Ray's contract as God's way of providing the means for Joshua to live the life of prosperity and victory which God ordained. I give all praise, honor, and glory to the Most High God! I did not have any prior experiences negotiating a contract, until it became finished business. God is awesome!

Personally, I received too much undeserved abuse which stemmed from others' insecurities, and money did not erase that pain. Besides, now, Ray could be afforded the opportunity to hire and pay his very own personal maidservant. Ray could do whatever else he chose to do with money, which is an object that can be easily abused. However, I am not an object. I am a human being, a child of the Most High God! I believe that you can see that previously I was blinded to this fact.

Although many people believed that Ray took extremely good care of me, this was not minimally the truth. Prior to Ray's huge increase in wages, I had everything that money could buy. I had a really good job, good credit, and the debt to go along with those things. Eventually, I became educated in chapter 7 bankruptcy. It was a life course, not one at a college but in a courtroom setting.

The fact remained, that nothing cost too much for my children. This is not because they are my children, but for as much as they wanted to please me and to see me happy, it was a no brainer to reciprocate the same. Seeing my children happy was enough to make me happy, but I needed to find that **the joy of the Lord is my strength.** Besides, as a parent, I tried to make up for the missing parent, but objects do not make up for another parent. I hope that you get that mistake too! However, a testimony came forth from this situation too.

I heard Corrinna tell many that she is glad that she was "spoiled" with material things. She did not have to become an adult to learn that material things do not make her happy. I did not only give my children monetary things. More importantly, I gave all of them my time, which I had much more of while basically raising Joshua alone for ten years.

Joshua signed up for basketball little league. This sport, we both loved. The community center did not have enough coaches, and I fearlessly volunteered, as I became the first female coach. My pain and my TENS unit joined me at every practice and game. The sufferings seemed lighter because I loved what I was doing, being a mother and Joshua's coach. The joy that I felt loving Joshua's face light up during and after he played his heart out cannot be described in theory. I loved seeing Joshua and other teammates smile as I screamed their names. I especially loved to scream Joshua's name and seeing his smile.

I loved sharing in the excitement that he felt after each victory. I loved encouraging my team even when we lost, which only resulted a few times. Joshua shined brightly, as the "beast" would come out of him. Joshua learned the art of being a true gentleman. The coaching experience did not take long to become such a reward. It was an invaluable, incredible, and life learning experience. I did not know what I was doing in the role of a coach. I selected Joshua and eight players that the other coaches did not choose. We ended up becoming the championship contenders both years, which no one would ever anticipate based on our team's limited talent.

The first year we were the red team, which is Josh's and my favorite color. The second year we became the orange team. Regardless as to the color of our t-shirts, we gave everyone that we faced on the court a fair challenge. I felt very little, if any remorse about the playing time that Josh received. Generally, each coach selected ten players, but I only had nine players each year; thus, I did not cheat anyone out of playing time. Besides, as a parent we are all biased, and we believe that our child is the best. I believe that we should! All of the other children were evenly rotated.

Some people did not like the fact that Joshua rarely was benched, but my feelings were that if any parent had a problem with the way that I coached, I felt as though they should volunteer their time to coach as well. Certainly, many parents were healthier and perhaps, they were more experienced too. Regardless, I received so much joy from this practice. Now, as I reflect on this awesome playing field, I have so many wonderful memories.

The extreme joy was not in the winning of the game, but that each player on my team felt like a winner. This became evident even when we lost, because they each learned to become so proud of their strengths and they were building on their weaknesses! Winning became the bonus.

No one, including myself, imagined that our team would be among the champion contenders both years, as that was not my priority goal. A proud smile *still* appears when I am reminded that some parents referred to me as Larry Brown because of the type of team that I began with and where we ended in the final championship. We fought really hard. Even though we placed an overall second, my team was number one. My least talented player felt like a star by the end of the season.

During one of my basketball coaching years, my first son-in law, Manuel, joined me as the assistant coach. Yes, I taught Manuel everything that he knows about coaching, and I hope that you are smiling too. As head coach, I sacrificed the championship game both years by choosing not to enter my best five players in at the last quarter of very close games.

If Manuel does not sacrifice the championship game for the children's self-esteem, I taught him better than that! I realized that the other parents and grandparents came to see their children/grandchildren play their hearts out, and it could only improve each child's self-esteem if they played equal time in the all of the games, including the championship game.

My belief is that self-esteem and willing hearts have what it takes to win any game, even with limited talent. This is a perfect example as to why I believe that sometimes you can give that which you did not totally master. It makes giving even more of a gift. I believe that these events helped the development of the God given self-esteem that others attempted to suppress inside of me!

One evening, I was in excruciating pain, and I allowed my first year assistant coach to be the head coach. When this alleged adult, who was not Manuel, confessed that Cathy sat the bench the last quarter because he thought that he could win the game, I was terribly angered.

On that date, I resolved that no matter how much pain I was in that I would never allow anyone to act as my team's head coach again; after all, we were a TEAM! *Still,* I believe that my team lost that game, but most importantly, Cathy's self-esteem could have been dented, and what about how her family felt?

I pondered these questions: had God birthed me with self-esteem that was there all along, and did I allowed people that Satan used to hide it inside of my secrets and by the demises? I had very little, if any noticeable self-worth. I thought that it was a part of humility, but I wanted to give my best to any who came into my life.

I wanted to make sure that my children and my players had what I believed was missing in my own life. I understand now that I carried a tremendous amount of faulty guilt which weighted me down. There are some things that I take full responsibility for and I have learned. I tried to treat every player as if they had a mark on their forehead too, because they do.

The sacrifices of allowing everyone their regular playing time were worth the losses of any games, because each of my players contributed at least one basket while in the championship game. They each scored points in my heart as I got to know them. They each developed some more skills and their weaknesses, and they became better players with more self-esteem. In the second championship game, each player scored at least one basket, even if it was at the foul line. I was the happiest coach that day! The final results made me feel ecstatic. I am elated to have the opportunity to coach Joshua and the other children during these periods of my life.

In addition to coaching Joshua, I had the awesome opportunities to be my daughters' youth cheerleading squad, their Brownie Leader, Cookie Mommy, and Girl Scout Leader. Eventually, this endeavor led to being promoted to the first African American Service Unit Director for one of the finest Girl Scout's Council.

While coaching Joshua, I yelled, jumped up and down, and I had so much fun watching my son score, score, and score some more points in my heart! It was so much fun to slap him five or ten, hug him, and to be his number one cheerleader/fan. Watching Joshua grow in ability and strengths and having so much fun while we both had new wonderful learning experiences, resulted in so many precious memories. At the end of the season, I hosted a sleepover party for the team at my home, while we shared so much joy, even without the victorious championship. Each player received trophies and awards.

Only one team player could not sleep over, but she only attending the party because she was the only girl on the team. Joshua received the Most Valuable Player award, as he was the most valuable player on my team and one of seven MVPs in my life. Now, I realized that I needed this fun, because in 2003, another unexpected twist occurred again in our lives.

Chapter 8

After Corrinna settled back in the normal military routine, our lives reverted back to some type of normalcy. I began to see a change in Joshua. Fortunately, it was not too drastic, but nonetheless, I recognized a change. Often, Joshua would inform me of his belief that I had eyes behind my head. When you really examine/study your child, you will know when something is not quite right with them, even if you don't see, touch, or hear them.

With all that we dealt with since his birth, I became concerned. The wisdom that I gained taught me that I had my "turns;" and now, I recognized that I needed to look at him the same way that he looked at me while I was growing through changes, which was wholly with eyes of love. God gives us grace and mercy.

Certainly, Joshua showed me much mercy and gave many reassurances, and I only wanted to reciprocate the same to him. Love really is an amazingly specialized gift, and relationships should be a method of giving and taking, which is never one-sided. Also, I noted that Joshua's age was a factor as he was in a transitional stage.

Joshua was prepared to experience Junior High School/Middle School. New people moved into the neighborhood, but I felt uncomfortable for Joshua to keep company with one particular male. Demanding Joshua to stay inside of the house was an impractical choice. The opened lines of communication remained intact, and we were able to talk candidly about our concerns. I believe that it really is an instinctual thing; that a mother can sense certain things about their children and the company that they keep.

Joshua and his best friend Mark were not "seeing eye to eye" either. This was a difficult time for both of them because from early childhood they were a tagged team. I asked Joshua what I could do to assist him at this difficult time of his life. Joshua requested that we move to be closer to family. Many stated that I acted ridiculously and that I was far too flexible, but they did not know what I knew. Nonetheless, I agreed to move, but only to the extent that we would relocate to the surrounding area which has a good school district.

I believe that the environment of people around you can affect you just as a dangerous chemical spill can infect you internally and externally while seeping through the air. It is my belief that one's surroundings and people that you allow to encircle your life can impact your life in many different ways. This list includes family, friends, community, school, and those involved in activities.

I do not believe that I ever hesitated to look for another place to call home. The only thing that I was unsure of was my credit score. I thank God that it was repaired just in time. Within a few months, we packed and moved to the outskirts of the town that Joshua was born. I was adamant about education, and as a Board of Director I learned too much about the educational system and the inner city mentality in the town that we once lived.

Now I laugh, as one neighbor sarcastically asked me, "What man did you meet now that you are moving?" The answer to that question is his name is Joshua Wayne-Anthony Brown, but at that time I just smiled and kept my thoughts to myself. However, I was not laughing internally. No man has ever had the responsibility of paying the bills of our household. At that time, I remained silent as to the real answer, and I just put a smile on my face. Nonetheless, I did not allow anything to stop me from moving, with hopes of bettering my son's life in every aspect, with a quality education *still* in my view. We moved into an area which was another excellently rated school district.

The first day that we arrived, Joshua readily made two new friends. As we were unloading the truck, two handsome young men introduced themselves to Joshua, and they invited him to play basketball. Instead of playing ball, the three young men began unloading the truck, and life seemed to become normal for Joshua.

The apartment complex was well kept and professionally managed, as my credit was restored. We had many viable options. We had access to a many things such as: a swimming pool, weight room, tanning room, game rooms, and a pool hall were located right down the street along with a movie theatre within walking distance. The mall is across the street.

I did not meet a lot of neighbors, as Joshua and I were busy most of the time. We only lived here for about a year. The two most amazing young men, who Joshua and I met on the day that we moved in, Zach and Michael, remained in our hearts. Eventually, Zach and Michael became two pallbearers at Joshua's funerals because they are two of his true friends.

With all the excitement that surrounded our new environment at the apartment, many valuable lessons were instilled in my and Joshua's lives during this shift. After we got settled in the apartment, Joshua began attending a new school, and he continued hating mathematics.

Absolutely, with Joshua's level of intelligence he could do anything that he wanted to do. Even if he did not test at a high level, he could do anything that he put his mind to do, and he proved that in many areas. Joshua jokingly blamed his dad for not paying attention in algebra, and I did too, as we laughed! That is just a joke, and my only hope is that you laugh.

About three months after the move, Joshua stated, "Mommy, I want to move back home; I am just a country boy." I laughed and said, "You must be kidding." Joshua was not kidding, as he was very serious about the next shift in our lives.

Adamantly, I expressed my concerns to Joshua, and I stood my grounds that I had no intentions of packing up during the middle of a school year. Rather, I resolved that he would have to wait until the summertime. Joshua knew that I "had his back, and was always in his corner," as these words he mentions in his song, Wipe Your Eyes.

During this time, Joshua was extremely patient, and he did not give me a hard time about finishing out the school year. Recall I Corinthians 13 states that **love is patient,** and what a virtue! Joshua calmly waited for his time to shine again back home while having fun and always shining brightly in my eyes and heart. He also found puppy/crazy love on a two way street.

As Joshua grew I saw other changes. One change in Joshua came as girls came on the scene. I know with all of my heart that Joshua believed that he loved Alice, and I do know that he stated desires of marrying her one day, as I read his written vows to her. They talked on the phone all hours of the night, even though they were cautioned not to do so. Alice's parents were strict, and she was not allowed to talk on the phone very much. I am unconvinced that dating is for immature teens.

Joshua befriended her little brothers, as if they were his own little brothers. He hung out with them just to get a glimpse of Alice. I must admit that I fell in love with her too. I knew too well how important she was to Joshua. It did not take me very long to realize that Joshua had his heart set on marrying this young lady one day, but many girls liked Joshua which became too problematic for their puppy love.

Eventually, He and Alice broke up, but I do know that Joshua continued to be crazy about Alice. Finally, their relationship was severed. Alice no longer was inwardly gorgeous to me, as she got another male involved who came over to the apartment. He and Joshua fought.

I became disheartened that Joshua would fight anyone; although, I tried to understand that Joshua felt that he needed to defend his "manhood." I always expressed my concerns to Joshua that I could never explain to him what it was to be a man, and that was a task that I did not have any talents to offer him any advice. I did the best that I could to teach Joshua good morals and values as a person, but I believe it is a man's job to teach/model how a boy is to grow into a man. I will allow this subject to rest because I could go off onto another philosophy, but that would not be very good.

The saddest part of Joshua and Alice's situation is that Joshua attempted to talk to Alice many times before his exodus, and she declined. **Let not your wrath go down with the sun.** Although Alice was absent, there were many other people who truly loved him. Joshua had many other female friends, but I do not believe that many were as special to him as Alice.

While I am biased, most would acknowledge that Joshua is very handsome, compassionate, and he had at least a smile to share. Joshua loved to eat, but he would even sparingly share his food with selected few friends. Joshua had a huge heart for people, and he was a respectable young man. As he grew in stature, I identified more deviations from his normal character.

In March 2007, I recognized another change in Joshua that I had not witnessed before. Generally, Joshua was a very compassionate young man. As I write, I am reminded of a conference with one of Joshua's elementary teachers. She called me in to warn me that Joshua's huge heart for people may cause other children to take advantage of him. She was concerned that this might make life hard for him. I already knew this syndrome too well because of my own life lessons, and I knew that Joshua really did have a huge heart for people. I believe that he received that honestly, as another gift from God.

Meanwhile, in March 2007, Joshua's father, Ray, became severely ill. His wife, Shirley telephoned Joshua's cell phone, which I was upset that she did not have the decency to allow me to inform Joshua of this delicate matter. With no further explanation other than the hospital Ray was ambulanced. I witnessed and wiped the tears that streamed down Joshua's face while his hands were placed over his eyes.

The only call came from Shirley early that morning which was placed directly to Joshua. Neither Joshua nor I were updated with any information other than that which we received through the grapevines. Additionally, I learned the hard way that the child support was instantaneously amended without going to court. I continue to believe that this was done illegally; nonetheless, it was done. I did not totally fight the issue, and I granted that all arrearages charged to Ray during his illness be forgiven. Joshua and I made it through this difficult time. Besides, with Ray's condition, he did not need additional stress.

Prior to Ray's illness, he and I spoke about all that he was responsible for. He barely got any rest, as he took his stepson to work, and then drove his wife to work. In addition, he worked until midnight. Many times, he drove to pick up Shirley's granddaughter.

Joshua received the phone call on the morning of the ninth grade formal, and I was uncertain if Joshua would *still* want to attend, but Joshua did attend the formal. Joshua could wear basketball shorts, a baseball cap, and moccasins and *still* look sharp!

Prior to the formal, he and his date took pictures. I smile every time that I look at them. Despite how the day began, Joshua appeared to have a good time. I attest that Joshua looked sharp with his brown suit and shoes, shades, cream shirt, hanky, watch, and "Kango" cap. I always reminded Joshua that he was handsome sharp, and he knew it too! I will never forget the day that Joshua came home very excited because he was listed as one of the top ten most handsome males at his high school. His personality was more beautiful than him. To really have known Joshua was to have loved him!

When the modeling agency spotted Joshua, they alerted me that he had everything that they were looking for, even his "pointy ears." His peers made fun of his ears until he grew into them. I used to tell Joshua to tell them that his ears were very valuable to him and that God gave him those ears for a reason. One good reason was that most of the time, Joshua listened very well. He could hear and understand that my instructions were for his best interests.

One thing about Joshua, no matter where he went or what he did despite any of our afflictions, you can be sure that Joshua enjoyed himself. If Joshua did not have fun, I knew too well that something was going on internally with Joshua. I am so proud to tell you that Joshua was who he was, take him or leave him alone, and he had fun in most everything that he did, with the exception of homework.

Joshua has a song in which he states, "It's my time to shine." He knew that he had "haters," which is defined as people who were jealous of his abilities. More importantly, Joshua knew who he was, which speaks volumes of his self-esteem. I always say when I grow up; I want to live just as Joshua lived.

Later in the week, I asked Joshua if he wanted to go back to the hospital, and he adamantly replied, "No!" This was the first and only time that I can say that I saw some of Ray's qualities as a male come out in Joshua. I did not push him. I did not play tug of war with him, but Joshua concerned me when he said, "Now he will know what it feels like!" I knew without inquiring what it was that Joshua had just spoken. I did not get angry with Joshua because he was expressing his feelings, but I became very concerned.

I always expressed to my son that no matter what Ray did or did not do that Ray was *still* his father. The Bible tells us to **honor your mother and your father**; although, I did not always totally recognize this scripture in my life, I knew that it was my job to instill it in my children. However, now I also appreciate that kindness can be not saying a word. However, I caution you too, never let anger consume you because of anyone else's actions.

Ray had all the responsibilities that I once owned. He cooked, cleaned, and took take care of most of the responsibilities that I once did for his wellbeing. Shirley did not drive, and he had to make sure that she was taken everywhere that she needed to be. I felt badly for Ray, but at one time I did all of that for Ray. Now the shoe was on the other foot. Ray admitted that he wished that we had worked things out. I was sorry that Joshua went through the things that he dealt with being a product of a broken home. For Joshua's sake I wished that LOVE was present.

Due to the disruption in child support, I did not have an available option except to find another job once again for the purpose of survival. God knows our needs before we even ask! God put a job right into my hands. I was hired on the spot after being recommended for the job by my friend Anthony.

Upon my pre-employment interview, I warned my potential boss that I would not, under any circumstances, take this job if it interfered with being absent from Joshua's basketball games. She has a son and understood my stance. She kindly made provisions that I would have the job and that I would *still* have the ability to be at each of Joshua's games, and for this I am grateful.

In more ways than one, this was a crucial time period of Joshua's life, and I really needed to be at home, but not working may have cost us our home again. Joshua needed all of the emotional support that he could get, and bad influences during this time were not beneficial, which are always present.

Prior to this illness, Ray made one attempt to be part of Joshua's life besides picking him up on court ordered visitation. I do apologize; Ray did come to one football game when Joshua and I moved in 2004. After I regained my composure from almost completely losing my balance, Ray laughed at himself.

On the way home from the tryouts, I asked Joshua how he felt about this experience, and he replied, "That's one." To say the least, the father-son "relationship" was very strained, and I am unsure that his father ever understood or attempted to understand. My personal belief is that after Ray's illness, Joshua feared for Ray's life and any possibility of a relationship. I believe that Joshua established what he may have considered the easy route, being angry at his dad for all of the things that he could have done, but did not chose to do.

I shared with Joshua my confessions about the wasted time that I spent being bitter due to a lack of relationship, and I pleaded with him to not take this approach. If the other person really does not want a relationship, he or she goes on with his/her life as if nothing has transpired, while the angered person really does unnecessarily suffer.

However, I tried my hardest to ensure that Joshua knew that it simply was not his fault. It is funny how I could identify this to my son, but I needed someone to demonstrate it for me. Also, I understand that **you can be angry**, which is identified in the scriptures, **but** the other part of this scripture is *to* **sin not.** I was more concerned about Joshua's wellbeing, and I knew too well the damage that was being created without a father-son relationship.

During Joshua's youth, he rarely wanted to go to his dad's home because he complained that there was nothing to do, but I explained to Joshua that it was court ordered and he did not have a choice until he was old enough to make his own decisions and/or speak to the judge himself. I would allow Joshua the flexibility to come home early if his dad agreed, which he did most often.

I believed that a relationship with his dad was of utmost importance, but it was not in my power to force a relationship between the two of them. However, I knew too well the difficulty of having and essentially being only one parent, but in any relationship there has to be a mutual decision for any relationship to exist. According to Joshua and other witnesses, when Joshua would go to his dad's house he would play video games in his room, and at times he took a friend.

At times, friends went along if his dad did not state that he lacked money to feed anyone else. This made me terribly angry and embarrassed. I was so mortified when one of Joshua's associates asked me to borrow twenty dollars so that he would have money to eat while going with Joshua to his dad's house. I told the teen to keep the money, but he stated that his dad wanted to pay me back.

My heart sank, but others knew exactly what was going on. Ray always accused me of being the one who cared about money, which I later learned that Ray was projecting his own feelings about himself onto me. Recall that this radio announcer gets paid a lot of money and after negotiation of his contract, I bailed out! Regardless, to my knowledge, and based on my conversations with Joshua and his journaling, Joshua and Ray rarely did anything together and this was a huge void for my son. However, I could relate to Joshua's pain, because it was the same while Ray and I "dated." Joshua went to work with Ray during visitation, and he was so absent as a husband.

Joshua mentions his dad in his music giving him props for being his parent, and Joshua even accredited Ray for his talents in the field of music. I am unsure if Ray heard Joshua's CD or not. I do know that Joshua was terribly upset that Ray did not attempt to help him in this musical endeavor, but God sent William and Will into Joshua and our lives.

True men would make remarks and ask what kind of man does not have his son with him all of the time? They would express how they would desire for their son to be just like them. Maybe, that is the answer to their question. There are many "men" who do not operate in the lives of their children, because other people or they themselves are too important, i.e., selfishness.

By the age of 16, Joshua no longer visited during most of the court ordered visitations for the weekends or the summers. The lyrics to the song that talk about the cat and the cradle and the silver spoon seemed to become Joshua's theme song concerning Ray. The last summer that Joshua lived on this earth, he and I spent the entire summer together. The exception was when he spent the night at his friends' homes. I am saddened by the fact that there was a missing piece in Joshua's life, but I am grateful that we had the whole summer together and that Joshua lived a full life. However, this earth is not heaven. We are by no means perfect. We all have issues!

My heart ached for Joshua, when I offered my two damaged red cents to him. I suggested for Joshua to call his dad to make Ray aware of Joshua's basketball or football schedule. The pain greatly masked Joshua's appearance, as it oozed out of his pores. It is very likely that my painful reminders soured his normally healthy smile. Joshua expressed to me that my request to him to offer Ray his sports' schedules ruined the possibility of him telephoning Ray at all, but that was anger speaking as Joshua eventually attempted to contact Ray.

I felt horribly and helpless as I watched my son taste pain. It caused my heart to be stroked with soreness, but my hands were tied. Yet, I knew too well how Joshua felt. Joshua was a product of a broken home from the moment of conception, which can lead to a broken spirit, if we as parents do not carefully handle our gifts. I am reminded of times during Joshua's youth when Ray attempted to pick Joshua up for visitations.

One time in particular, Joshua took off his seat belt, as he piercingly screamed. Joshua was trying to get home. I assume for Joshua's safety, Ray spanked Joshua's behind in the car, and he buckled Joshua in and drove off. That evening, Joshua came back home. Eventually, Ray no longer had the power to force Joshua to go to his house. Joshua's statue was 6' and he weighed in at 170lbs. Joshua is the tallest young man in my world, heart, and eyes.

Many times in Joshua's early youth, by the end of the evening, Ray ended up bringing Joshua back home. Most of the time, Joshua was not that extreme to necessitate a spanking, but often Joshua was brought back home the same night that he went to Ray's home. Joshua suffered terribly from the illness of homesickness. I assume as Joshua grew in statue and age, that Joshua informed his dad when he wanted to come back home.

In 2001 due to many ill factors, I had my morphine pump turned off. I should have been hospitalized much longer, but Ray only afforded me a ten day period to keep Joshua. I think that is the lengthiest time period that Joshua ever spent at Ray's house. I became terribly ill after this event, but by the grace of Almighty God, Joshua and I made it!

I provided Joshua with a cell phone mainly for his visits at Ray's house to stay in contact with him without calling Ray's house and for emergency purposes, but as Joshua got older, he and I did not have the same goals concerning the cell phones, as he loved to text! A cell phone did not aid in the strained relationship between Joshua and his dad.

Eventually, my lips became sealed concerning reminding Joshua to telephone Ray about his games, but I often asked Joshua if he telephoned Ray. There were times when Joshua would call and if Ray did not return Joshua's call and that stunned Joshua as well. I made a point to keep my ears and eyes widely opened, in case Joshua wanted to talk. I can tell you that my brows were heavily weighed down. I limited input into the deciding factor of Ray being Joshua's dad, but I do not have any regrets concerning God's choice. Without Ray's donation, Joshua would not have been who he was. Surely, I hope that you get that point.

During Joshua's inadequate behavior due to his stage of crazy love, he called his dad's home and asked if he could come over there to chill out. Ray's wife, Shirley, was on the line as well. I listened over the speakerphone, and I heard her rudely ask, "What does he want to come here for?" My heart sank really, really low. Joshua and I talked briefly about it later, but to Ray or Shirley I did not say a word. As Mr. Jefferies suggested during Joshua's funeral, Joshua was not one to hold grudges, and I do thank God for the clear vision that He gave to Joshua.

Joshua mentions in one of his song: "Don't talk bad about your dad, remember that?" I had several conversations with Joshua explaining that his dad played a much more active role with him than any of his paternal siblings. There was another daughter, named Shannon, whom I never met. I was married to Ray for at least eleven years. While I was married and living with Ray, I often petitioned for his oldest daughter, Renee and our granddaughter, Niece, to come to visit. After Ray and I divorced, it became knowledge to me that their relationship ended, until just recently.

I treated Renee as I wanted my own treated. For Father's Day, Renee, Niece, Corrinna, Maria, and I dressed in red and black and took pictures. We presented this picture to Ray for Father's Day. In addition, when the Catholic school stated that Renee would not be marching, I fought for her rights. Renee and I both can tell you that she proudly wore her white gown draped with light blue and gold as she marched to receive her diploma! All praise belongs to God! My main focus was my children's self-esteem, not that of his dad, Shirley, or anyone other adult, for that matter.

The Friday evening prior to my son's death, Joshua laid on our cream colored leather couch with one tear running down his cheek, and he asked me this question, "Do you know what it feels like to be rejected by your dad?" After grasping for air, I answered, "No, Joshua, my dad was just the opposite." Although, I knew these feelings too well, as I was rejected by Ray, as well as others, it was neither the time nor the place to engage in those conversations, as my son was severely wounded.

Much later, I read many of Joshua's writings later, which disclosed many of the pains that Joshua had experienced, and it explained how he felt as a result of the lack of relationship with his dad. I dare not share with you the all of the things that I read because they may just make you cry as well, but my son was internally injured. I could see and feel it along the way.

One thing is for sure, Joshua may have felt rejected by his earthly dad, but I am sure that his heavenly Father has made up for that rejection by receiving Joshua safely in His widely opened arms! Another thing that I am one hundred percent clear on is the fact that if God gives you a gift, no matter if it is; a son, daughter, husband, friend, grandchild, cousin, aunt, or uncle, no one has the power to take their love away from you.

My children appeared to always in the "middle" of my marriages. It was obvious to me that neither of our spouses really wanted Joshua in their lives, as if he was clutter in their space. It appeared to me that Joshua was viewed as a mere inconvenience to the other spouses than the blessing that he really was. Certainly, Ray made it no secret that Corrinna and Maria were to be hiding at all times, but this was not a game of hide and seeks; rather, this was about my children's lives and livelihood. Often, I reminded Ray that I did not hide my girls inside of a closet while we were "dating." I encountered so much agony because my children appeared as a burden rather than a blessing.

The emotional torment that my children watched me suffer is one of the greatest pains that I wished that I could have spared Corrinna, Maria, and Joshua. Before you make a move, please look at the effects that it will have on everyone around you. Also, be mindful as to who you give your time, as a lot of our time was wasted in pure foolishness. One thing that you cannot get back is the time that you have lost. All of the tears that my children, and especially my son, witnessed could have been smiles, happy, and good times rather than tears from unnecessary pains of life.

I learned the value of how precious time is, and it is important to only share that time with people who treat you as though you are precious. Please notice that I did not say as if you are perfect. You can repurchase monetary things, but you cannot make up for lost time. So, I encourage you to use your time wisely with those who matter and on things of importance.

From my point of view, there were no questions, my children were there first, and we were a packaged deal. No one that I chose to be in my life was going to interfere with their livelihood because of my bad choices. By this I mean that no one was going to mistreat my children, which included their natural fathers, if I could help it.

Sometimes, helping it meant that we needed to exit the situation. If my children could not be accepted, the other person had to go. They had no place or space in our home. I can tell you that I have no regrets! Certainly, my children could have been corrected in love, but not because they were merely born. Their birth was not a mistake. As a matter of fact, I thank God for that mindset, especially on this day.

I am reminded a confrontation of my daughter's coach. My daughter was upset, as she reported that the coach always referred to them as little B's. Boy, did I become inflamed! At this time, I was on the school board. I confronted this coach, and it is my belief that my daughter suffered because of this altercation. She sat the bench most of the season. So be it, sometimes you have to sit the bench to see what is really going on. Corrinna maintained a positive attitude, and she practiced hard. Ironically, Corrinna earned the coaches award that year, as she was maturing gracefully.

Strongly, I believe that the most challenging job that I have ever had; yet, the most rewarding job, is that of being a mother. The years of rebellion were not easy, especially being a single parent with limited involvement from the other parent. No matter what, I attempted to make each of their games and support them in any way that I could. In January 2007, I was terribly upset at myself that I was asked to be a replacement for Victoria's guest who could not attend the function, and I made a last minute decision to fill in and go along with Victoria to see Celine Dion's Las Vegas performance for her birthday. This meant missing Joshua's basketball game.

Joshua played basketball since he was around the age of eleven, and I think that the total count that I missed all the days of his life was only four games. The third game that I missed, Joshua asked me not to drive one and half hour trip alone in the dark after working late, for fear that I may get lost, as my GPS took the school bus with his teammates. After working, my neck ached worse because of holding it down while tutoring students and air conditioning has an effect on my neck, as it pours out of the college's vents. The other game that I missed you read about, as it occurred while I was coaching.

I do not believe that I ever missed a baseball game, and even though it was awfully cold, rainy and or chilly at most football games, I do not recall missing any of his football games either. I may have been late; but missing, I was not, because my son was in action. The same was true for my girls, I rarely missed their games, whether they were cheering or playing. Joshua and I got lost while trying to find one school and Corrinna was very upset because it was her best game. She does not know how saddened my heart became because it was my desire to be there more than she will ever know, but I was very lost in a back wooded area without any knowledge of how to get there. Finally, Joshua and I arrived, but the game was practically over.

I did not always handle every situation perfectly and there were times, that I had no choice except to give "tough love." When my children put themselves in dangerous situations or absolutely defied what I stated as a rule, there was only one choice, which was to show tough love. I did not share with anyone all that I have dealt with, but love protects. Surely, I believe that being a grandmother is a much easier job than being a mother.

We all heard the old saying that the apple does not fall far from the tree. I believe that if you are a decent parent that more than likely, your child will do an even better job than you did as a parent, because our children learned from our good, bad, and ugly too. So, the rewards become even more wonderful as one enters grandmother/grandfather hood.

After my grandson, Tony, turned six months old, Maria returned to work. Daily, I babysat him while Maria and Manuel worked. Also, Maria returned to school. I enjoyed having Tony with me during the days, as well as some evenings/nights. I began to see all of his first moments, and some days and nights were extremely long, especially due to the pain I suffered. One of Tony's first words was Josh. Every day, I pointed to Joshua's picture and repeatedly said his name. What a proud moment and precious memory! Tony's other first word was hot, which he pronounced as hop, but we all knew what he was saying, and we all laugh about now!

I never advised my daughter to quit her job, but I encouraged her to think about all of these precious moments that she would miss by working full time and attending school. I will share the same topic with you. Money comes and goes, but precious moments cannot come back and they are priceless even if you have to go without for just little while, which is what I learned from being home with Joshua most of his life.

I learned the beauty of living largely on a very small amount of money, which can be so rewarding and fun if you view it that way. To find a true bargain provides me with so much joy! Today, I do not need a lot to live comfortably, and I am grateful for that blessing.

Eventually, Maria did terminate her employment status and she became a full time mother, as Manuel does well in his career. According to Maria, she is grateful that she has this time with her children, and I am so happy for them collectively and individually! Even while I watched Tony; *still*, I was contending with monstrous amounts of physical and mental pain, and the pain of my buried secrets.

I felt that one of my biggest problems was that I allowed Joshua to witness my depressed and painful conditions. Some have silently and verbally rebuked my behaviors, but it was not something I could always hide; regardless as to how hard I tried. I suffered from depression most of my life.

Often, I shared things with Joshua because I wanted him to know that it was not his fault that I was sad. I went through a lot of hurts, physically and mentally that did not have a thing to do with Joshua. On the other hand, I wanted Joshua to know that through his life God gifted me with so much joy and happiness despite my battle with depression while trying to figure out who I am in Christ Jesus.

No matter how difficult it was to be a single mother, added with illnesses, I believe that God knew that Joshua's life would be what would keep me alive long enough to continually survive; until eventually, I would learn how to live. There were many days when I did not know how I was going to make it, but I can attest to Mr. Jefferies words that Joshua always gave that reassuring smile, which was just enough to get through that day and know that everything was going to be alright. *Still*, I visualize Joshua's smile every day, which brings me so much happiness and allows me to open up with you even the more!

I have another confession; I apologized to Joshua about a week before he died for being so dependent on him for a lot of things. You see, I felt that it was wrong to depend on his birth to save a severely broken "marriage," which was a ton of weight to put on an infant's life, and it was impossible. Additionally, I depended on Joshua for many things, as I felt at times that he was all I had in the flesh. Yes, I had my daughters, but they have their own lives to contend with. God made me extremely happy by giving me Joshua.

The glory belongs to God for the things that He has done. Without God, it would be impossible, according to man, for my son to walk this earth and live as long as he did! It was only God's grace and mercy and I thank Him so very much for the seventeen years of Joshua Wayne-Anthony Brown's life, and for each person who God brought into our lives!

An eventual encounter with my counselor, Dr. Johnson corrected my mindset. Dr. Johnson softly disciplined me as he let me know that no crime was committed by depending on Joshua. Previously, other than my children, I did not have this human experience completely. When I or others got tired, we bailed out. **Love never fails.**

Today, I can state that I am grateful that God gave Joshua Wayne-Anthony Brown when I had no other human male to depend. I am also grateful that I did not have any human to totally depend. If I had others to depend on, I probably would not have the relationship that I am establishing with God today. Even **when mother or father forsakes us** God always stands by our side and carries us through every storm and through every misunderstanding.

All praise, honor, and glory go to Him and to Him alone.

Upon this new awareness that Dr. Johnson brought to my attention, I became so thankful that Joshua did have me to depend, as we depended on each other, because that is what love does! More importantly, I am grateful that he listened. If Joshua and I did not have the relationship that we had, I am unsure if he would have paid the words any attention.

Joshua knew and recorded in his music that I was in his corner like no other and that I was the only one that he had! Although we had each other, Joshua also had many friends and things that he loved. Joshua loved music, and he began writing rap music at a very early age under the name KINGZ. Certainly, he had a king inside of him. I was not a fan of rap music, until Will and Joshua flourished.

In August 2007, Joshua came home from the studio after recording the CD, and he took me for a ride. He asked me to listen to a song, and he gave me specific instructions not to cry. What a task? Can you identify that my son always challenged me in a good way, but that he rarely challenged my authority? After you hear the song entitled, "Wipe Your Eyes," you will understand why this was such a challenge.

I did not only want to wail; I wanted to sob, as the lyrics are simply beautiful. Immediately, I did not bawl. Once I went out of Joshua's view, I went in my room, and with my head under the covers, I wept like a baby. *Wipe Your Eyes* is the most beautiful song that I ever heard, and it is the only song that was ever written just for me.

Within Joshua's writings, he tells me thank you and to know that he really appreciates it even if he doesn't say it all of the time. Those are not the exact lyrics of his song, but these words were within the last Mother's Day card that I received from Joshua. In his recordings he states, "You were in my corner like I was a boxer." Also, Joshua reminded me to "never wonder why his name is on his shoulder." Yes, I allowed him to have a tattoo at the age of 16, and he chose to put my name on his shoulder. While I was heavily in grief, I had the same artist put Joshua's name on my left shoulder, and I did not feel any pain. I am not recommending that you do the same.

Joshua describes me as "his rock, his strength, and his boulder". Then he says, "I love you mom." In addition, Joshua states the words, "I just want to thank you, even if I brought you a mansion, I could never repay you." In addition, many of Joshua's words throughout the CD allowed me to see just how diligently Joshua was listening while we shared in conversations. To know that he gave me his undivided attention even when I may have felt as though he really did not want to hear what I had to say. You do know how teenagers can give you those looks. Please let this be a reference to you that chances are *if* we are talking, chances are that our children are listening.

More importantly, I believe that our children are watching. However, they may not say thank you every day. Eventually, they will say thank you if you taught them their manners. I did not just learn these things that I am sharing with you from Joshua's song, but I am so grateful to have these words recorded! The strangest thing about this song, *Wipe Your Eyes*, was that this particular summer was one of the longest summers for Joshua and me because of his struggles with that crazy love for Alice.

Joshua and his best friend, Mark, from early childhood reunited in late 2007. I always reminded Joshua that any relationship that was validated would return. I do not know who coined this next phrase but my belief is that they may be correct, if you love someone set them free if they come back, they are yours if not they never were. Although Alice did not return, Joshua and Mark's relationship was reestablished.

Mark and Joshua picked right back up where they left off, as if they never parted from being friends. That is what true friends do. Although they went in different directions, the friendship never ended, just as true love never ends. It was a pleasure to witness their interactions again in each other's' lives. Joshua never volunteered any negative information about his friend Mark, even though Mark's absence spoke volumes, which made me aware that they had some type of disagreement. Joshua and Mark always were two clowns together. They shared much joy as they always laughed, wrestled, played and experienced new adventures together indoors and outdoors. Wherever you saw one, you saw the other one. The only exception was at football little league practice.

Mark always has been a serious fan of football, and he always wanted Joshua to play by his side. As I mentioned earlier, Joshua would always quit the little league football after he had enough of one or two weeks of practices. Joshua hung in there with wrestling, basketball, and baseball, until the seasons finished.

In Joshua's junior year, he was determined to play football and he remained on the team until the end "giving 110%," as one of his teammates was quoted. Joshua and Mark were so dedicated to football that occasionally they walked a good distance to practice. There were days during the hot summer that I or Mark's grandparents were working and practice did not end until late in the afternoon. Once Mark and Joshua reconnected, they were not easily broken.

Joshua and Mark shared many things in common; they both had at least one tooth broken while together, and Joshua was the cause of one of the incidents. Joshua and Mark have many memories that will live on forever. Joshua and Mark had a wonderful friendship that either could say whatever was on their minds to each other. The other would shrug it off as each of them was very different, yet so much alike.

Truly, Mark was Joshua's best friend, and this I will never doubt because Joshua adamantly reminded me the week before he died. It was just as if he wanted me to make sure that I had it just right! Joshua shared in detail who he believed were his truest friends, and they became Joshua's pallbearers on the date of his funeral, as Mark took the lead. There were a total of seven pallbearers, and each had great significance in Joshua's or my life.

Mark and Joshua's relationship always amazed me and it continually amuses me, even today. *Still*, I continually receive a lot of joy when I think of their friendship. Even though Mark and Joshua are of different skin colors, other than that, one might believe that they were blood brothers. Upon their reconciliation, Joshua and Mark were together every chance they got and especially every weekend. Either they were at our home, Mark's home or at another friend's home named Jake, just as they were when they were younger; inseparable.

During Mark and Joshua's period of dispute, Joshua made several attempts to allow others into his life, but he found no substitute for his friendship with Mark; although Jake made his presence known and he became extremely close to Joshua.

Although Mark and Jake assisted in lying Joshua's body to rest, I know that many others will always hold a special place in their heart for Joshua, just as we do! In addition, I do believe that Mark and Jake will see Joshua again. I did not know the day, or the hour that my son would die but God gave me warnings in my dream that I needed to pay even closer attention to Joshua's life.

Chapter 9

Early, during the month of September 2007, I had a dream that I received a phone call from the principal's office because Joshua got into an argument. I awakened that morning, and I recall looking at Josh, and I shook my head that morning while thinking; no it was just a dream. At 8:36 AM, while on the phone with an acquaintance, Richard, I received a beep which indicated that another call was on the line. I recall looking at the caller identification; immediately, I clicked over, and I heard the vice principal state that he confined Joshua to his office. Joshua got into an argument with another student.

I recall this terrifying call, which did not have anything to do with the argument, but it did have everything to do with the dream. I spoke with Joshua while he was in the principal's office, and I advised Joshua to apologize. I warned Joshua that we would speak later that afternoon, and we did just so.

Later, that evening, I shared the dream with Joshua, and I told him that I shrugged it off while thinking that it was just a dream. It was extremely rare to have many problems out of Joshua, and certainly not in school. There can be a first time for everything, but I knew that this was a warning that I needed to pay attention to my dreams. One of my fears always has been of my dreams because I did not recognize the gift therein. Later, Minister Sharon identified that these dreams are considered special gifts from God.

Pastor Paul stated that the gifts are probably in our bloodline because both Joshua and I share another commonality with my mother. See I Corinthians chapter 7 to read about spiritual gifts.

Today, I know for a fact that Joshua was gifted in this area as well too. I read many of his sealed writings within his journals. He explains his fears and how he felt about knowing some things that were going to happen before they happened. Oh, he did have many special gifts. It is believable because he was a special gift from God.

In Joshua's CD, he speaks about the death of his aunt. None of his aunts died while Joshua lived, but Aunt Louise died soon after Joshua's exodus. In addition, Joshua states in another song, that "any day my body could be riding in a Hurst." Recall this CD was produced in August 2007. He continues stating, "I take nothing for granted, not even my last verse." I did not recognize these as special gifts from God, I shared with an ex-boss the "connection" that Joshua and I had.

I always referred to the connection as a "weird connection." Today, I know better, as I realize it is a Godly relationship, which is even deeper than a mother/son bond. Most of the time, Joshua would already have the apartment door opened for me to come back in because he already knew that I forgot something. Joshua did not have any physical way of viewing me. We lived on the third floor and our windows pointed towards the street but not the area of the parking lot. Later, another dream paralyzed me.

During the early months of 2008, I had a very concerning dream that Joshua was on a motorcycle. He was wearing blue and white, which were his high school colors. While on the motorcycle, Joshua was properly suited. Joshua came to a cliff, but I did not see him go over the cliff, but what happened next in my dream is what freaked me out. I had a similar dream concerning my Aunt Louise who was diagnosed with terminal cancer and that alerted me.

At this moment I recognize more significance of my dream. Joshua was fully equipped to meet His maker, as in my dream, he was properly suited! The Bible tells us *to* **put on the helmet of salvation, the breastplate of righteousness, and to** put on the whole armor of God. The word is our sword and it is alive and it exerts power! *Still,* I can hear the echo from recalling being fully awakened and loudly and fiercely screaming, "NOOOOOOOO!!!!"

I will never forget the feelings that overwhelmed my body, soul, and mind. Instantly, I realized that Joshua's life was in danger, but I did not know how he was endangered or what I was supposed to do with this information. So, I prayed and cried; then, I prayed and cried some more. I did not doubt that a spiritual war was inevitable concerning my son, and I was adamant that Satan was not going to win this battle.

I prayed as if I never prayed in my life. I prayed more fiercely than I prayed for Joshua's conception but this time, I was fighting mad. Satan was not going to have my son's soul, as Joshua belonged to God from day one! *Still,* I continue to be angry with Satan for all of his evil acts, which is another reason this book must get out! You see, it was because of Satan that death was pronounced on all of our lives back in the Garden of Eden. The victory of my life story only goes to God!

Before Joshua left home, I decided to speak calmly to Joshua concerning my dream. I did not know how to begin this conversation but after I began, I believe that the spirit of God gave me the words to share with my son. In my best mindset, I could not have chosen more appropriate words. The deeper issue was the words that Joshua shared with me.

While I shared my dream with Joshua, I came to the climax of the dream where Joshua was at the cliff, and before I could complete the dream, Joshua responded, "And I died, didn't I?" My eyes widened, my mouth gaped open and my heart stopped; once again, I screamed, "No!" Only a split second elapsed by the time that Joshua rebuked me and said, "Yes, I did." How does one's life go back to any type of normalcy after this type of communication? I expressed my concerns to Joshua that I believed that he had some serious decisions to make. Joshua listened in more ways than one. I do not believe that I was the one choosing the words myself or even the timing that I spoke with Joshua. Even as I write these words, it seems so surreal as if I was not present or speaking.

Carefully, I listened to Pastor Paul as he ministered at Bible study that Wednesday evening. I was scheduled for a mandatory class that same evening. I went to my advisor and told her that I needed to be at Bible study, but I did not want my grade to be affected because of being absent. God provided that I could be at Bible study that Wednesday evening! I forget the actual topic for that evening during Bible study, but I do recall that we were studying the book of Joshua. That Wednesday evening, we received specific instructions from Pastor Paul to discuss our milestones with our children, and that is how the conversation began.

I reminded Joshua of how I prayed and asked God for a son, and that I promised God that I would name him Joshua. I had shared this story with Joshua at least ten thousand times over his lifetime. I mentioned to Joshua that one day that he would lead people, but I did not know what this meant until later, and I hope that you will understand before the end of these writings.

In addition, I shared with Joshua how badly I was railroaded off track and some of my reckless behaviors, while sometimes wondering if God was really real. This was especially based on some pastors/preachers' actions. Also, Joshua and I talked about our different religious experiences, but I expressed to Joshua that on this day that I knew for certain that God is real and he needed to make some serious decisions.

Ironically or I beg your pardon, as God would have it, I taught the praise and worship team the song *Yes God is Real*, and we sang it the next Sunday morning. Joshua willingly drove to church that Sunday. He was on his feet praising God during all of the songs while I played on the piano, even though this week was not the easiest for either of us.

I have the wonderful testimony that I witnessed with my own eyes Joshua personally accepted Jesus into his heart. I know the confession from Joshua's mouth prior to communion that he believed that Jesus died and rose after the third day. Later, Joshua was watching a preacher on TV with Maria and Manuel and the topic was on death. Joshua asked some questions, and then he stated, "I am not afraid to die."

Some of you may ask was Joshua baptized. I will answer that shortly but please know that baptism is not what saves a person. Baptism is an outward expression that one has accepted Jesus Christ into their lives. The answer to your question is yes, Joshua was baptized at the age of two months. Ray and I had Joshua baptized through sprinkling and dedicated him to God for His services. The fact of the matter is as his parent, I made a decision a long time ago, but my son had some decisions to make for himself. Recently, I ran across a scripture in the Bible that explains that **sudden death will not come without warning to the believers**, and I know that to be so true. I bless God because He is so faithful to his word, if we just believe and trust Him!

Undoubtedly, the last two weeks of Joshua's life were the hardest two weeks that Joshua and I ever endured with each other. The weeks were durable. In actuality, I consider them to have been two of the most powerful weeks of our lives. We were able to get real with each other in ways that never needed to surface. Our talks were intense but absolutely respectful. We even had the opportunity to go shopping and to dinner alone on two separate occasions. Joshua did not only give me specific instructions within the song Wipe Your Eyes, but during these two weeks he instructed me that I needed to be strong enough to let him go. Instead, Joshua used the words "You need to man up just as I am manning up."

In addition, he told me that he wanted me to relax and be happy; none of which I never dreamed possible. Eventually, Joshua's words, which I thought would never be a possibility, are becoming a reality! I warned you that my son always challenged me unlike any other man in this world to get real. It is rather amazing how God used my son's life and love to help me understand Him! How many special gifts can you see within these writings?

Joshua asked me some very personal questions, while he continually stared at me with an eerie technique. This was also noted in Minister Sharon's email because of her observations at worship one Sunday morning. The way that Joshua stared at me responded a personal inquiry from me concerning his motives, but he did not answer. I questioned Joshua why he looked at me with that stare, but even though Joshua never answered that question; today, I know the answer. The same exact intent stare that Joshua gave to me is the same intent gaze that I gave to him as he laid in his silver coffin which is lined with a cream cover, as I seared him in my memory forever.

The Friday prior to Joshua's death, my son summoned many who played important roles in his life, as though he was tying up loose ends. He even attempted to make amends with his dad. When his dad did not respond as Joshua expected, Joshua telephone two associates that he disagreed with, but only one responded. Joshua seemed to prepare to get ready to get to the next level. He telephoned at least three people that weekend, one was his best friend Mark, and he asked them to get together on a Friday evening.

Mark and Thomas responded to the invitation, and they spent the night that Friday evening. After staying at Maria and Manuel's home, Joshua hugged Maria unlike he ever hugged her before but he said very little. Prior to going to the movies the weekend prior, Joshua also hugged me in a mannerism that he never hugged me before, and Joshua had hugged me many times before. Often, Joshua was a man of few words, but his actions spoke volumes.

I requested that Joshua not make plans to go out that Friday evening. Joshua was supposed to have helped me with my grandchildren/his nephews and niece that Friday night, as I was in much pain. I agreed that others could spend the night. I hid the fact that I got very upset when one male suggested that they go to the Chinese buffet. Joshua asked to go out. I reminded him that I asked him not to make plans.

Eventually, I caved in and granted Joshua permission to drive to the Chinese Buffet. Instead, Joshua made a choice to have Chinese delivered to our home, which turned into an empty apartment by 5:04PM. The next day, Saturday morning, I was ordered that I would be in attendance at a conference. In all honesty, and with an opened heart, I confess that I did not want to attend the scheduled church conference on Saturday morning. I Samuel 15:22 states **that obedience is better than sacrifice**, as Minister Sharon pronounced to me via email, "You will be there."

Early, March 15, 2008, I opened Joshua's bedroom door, but rather than disturb him and his friends' rest, I quietly looked in on him. I recall wondering where Joshua got those red and white striped boxers, as I did not recall purchasing them. My mom rose early Saturday morning to pick up our three grandchildren. I was babysitting our grandbabies because Maria and Manuel went to Allentown for a convention.

After they departed, I looked in on Joshua. Then, I drove to the church conference. I reached my destination on time. The conference was held at a place which is located near the fancy apartments we moved from only two years ago. As the conference was about to conclude, my cell phone rang, but I could not get out of the meeting room in time to answer without disturbing others. Joshua was ringing my phone. Immediately, I excused myself, and I went into the ladies' room to privately return Joshua's call. He answered the phone, and he said "Hey mom, can I go to the St. Angus Park to run ball? I said, "Sure."

Joshua's call came in around 2PM, and the convention was just about to end. Do you see God's hand in our situation already? After having a high time in the Lord, while dancing, singing, praying, reading scriptures, and dealing with church business, I said my goodbyes to my beloved church family. Then, I got into my vehicle to head home. Thirty minutes could not have passed when I received a phone call from one of Joshua's friends. He said that the EMT was at the basketball courts performing CPR on Joshua. I am sure that we both sounded confused, and I asked to speak to the EMT person, but that did not happen. Instead, faintly, I heard another frightened and concerned voice on Joshua's cell phone. It was another friend. Prior to the calls, I was on my way home, but I became more confused as to where I was and whether I was coming or going.

Next, a police officer telephoned from Joshua's cell phone, and he identified himself and told me that I should meet the ambulance at the emergency room entrance at the Hospital. Immediately and without hesitation or thought, I telephoned my mother to notify her that I was on my way to the hospital to see about Joshua and I told her that I would have to get the grandchildren later.

Then, without a second thought, I telephoned Ray, who normally does not answer my calls, but Ray answered. I told Ray what I knew at this point, and I alerted him that he should come to the hospital. Somehow, in the midst of confusion, I thought or perhaps I just called Minister Sharon. I requested that she meet me at the hospital.

I was alarmed, to say the least. I assure you that I was driving really fast, but it felt as if I was driving in slow motion. I could not even recall how to get to the hospital or the location of the hospital, but by the grace of God, I arrived safely at the correct hospital.

A short, petite lady who was robed with a dark jacket politely asked, "Are you Ms. Brown? I replied, "Yes," as she handed me a folder. She began leading me to a family room. Immediately and respectfully, I stopped and asked her for the location of the ladies' room. It was urgent that I get to the restroom. I doubt that you will understand this, but confirmation of my dream was without a doubt at this point. Without question, I knew at this moment that I was about to lose my son. You can believe that I was praying.

I returned from the restroom. The nice and notably concerned lady began leading me to a family room. Politely, I responded, "No, where is my son? I want to see my son." She answered, "Follow me," and without any hesitation, I did obey. Later, a chaplain of this city's police department, informed me that it is very unusual for the hospital staff to allow anyone back in the emergency room while they are working on patients. Gracefully, she reminded me of the goodness of God.

Daily, I thank God that the nice woman dressed in the dark jacket escorted me back to the room to my son, as I am unsure if the witness would have gone forth as it did, God really does know best. I will never forget the look in Joshua's eyes when my eyes met his eyes. There appeared to be at least fifteen to twenty staff members working on my baby with all types of instruments and tubing, while their hands performed CPR, as the emergency team quickly and readily changed places. I watched as they shocked Joshua's chest. I recall feeling as though I was in the way, even though I knew that I was in my correct position, right beside my baby.

I did not witness any appearance of an attempt to give up on Joshua's life. I began softly speaking to Joshua, and then to God as I laid hands on him, and I prayed for healing in the name of Jesus. I did not have time to care what others thought about me at that moment. It was praying time. The lead physician alerted me that Joshua's heart activity increased while I talked with Joshua and prayed to God.

At one point, I looked at the general practitioner and I said, "His body is warming up?" The only problem was that it was cold in the emergency room. I was cold and did not take off my black leather jacket. I was hopeful that the lead physician would have said yes, but respectfully and sorrowfully, he replied, "No, he has no pulse." Without a right or a desire to give up myself; again, I laid hands on Joshua, and I prayed louder for healing in the name of Jesus; *still*, there was no response. Major silence was in the air. While the doctors were continually working on my baby boy, I stepped over to the counter with my head bowed and my heart humbled; admittedly, I am angry as heck with Satan, but silently and in love, I prayed to my Father.

Then, the strength of God rested upon my shoulders, and it was then that I found the strength to pronounce these words, "God, whether Joshua lives or dies, I will serve you for the rest of my life." At that moment, Satan did not hold any power at all! He lost the battle for both my and Joshua's life forever, and we are both safe in God's arms! Eventually, each staff member humbly apologized, as I thanked them individually and collectively.

Minister Sharon arrived before anyone else, and I told her to go in the room and lay hands on Joshua. I sat in the chair, as I was extremely exhausted, as if life had just left my body. Actually, I knew before I requested for Minister Sharon to pray for my son, that Joshua's spirit was in God's hands.

I will never forget the look on the police officer's face, when I politely asked him, "How did this happen?" His response was a shrug of his shoulders. Just because God did not immediately heal my son; do not be deceived, it does not deny the power that God has to heal. Do not ever discount the fact that God does hear and answer our prayers. At times, the answer is simply, not in the natural. One of the most profound things that I heard since my son's death, but even more importantly I understand since the death of my son, is that this world as we know it is NOT heaven! Although, I would advise you again *to* **be careful not to entertain a stranger, for they may be an angel of the Lord!**

Prior to Minister Sharon's entrance, the chaplain of the hospital came into the room where I stood and Joshua's uncovered body laid. The chaplain touched my arm with his hand, as if he was in agreement with me, as I continually prayed. The Bible does say that **wherever two or three touch and agree that God will be in the midst.** Even though my son's spirit went from his body, God was in the midst! There is no way on this earth that I could have gotten through all that I dealt with if it was not for the Lord on my side!

Surprisingly, Joshua's father, Ray, arrived at the hospital, but unfortunately, Joshua was pronounced dead before his dad was able to see or talk with him. I understand that there is a reason for everything. Ray asked me if Joshua shared the last words that he spoke to Joshua night before. I silenced my abrupt answers with the quickness, because I could feel myself getting ready to explode! Joshua had share his last conversation with his dad, and it made me mad. I was already angry because the coroner arrived, and he asked Ray and me some questions. Ray was absolutely clueless; although, he tried

Shortly thereafter, the Chaplin requested for Minister Sharon and me to go to the room to help many students/teens/friends and to have prayer with them, and we did just so. Minister Sharon said these words to me, "I cannot believe what is going on here. This is about you." I don't know what happened to Ray. However, he did not come into the room that was crowded with students and Joshua's friends.

The coroner officially took custody of Joshua's body, which neither of Ray nor I had any control. Joshua's death is undoubtedly the most helpless moment that I have ever experienced in my entire life. Still, I am shocked that I lived through this entire experience. No one ever took custody of my baby's body, but I understood that an autopsy needed to be performed. No one knew why Joshua died. Besides, Joshua's spirit belonged to God, and **to be absent from the body meant that Joshua was present with God!**

Many conformations came to my heart immediately that Joshua was safe in God's arms!

Seventeen years ago, two months and a few days ago, I dedicated Joshua to God. Seventeen years later, four months ago, two days later, one minute Joshua was playing basketball, scoring the winning basket, grabbing his arm, and speaking his last words, "*Oh Lord.*" Now, all I could say was, "Oh Lord." What a testimony for someone's last words, especially a teen's last words to be "Oh Lord!" Joshua spoke the words that could save him. **Those who call on the name of the Lord shall be saved!**

Before Ray and Shirley left, out of respect for the order of the court or out of my anger, I requested permission from my ex-husband's wife, Shirley; to contact her husband. Although, she and Ray were married the year we divorced in 1996, this was the first time that I ever laid eyes on this female's face. Previously, Shirley cursed me out on the phone, but I did not have any idea what this woman looked like. Today by the way of the grapevine, I may be semi convinced that Shirley was partially responsible for my inability to call their house. Joshua's dad always instructed me to just call his job to avoid the drama, and that is what I did until his illness. However, being a male does not make one a man.

Ultimately, I believe that it is the male who has the responsibility before God, regardless as to what a woman wants you to do, and I believe the man is supposed to be the head of the house. God put the man as the head of the house. Remember that it was Satan that deceived Eve, but Adam was ultimately held accountable before God. Eve caused all females the longing for a husband. *Still*, we continue to suffer from those consequences.

One of my concerns about Shirley's cursing me out was that my child would endure repercussions for any wrong that I did or said. Generally, I only replied with sarcastic questions, "Are these the types of things that my son contends with every other weekend and during the weeks of the summer? Then I questioned, "Are you a Christian? When I questioned Ray why Shirley cursed me out, he replied, "I guess she is just frustrated."

When there was an atomic notion of any idea that anyone hurt Joshua or any of my children, then I did not have any qualms of following through to the nth degree, even if it caused others to refer to me as a witch, that was their problem.

Strongly, I believe that God holds us accountable for our children's lives. He gave me the responsibility to take care of my children until they became adults or are returned unto Him. I am unashamed of the mother that I am, and I take this responsibility very seriously. I am very grateful that God knows the full truth.

Ray misstated the amount of times that he was married on our marriage licenses. It states that he was only married one previous time. Does that make our marriages null and void according to the law? In one complaint to the court it states that I cursed Shirley out. I am unsure who is responsible for that lie, but I think that they both may deserve each other. Nonetheless, while at the hospital, Shirley gave her approval to allow me to telephone Ray without confrontation concerning the funeral arrangements.

Meanwhile, at the hospital, Minister Sharon requested a private room for me, and she went into the private room with me after we prayed with Joshua's friends. Now, I heavily anticipated the most appropriate time to notify my daughters. I was "taking care" of others' children prior to taking care of my own. Finally, I figured out what Minister Sharon meant by her words this is about you. Oh my God, how was I going to tell Joshua's sisters, my daughters, the awful news?

Maria and Manuel were in attendance at a convention in Allentown. Recall that my sister was at a symposium when our father died. The conference that I was attending had just ended too. The difference was that this time both of these conventions were spiritual. Actually, Corrinna gifted Maria and Manuel with this trip to the convention.

I believe that God has a way of putting us in the right places at His appointed times. Somehow I realized the need to calmly speak with my daughters, but someone already telephoned Maria and informed her something about Joshua before I could break the news to her myself. At this point, I did not cry, scream, yell or say much to anyone. Silence was the only thing in my vocabulary until I spoke with my daughters. Upon speaking with Maria, a huge pain/anger trigger and extreme agitation; perhaps, it was the first notion that I began to deal with my anger concerning the death of my son.

The next necessary baby-step was to call my baby girl, Corrinna, which was very tough for me. I knew that this most difficult call needed to be made soon, as experience quickly taught me not to wait any longer. Certainly, I did not want the same thing to happen to her that just happened to Maria.

The dilemma was that Corrinna resided in Florida, and having to tell my baby girl her baby brother had expired via the phone and at a distance became more difficult because I was not in Florida at this time. Corrinna was not only an hour in distance; although she always remained close in my heart. I did not have a choice except to tell her over the phone. Then the weight came of having to witness her pain stricken being. Corrinna was expecting our arrival on Tuesday, not notification that her baby brother departed his life from this earth.

Joshua, Mark, and I planned to visit Corrinna and Joe in Florida the next Tuesday. We all just talked about it the vacation that Friday evening. Joshua and Corrinna were texting back and forth making plans, and their last words were "I love you." I thank God for these last words between Corrinna and Joshua, but that did not make it any painless to tell her. Finally, I made the call, and Corrinna's scream and cry pierced my heart even more. By now, I felt overwhelmed by my own heartache, the aches of my two other children, three grandchildren, the rest of our family, and the aches of a community that really loved my son.

Please God, have mercy on us all.

Mark arrived at the hospital while uniformed in his work outfit. Upon hearing the report, he began viciously vomiting and punching the wall asking loudly, "What am I going to do now?" I thank God that his mother and grandmother were present to comfort and assist him, because at that time, barely, I could help myself. No one knows what I felt! All that others appeared to see was the strength of the Lord was on my shoulders. When I look back, I am amazed that I did as well as I did.

It is habitual for me to call Corrinna and Maria about minor things. I cannot fathom or explain to you why I did think to telephone Maria and Corrinna when I received the first phone call. I never call Ray during the daytime, and rarely at night, but I guess God was having His way. I was not in charge that is for sure. Certainly, I did not have control of the situation. I did not even call my mother once Joshua was officially pronounced dead, which is strange. I did not cry, scream, yell or recognize that I was alive.

Man really does looks on the outward appearance but God looks at the heart. My heart ached for everyone, but I was unable to cry, scream, or say a word, except to God, silently in prayer. Eventually, I left Joshua's body in the care of the coroner. I never met this strange looking man, and he was going to make decisions about my son which I had very little if any input. Subconsciously, I knew that Joshua's body was about to be violated, but I did not thoroughly think this through; until, I eventually read and cried while I examined the autopsy report.

It never crossed my mind in a million years that I would have any dealings with a coroner's office. I will never forget the thoughts that came through my mind the evening that the coroner telephoned me to inform me about the scheduled autopsy. Finally, I screamed at this point. The coroner asked me if I was alone, and I replied, "Yes." Literally, I begged this man to please just tell me this was a dream." He politely apologized and said, "I am sorry Mrs. Brown but I cannot do that; *THIS IS NOT A DREAM!*"

I remember laying the phone to rest and quietly feeling the introduction of intense pain, as I have never felt before. You and I may have thought that I was in pain before, but I have never experienced this level of pain in my life. Nothing that ever happened to me, which includes the death of my father, many episodes of physical, mental, spiritual, emotional, and financial abuses mattered. The number of accidents is more insignificant. The surgeries or even childbirths will never touch the pain that I felt on this day of March 15, 2008.

Immediately, after I spoke with Maria and Manuel, they rushed to the apartment. Recalling the memories of the tears that fell from both of their eyes is as vivid as yesterday, even though it was only twenty months. Manuel asked, "Why Josh Mom, why? I never witnessed my son-in law's cry or tears. At that moment, I cautioned Manuel not to become angry with God. Maria looked like a puzzle in pieces without a picture to put her back together, and the pain trickled out in her tears. Although, I was not in Maria's body, I could feel her heart, and I read her mind intensely. Our thoughts and our hearts ticked the exact same way as if she was in my womb once again, right underneath my heavily broken heart.

Immediately, I began to pray for more protection of my daughters and my grandchildren than I have ever prayed in my life, and that is a lot! Maria and Manuel departed from my residence to pick up their children. They attempted to explain that their Uncle Josh died, and bring comfort to my three grandchildren's little hearts, whose ages were six, thirty two months, and sixteen months. Nonetheless, another task needed to be accomplished; although, my grandchildren, just as adults *still* do not completely understand death and all that it brings to one's door. Before I could get out of the hospital, a woman named Victoria, called my cellular phone. She called nonstop, at least five times. Finally, her mother, Rita, rang my cell phone, and it was then that I finally answered, as I arrived at the gas station. While at the gas station pumping my empty tank with fuel, I answered the phone. Openly, I admitted that I just needed to be alone to feel my aloneness and absorb my son's death, but it appeared that my feelings did not matter because her son, Luke, desperately needed to see me. As a general rule, I never answer my phone while pumping gas, but I was tired of its ringing sound and I answered. The request was made to visit me. I was not home from the hospital yet. I asked if they would give me an hour.

Instead of standing my grounds, I requested that they give me an hour. I knew that Maria and Manuel were coming to the apartment first. Obviously, I did not persistently state that I just needed to be alone to absorb the shock. Articulations of my words were unavailable. I needed to try to digest what I experienced, the death of my one and only son. People may have thought that I did not need to be alone. I only wanted to speak with my Father, who is in heaven.

My house phone and cell phone did not stop ringing. I just wanted *everything* to STOP! The phone rang, and it rang; finally, the disturbing sounds no longer affected me. I was so comatose that sirens did not affect my hearing. All that I know is that God heard my prayers. At times, I only offered my thoughts and sighs in silent prayers. This was only the beginning of the longest and lowliest days of my life. Still, I am unsure if I spoke with my mother, but company arrived.

About fifty minutes later, a startling knock came to my door. I am sure that I opened the door because they entered into my apartment, and the first words that I heard out of Victoria's mouth were, "What am I going to do?" A feather could have knocked me over, because she asked the wrong person this question, but the true questions in my mind were, what all do I need to do….and finally; how do I deal with this pain? I experienced another level of anger only an hour into my grief. However, blessings did come out of this visit.

Rita, Victoria's mother also came to the apartment with Victoria and Luke. She began taking mental notes as to what needed to be done, which at that moment I could not even think about. The next day, Rita telephoned the principal, Mr. Jefferies, who gave a suggestion of the best local funeral parlor and he kindly asked Rita to give me his cell phone number. Also, Rita made the first contact with Mr. Walker and she took charge of setting up the appointment to begin the funeral arrangements, for which I am grateful.

In addition, Rita is a retired employee of an airline, and she compassionately sacrificed her buddy passes and collected enough buddy passes so that Debra, her husband, and my two nephews could fly home at a much cheaper rate, which was a tremendously appreciated blessing. A flight for four from California to Pennsylvania is extremely expensive; especially, at a last moment notice. I thank God for the blessings from Rita because my sister and her husband were financially able to pay the low premiums for their families' ticketed prices.

It was not until much later that I even realized that I *still* continued to deal with the antagonizing unfinished grief of the death my daddy. Cautiously, I observed those who could not keep their distance at a time like this. As a child, I was an eyewitness to very needy people who tried to lean on my mother's strength during Daddy's death. There were constant phone calls, people everywhere, and no rest in sight, but after the funeral was over, where did all of the people go?

Victoria shared with me that her son, Luke, was experiencing an enormous amount of guilt concerning Joshua's death, and many other disturbing things which resulted in a lot of attention too. Upon my opening the door, Victoria immediately exposed her fears that she did not know what she was going to do concerning Luke.

Perhaps; the second day after Joshua's death was the first date that I recall being totally aware that I acted selfishly, but I did not get too upset with myself. I also realized that I should protect myself in the flesh. I did not know how to relate to Luke's feeling of guilt, as our guilt issues were entirely different. Actually it was not until later that I recognized any hints of guilt.

One time was too many times, but Victoria constantly brought her son to me for consolation and she persistently cried on my shoulder in person and over the phone; despite the fact that I already had enough on my plate.

Certainly, I did not have room for anymore or anyone else's issues. It was not a true relationship from the beginning. Now was not the time to form one. Luke is her son and her problem at that particular time. She needed to deal with her son, just as I needed to take care of my son. After all, this would be the last thing on this earth that I could do for my son. Luke attended grief counseling at the school as I spoke with many students on that Monday. Please note that I shared these words with Victoria, and though it may have come as a surprise to you, it will not be a surprise to her.

I really attempted to be patient, loving and kind, even though my attempts did not always manifest. I offered the name of a therapist. I did not want to be rude. I did not want to say do not bring yourself or your son back here for comforting; finally, I did not have any other choice, as I politely closed the door. *Still*, important matters of the heart needed to get done in a timely fashion.

Immediately, Corrinna and Joe purchased their airplane tickets, and they arrived home shortly after midnight, Sunday morning. Serving in the military definitely has many advantages. Corrinna was extremely emotional at a distance, but my heart sank again, as I witnessed her painstaking being. As I think back, tears come into my eyes as I recall how devastated we all were at these moments.

As Corrinna entered Maria's home, I shall never forget the soft hug that Corrinna gave to me, as if she knew the extent of my physical and emotional pain. We stood in the kitchen and silently cried, as our tears poured down our faces the Pergo floors were drenched. Our 'family' was together, but Joshua's body was not present. His absence was burly clear and painful. The loss that we suffer is huge, just as huge, if not larger than Joshua's heart.

I can tell you that I was afraid of my two daughters' being in the same vehicle together. I would wonder what if something happens to them both at the same time, but God is a deliverer. Death brings thoughts to your door that you do not think about on a daily basis. The reality was that we knew too well the plans that were made for the next day. We had to meet with the funeral director the next morning.

Corrinna and Joe's flight arrived very late.

After sharing our loss, emotions, and expressions of love, we went to bed. I am unsure if being extremely exhausted; emotionally, spiritually, and physically helped us to sleep, but I think that we managed to sleep at least for a few hours.

At some point, I was in contact with the Joshua's principal, Mr. Jefferies. He scheduled grief counseling to be available at the high school on Monday. May I assure you that the administration of this school district did an amazing job handling the death of my son?

I assured Mr. Jefferies that I would be at the school on Monday afternoon, and that I would speak with some of the students. I cannot tell you the amount of people that offered to do anything that we needed to be done, but they kept themselves at a distance. I knew that they said these words from the bottom of their hearts, but I could not think of what anyone could do to help us at this time. The following Sunday, we attended Pastor Paul's church, as we praised the Lord through our pain.

I do not know what I was thinking or why I volunteered to go to the school for the day of grief set aside for Joshua, but on this day I recognized that that I was a preteen when Daddy died. In addition, I recalled some of the things that I would have rather heard than those that I did hear. The things that we shared at the school on Monday, March 17, 2008 were things that I would have preferred to hear about my daddy, and the rest I stated at my son's funeral.

Different students, faculty, and our family gathered in a room. We talked about many of the positive things that we easily recalled about Joshua. There were many positive stories that I did not hear before. Some were funny, but more importantly we encouraged each other on that day. One of the best things that I offered thus far just occurred. It was not because of what I gave; rather, I received so much from the giving. In addition, I heard some things that made me exceptionally proud to be the mother of Joshua Wayne-Anthony Brown.

I almost cried when Candace mentioned how Joshua would not allow her to stop practicing dribbling with her left until she gained confidence. Joshua politely told her dad that she had to work on it just a little while longer. Joshua always wanted others to do their best; yet, he stated that I was hard on him for requiring that he give his best. Now, I chuckle at the thought.

I know that Joshua is very special to me, but I am his mother. However, I did not know just how special Joshua was to more people than I ever dreamed. Once the vacant hallways of the school were cleared of students, our family, some of Joshua's friends and associates, and Mr. Jefferies walked to Joshua's locker. The responsibility of cleaning out Joshua's locker for the last time was given to me.

Actually, I thought that I was impressed with cleanliness of his locker. I am unsure why I thought that I was impressed; generally, Joshua kept his room clean. While I worked on Sunday afternoons Josh did not hesitate to clean the entire apartment without a request being entered or demanded.

While at his locker, I carefully sorted through and touched each book with a page; then, slowly, I returned those items that were to remain with the school back to Mr. Jefferies. The private matters went in a bag that would go to the apartment with me. Purposely, I took my time because I did not want to close Joshua's locker, which I knew that Joshua would never open again. Yet and *still*, I could not believe the impressions that Joshua left on so many hearts of students.

As we slowly and silently walked down the hallways, scrolls of cream paper inscribed personal writings on them about my son.

My tired eyes opened wider on this date. I reviewed each written word, as I carefully noted each signature one by one, and I took each moment by moment. I attempted to seal each word and signature into my worn brain.

Although I was not searching for a negative word, location of a negative word went undiscovered between the schools' walls. Joshua's smile, warm personality, and how much he would be missed were carefully and painfully written all over the walls of his former high school that he once stood proudly between, but his impression will last a lifetime.

Recently, I expressed my concerns to a woman; it is hard enough to get through a day dwelling on the positives of Joshua. Certainly, I do not need to hear any negatives. As his mother, I know that Joshua was imperfect. I choose to dwell on the positives.

While we were at the high school, channel ten news arrived. Mr. Jefferies politely took the reins, and he spoke with the news reporter. I became very pleased with the news coverage and the principal. It took several months to review the footage. Mr. Jefferies stood very tall and proudly, and he spoke very highly of Joshua.

At some point, Mr. Jefferies also remarked about how society views children. On this day, he stated that this was one case that teens spoke very loudly and did things in a very respectable manner. I contribute the students' actions to the fine leadership at this School District, and of course their parents! Channel ten reported one of Joshua's friends who stated, "Joshua scored the winning basket." Another friend reported "That Joshua grabbed his arm and said, O Lord." Oh, did I mention that in one of Joshua's songs he prophesized that he scored the winning basket at the last second?

Some of the young men that were playing the pickup basketball game on the blacktop court figured that Joshua was only joking after he scored the winning basket. They soon learned that this was not an on stage performance. In the High School talent show that Joshua had recently performed, the audience was on their feet dancing and yelling his name; rather, Joshua really needed help.

Upon this realization, someone phoned 911 after 2PM on this Saturday afternoon. Some students reported that the ambulance took forever to get there, but the coroner checked the timing of the call. He established and reported the amount of minutes that it took the ambulance to get to the park. I can only imagine how the teens felt that witnessed Joshua collapsing on the black top. I think of them often and pray for each of them; although, I do not know each of them by name.

The last day of the week came on the day that I felt as if my life ended, which a part of my life did end. No longer did I have a child at home to take care of, but there were many tasks that needed to be completed before anyone of Joshua's family could rest. The next necessary step was planning of the funeral arrangements. I did not know the necessary planning involved in preparing for a funeral.

I played the piano, sang, and attended many funerals, but the only funeral that I had any major input in was my ex-mother in-law's funeral. I helped, Ray's sister Linda, plan and orchestrate the funeral of their mother, but Joshua's funeral would be my first experience planning an entire home-going service. I did the only thing that I knew would work, as I began to **pray without ceasing.**

Chapter 10

Another brash statement that Victoria offered earlier was, "I cannot believe that you are not sedated." If I was not already rare, it was at that moment that I immediately became raw. If I was sedated somewhere, even if I needed to be, who would make Joshua's funeral arrangements; her? I do not think so! Regardless as to the difficulty of burying my son, personally, I do not know how any family member allows someone else to plan a loved one's funeral.

Perhaps my daughters or my mother would have taken charge, but I think that would have been one of my biggest regrets. I did know that we, my daughters, their husbands, and I, needed to get through this somehow. I know some of that resulted through my mother's and others' prayers, but the only method was total oneness, with God's covering. At least five people became one on March 15, 2008. Prior to doing anything, we held hands, and we prayed our way through it all. Thank God that we prayed prior to making Joshua's funeral arrangements.

I requested that my ex-husband, Ray, not bring Shirley to the funeral parlor to make our son's final arrangements. The first time that I ever laid eyes on this woman was at the hospital on **March 15, 2008**. This stranger of a woman walked up to me with her arms extended and offered her condolences. She said, "I am sorry." I asked, "And who are you?" She replied, "I am Shirley." Although I heard Shirley curse me out previously and the childish name that she allegedly called me which came through the worn grapevine, this woman was unknown to me. Yet, she wanted to be included in making my son's final arrangements, but that which I did know, I was not very pleased.

Nonetheless, if the request that Shirley be absent at the funeral arrangements could not be honored, the funeral parlor was large enough for her to have enough respect to sit in a different waiting area while we, Joshua's parents and his sisters, attempted to finalize the last possible doable rites on this earth. I believe that Joshua and I had that right!

To be even more honest with you, Ray was extremely blessed to be invited to make the final arrangements, especially, after one of the last conversations that my son had with me concerning his dad the Friday night prior to his exodus. Do you think this may be in part why Ray thanked me for the invite to the funeral arrangements? Already, our family and God knew the truth.

Some kinfolks offered the suggestion that I not allow Ray into the funeral. I taught Joshua that no matter what, that was his dad. If I did anything less that would label me as a hypocrite. My son in-laws' engines were steaming from many of Ray's absences during Joshua's life.

My son in-laws, Joe and Manuel almost allowed their anger to take them over by taking matters into their own hands. Kindly, but with authority, I requested that they allow it to rest. I reminded them, as well as myself, that this was about Joshua. The undertaker seemed grateful for this wisdom. Soon, Shirley became absent in my mind, just as she was from Joshua's life and during his funeral, even though she was in attendance.

Mr. Walker commended our actions as a family several times. We were not there to make Mr. Walker's job difficult. We were there to plan Joshua's funeral in a respectful manner. I recall Mr. Walker sitting very confidently, professionally, and politely, and he began with these words, "I went to the school to check out Joshua's reputation." At that moment, my heart skipped a few beats and my eyebrows rose because I could not fully comprehend why a funeral director felt the need to do such a thing. Without stating a word; perhaps, my looks said it all, Mr. Walker gently explained that we needed to break the funeral up into three days because of the outstanding reputation of my son. My mouth widely gaped open, as my eyebrows relaxed, and my eyes were filled with tears while my heart pattered softly.

I expected that Joshua's entire funeral would be held entirely on Saturday, but Mr. Walker reassured me that would not work well. I did not know how anything would work. At this point, I did not know where Joshua's funeral would be held. Mr. Walker addressed specific questions concerning Joshua to Ray and me. I became so disgusted, appalled, disturbed, and utterly angered by his dad's irrational responses, because most of his answers were totally inaccurate. Honestly, I did not have a clue as to what to do, think, or feel. Again, I wanted to scream, yell, cry, and perhaps even curse a bit. I did not say much, except to politely help correct Ray's errors as fashionably as possible. I am sure that my eyes verbalized an earful.

I am reminded of a day when Ray came to pick Joshua up as scheduled. I reminded Ray with these words, "You have a wonderful son." He replied, "Oh really." I became livid!!!! It is sad that Ray learned how true this statement was at his own son's funeral. I know if I was shocked by how special Joshua was to so many people; without any doubt in my mind, Joshua's funeral had to totally blow Ray's mind. Ray did not see the half, because he was literally absent from the candlelight vigil and Joshua's viewings!

I am sure that Ray did not know what to expect at the funeral. He did not choose one item, and he only knew a limited amount of Joshua's friends and associates. Ray did not ever see Joshua in his blue and white sports' uniforms. Ray's only concern was that his wife's name appears on the obituary during his son's funeral. As we began discussing the obituary, my ex-husband's only recommendation was that Shirley's name be listed on my, (excuse me), our son's obituary, which stated that Joshua was a miracle.

I recalled that Ray told me privately "I do not have any money for no funeral; I live paycheck to paycheck just like everybody else," which became another fiery moment. Who did have any money for a funeral, but this was our son's funeral! So, I inquired to make sure that my hearing was not totally impaired. At this moment, I did not know if I heard Ray correctly. Was I to become the responsible party to pay for this funeral, obituary, flowers, and any other expenses? He replied, "Yes, I live paycheck to paycheck, just like everybody else."

I became embarrassed for Ray and Shirley. I did not have much money either. Once again, money was not the issue. This was the last thing on this earth that we could do for our son. Rather than upset myself even more, I assured Mr. Walker that we would talk about the obituary later, and I told him that I would also bring back Joshua's social security number, even though I fully memorized most of Joshua's life.

Yes, with the exceptions of Mr. Walker, my daughters, and their husbands, there was room for a wealth of distrust in the funeral parlor on that day. I looked Mr. Walker directly in his eyes and committed to him that no matter what I needed do that every red cent would be paid in full as soon as possible. Mr. Walker did not appear fretful.

Already, my mind and heart overflowed anger during this stage of grief and many of Ray's reactions compounded that anger, and if I was a bank, assuredly, that rate was compounded at a daily rate on this day! Hindsight tells me that perhaps mercy is necessary and that perhaps Ray's wrong answers, lack of names of his other relatives, and lack of adhering to leaving Shirley out of the funeral parlor is related to his illness. I became sickened that he could not recall his own children or his grandchildren's last names.

The fact that he did not provide any of the names of his mother, great grandchild, children, siblings or relatives disgusted me as well. I don't know if Ray could have done anything right on this date after hearing my son's last encounter with his father, and the fact that he lacked the respect, decency, and responsibility. What did I expect?

A Special Gift

Maybe Ray was embarrassed. If he was not embarrassed, I was mortified for him and Shirley. I was too disgusted with Ray during this moment to recall that Ray may have been recuperating, but let's give him that benefit of the doubt; even though, as you have read, he has demonstrated this type of behavior prior to his illness. *Still*, let us apply mercy, just as I ask God for mercy daily.

I had only purchased an accidental life insurance policy on Joshua's life, and his father did not purchase any life insurance on his son. Well, with all due respect, not to my knowledge. When I logically think about it, perhaps that is why Ray only requested a death certificate.

I purchased and sent to Ray the death certificate. In addition, I sent Ray a t-shirt and a wristband, and a bond that the other radio station purchased for Joshua. However, I am unsure if Ray ever heard Joshua's CD. I am uncertain if Ray received the package because he has yet to say thank you.

I believe if the radio station knew that we were struggling financially that they would have offered help. Perhaps they did, but if they did, Ray received that help too. The radio station sent flowers to the funeral home. Although I purchased accidental life insurance, I did have many doubts that the insurance would pay the $5,000.00 face value amount of the policy. Yet, I trusted God completely!

At this time, the autopsy was inconclusive. I was unsure if the premium was paid, as I was not sure of anything during this time. The life insurance policy was in effect, but it was just that an accidental life insurance policy, which meant that the policy would only be paid for it if Joshua's death was ruled as an accident.

I was only working part time, and I was also attending school full time. It did not matter that I really lacked money for a funeral but Joshua's death necessitated a funeral. I could not believe it, and I became irate with his dad. Living paycheck to paycheck was not the issue. It seemed rather personal and perhaps ignited unresolved issues.

Ray took one look at the price of a coffin, and said, "WOW," and with that look, Ray kept his eyes towards the exit door of the funeral parlor, and Ray exited very quickly.

As sure as Ray released that gasp from his tongue, Ray walked out of the funeral parlor, and he did not return.

People only think this happens in movies, but believe me the idea came from someone. As Joshua's family we chose each item separately and very carefully to fit his personality, which is simply beautiful. Although the challenge was extremely difficult for all of us, Corrinna needed extra time to enter into the situational room that we all dreaded facing.

I recall telling Corrinna to take her time, as I gently reminded her that we needed to get through this protocol, because if we could not get through this part of the night, certainly, we would not get through the day of the funeral. Slowly; but surely, we entered into the room as a broken yet totally unified family as we needed to select each item necessary for Joshua's funeral.

My son-in law, Manuel, is a salesman at heart, and he began attempting negotiations concerning a coffin. Mr. Walker immediately informed Manuel that he planned to work with me. As I walked in the door, I saw the coffin that I did not want to select. I knew that I did not have a choice in this matter. Then, I peaked at the cheapest coffin available. In my heart and possibly on my face, I frowned immediately, while my heart said, "No."

Mr. Walker assured me that I would not be judged for this choice. I could not put my son's remains in that coffin; regardless as to what I needed to do to pay for another one. I would have cleaned 1000 dirty bathrooms with my injured spine bent over before I would put my son in that casket. Mr. Walker offered this particular casket to us for free, but I could not live with that decision. Maria and Corrinna and their husbands were on the same page.

Mr. Walker's alternate offer was to enable purchase of the coffin that I desired to lay my son's body in for a much lowered ticket price, which I trusted that we would manage to afford. I did not know that we were required to purchase a vault, and pay for many other things upfront, but I will say this again and again, God is so good!

Later, Mr. Walker gently offered his advice that I should speak to Ray and inform him of my financial position, and this became the one and only thing that Mr. Walker and I totally disagreed about the entire time that we worked together. I refused to ask Ray for anything while Joshua was living, and after Ray's remarks that he did not have any money for a funeral, I adamantly refused to ask Ray for a dime to help pay for his son's funeral.

Chapter 11

Blessings do not only come in a financial form! By the next day, I knew for certain that Joshua needed to be buried in a purple shirt and a charcoal gray suit, but that was only one thing that needed to be done. We needed to select and purchase a burial plot. I did not ever want to go to the cemetery. Especially, I did not want to go that evening. However, it was subtly insisted that we handle that task.

While totally fatigued, we drove by one cemetery, which I confessed prior to leaving the funeral parlor that I did not desire my son's remains to lay. Later, Mark informed me that there is another Joshua Brown already at the cemetery. Immediately, I knew that the second cemetery would be Joshua's final resting place. However, I became too exhausted to choose the right burial plot just then, but I did have a good idea as to where Joshua's body would be laid. The location that I spotted had a view of the sunrise and gracefully setting, and it is on a hill with a tree nearby for shading purposes.

Instinctively, I knew that this would be Joshua's final resting place, and it would be a place that I would be visiting often. No one that I know of in their right mind would ever want to select a final resting area for a child. It is so unnatural, but I am a witness that it really does happen. The next day, my daughters and I traveled alone to select flowers that would become shaped into the family spread. We chose white lilacs and white carnations. Some of the white carnations were slightly sprayed with a fuchsia color and the spread contained fourteen lavender roses.

The reason for the selection of fourteen lavender roses was that I thought of fourteen people that I wanted to give a rose in remembrance of the beautiful rose from God's garden, named Joshua. Maria made sure that the family spread was as perfect as a family spread can be arranged. The spread was simply beautifully arranged. Once again, Maria returned to her role of my right hand. Upon returning home from picking out the floral arrangements, I realized that God confirmed our next selection.

By the time that we arrived home, a floral delivery sent from Baltimore, Maryland, was made while my daughters and I were selecting the flowers that matched our selection perfectly. I recall asking Corrinna if she telephoned her friend who shipped these flowers to our family. She replied, "No mommy." At one of the most dreadful periods of my life, I already saw the hand of God in our selections at least three times.

The first time that this conformational process occurred, I almost faintly fell out of my chair. My daughters and I had just decided on the emblem that would be placed inside of Joshua's coffin would be prayer hands. The other choice was a music symbol.

The way that we handled all of our decisions was quite simple after we prayed without ceasing. First, as always, we held hands in unison and prayed. Next, I asked each of my daughters their opinions. If they were in agreement, then it became the final decision, but if their opinions differed, then I made the concluding resolution, but all with prayer.

Upon our arrival home from selecting the casket, emblem, and vault, William, who so kindly produced Joshua and his son, Will's CD, came to visit. William handed me photographs of Joshua and Will. I recall screaming as I almost fell out of my chair. The very first photograph of Joshua and Will demonstrated Joshua's hands in a praying position. I was floored to say the least.

My mom offered to pick up a purple shirt for Joshua to wear, but I could not grant her that request. I knew upon seeing the shirt that would be the time that I would know which shade of purple I needed to purchase. Purple was a very strange thing for a color because Joshua's and my favorite color is red.

Upon entering the men's department of a local store, I spotted the purple, (almost fuchsia), colored shirt that I intuitively knew needed to be on my son's body. I apologized to a lady that waited on me in the department store because I felt on edge. I offered an apology if I appeared out of character, but it was difficult to shop for my son's last outfit to wear on this earth. She grabbed and hugged me and said these words, "My family is praying for you daily." I will never forget that experience or that woman's face.

Later, my daughters selected a purple and gray outfit for me. The suit was light gray, and the shirt was a lavender shade of purple which they matched to Joshua's tie which included fuchsia, lavender, light gray, and charcoal gray. Joshua's handsome outfit needed to be at the undertaker's office by Wednesday because the private viewing was scheduled for Thursday evening. Wednesday prior to dropping of Joshua's clothing to Mr. Walker, and later that evening a candlelight vigil was planned.

Joshua played basketball and football for Senior High School that he attended. As a parent, I took an active role in the Basketball Boosters' Club. First, I acted as the concession stand coordinator, which generally meant that I would be in the concession stand when parents would not show up as scheduled, and that was often.

My next role became co-treasurer. I refused to remain in that role without the proper controls in place. Only one person needed to sign the checks, and statements were rarely brought to the meetings. When the bank records were brought to the meetings, they were bogus. No one was counting the cash prior to handing the box over to the other treasure at that time. The time came to end that position.

Prior to Joshua's death, there was an ongoing audit and an investigation because of suspicions that I brought to the attention of Alisha and Marissa. I believed, without a doubt, that funds were not properly controlled. I had reasonable suspicions that funds were possibly abused. Things were not adding up.

The evidence boldly spoke for itself that this in fact was an issue, and the meeting was previously scheduled. I requested that the meeting not be rescheduled. I knew that my co-treasurer hat was about to be laid to rest forever. That Wednesday morning, I went to Mr. Jefferies' office and met with him and the other ladies that were/are officers of the Boosters' club.

I was treated very poorly by some of the members of the Booster club because I shed light on my dark suspicions, which was unnerving. Anyone with an ounce of sense knows that you must have controls on your books. Even a silly and naïve, female like me knows that you do not hand over $10,000.00 plus budget of funds to anyone who has a prior history of writing bad checks, but I became the fall guy for the heat of exposing the demons.

At this particular meeting, I wore my co-treasurer hat and these are the words that I said for everyone to hear, "When I exposed this I was not trying to get anyone in trouble. I do not want to see this mother separated from her children. I only wanted controls on the books."

I told the Mr. Jefferies that I was leaving this situation in his capable hands, and I dismissed myself from the co-treasurer position. Eventually, the audit report revealed an amount over six thousand dollars was stolen by writing of illegal checks.

It is my understanding that the other co-treasurer, who had the checks in her possession when these illegal checks were written, made restitution for the missing amounts. Earnestly, I prayed for her and her family. Nonetheless, controls are now on the Booster club's books. The funds that were stolen had not been replaced as of Joshua's death, and this is one of the reasons that I requested that donations be made to this club in lieu of flowers. There is no proof of how much, if any cash was stolen. Cash was unverified prior to my role as co-treasurer, but my job ended, and I removed that co-treasurer cap forever.

After taking off that cap, my favorite hat will always remain on my head. This cap as a mother showed because I *still* needed to take care of my son's body. Confirmations of my intuitions were verified. After leaving the meeting, I returned home and gathered Joshua's underclothing, shirt, tie, suit, belt, earring, lapel, and shoes. Next, I took each garment to the undertaker, as Joshua's body needed to be dressed for the private viewing. After I took the clothes to the undertaker, I came back home and attempted to rest for the evening. A candlelight vigil was planned in Joshua's honor, and I did not know what to expect.

I never attended a candlelight vigil, and certainly not in the chilly rain. This was the first time that I openly held a candle outside because someone died, and it was in honor of my son. I did not know if this was scriptural or if it interfered with religious beliefs. I asked Grace, but I am unsure if I received a direct answer, but she attended as well. So, I assume there is not a scriptural reasoning to regret that this occurred. *Still*, I had no idea of what to expect.

I recall walking down a hill, and seeing the lights of cameras from a local television station. I turned around because I did not know what to do. I proudly wore Joshua's white retired football jersey with the number 14 visibly displayed. I was amazed at the size of the crowd, which amounted to about 700 people; even though it was a rainy, dreary evening.

The candlelight vigil was held at the park that the newspapers reported that my son collapsed at, but it was not at the park that Joshua requested to go to play ball. My spiritual mother, my daughters, son-in laws and three grand children were in attendance.

I believe that Joshua's best friend, Mark and a few other friends helped organized the candlelight vigil. I did not know that Mark was at the bank upon my arrival. Not knowing what to do or what to expect, I called out for the Mr. Jefferies or Mark. Neither of them answered. I did not know what was to happen next, but I did know that there were four undercover policemen on the scene.

After I was seated, Pastor Grace offered the opening prayer, and the next thing that I recall is one of Joshua's friends, Mariah, singing a song. I think that I wanted to cry when I heard her distraught voice crack while she fought back her sorrows and tears; besides, Mariah sang very beautifully, but I could not release another sound.

Often, I believed that if I ever began to cry that I would be unable to stop. Eventually, I learned that this was only a myth. One of Joshua's ex-girlfriends, who is not named Alice, read a poem and others said some things about Joshua. I recall some making remarks, and some people made me smile, some made me angry, and some things that were spoken were just plain ignorant. Some people were great actors while the cameras rolled. It became blatantly obvious who wanted the spot light that evening, while others' comments were extremely compassionate, kind and sweet.

Joshua's song *"Wipe Your Eyes,"* silently but profoundly met the airways, and I only wanted to hear Joshua and Will's voices and the silence that would capture the *still*, silent moments forever, but that did not happened, as someone already tried to take Joshua's place.

A female reporter, Tammy, was in attendance. May I report that she did a fabulous job reporting on the candlelight vigil? She wrote a four page story with detailed coverage on Joshua that includes an editorial about what she learned from Joshua's death. I felt it only fittingly to provide her the very first interview for this book! I felt rather embarrassed by some ignorant males who obviously exposed their own flaws and secrets while flaunting in front of the under-cover police officers. Now the officers know who to keep their eye on, as if they did not already know.

I could not believe that some parents did not teach their children how to act in public, especially while honoring someone's life that recently died. There were only a few who did not have any dignity, respect, and honor for themselves, out of the hundreds of hundreds of people who appeared to honor my son's life on that cold, rainy, and dreadful evening. It was definitely my first experience at any candlelight vigil.

Before the night passed to morning, surely more good than evil come out of this event. Just the fact that people loved my son and our family enough to plan such an event said more than words can ever express, along with the fact that people came out in the midst of bad weather! It was a mind blowing experience.

Mark was absent at the beginning of the candlelight vigil because he was at the bank. Mark, Joshua's best friend presented me with a check in excess of $1,000.00, which shocked me again. I was not expecting any money or such a large turnout from people on this evening

Mark and other friends of Joshua sold t-shirts with a logo, that stated, "In Loving Memory, Josh Brown" and "Forever in our hearts." The t-shirts inscribe his date of birth, date of death, and his name, and that quickly within days, I was presented with a check over $1,000.00. The t-shirts were sold at $15.00 each. Joshua's female friends had t-shirts designed with a picture that Joshua took of himself, with his name, date of birth, date of death, and his football or basketball number on the back. Joshua's friends did an amazing job coming together at the death of their friend. Even those who were not Joshua's true friends acted in accordance

Our family needed to rest after this event, as we prepared to see Joshua in an embalmed state and fully dressed in his purple shirt and charcoal gray suit at the private viewing the next evening.

I telephoned Ray to remind him of the private viewing for the family, but I assume that he did not consider himself or his relatives Joshua's family. They did not attend. Mom, Grace, Aunt Loraine, Corrinna, Maria, Manuel, Joe and I went into the funeral parlor that evening. When I telephoned Ray to remind him of the appointed time, the only question that Ray attempted to ask me was about the seating arrangements at the funeral.

I did not have time to give thought to that question, as we had a lot of unfinished business. Maria, Corrinna, and I gathered many items that belonged to Joshua. I was planning on draping the room at the funeral home with some of Joshua's things. I gathered Joshua's baby shoe, XBOX, name poem, trophies, and family photos, along with other items to be placed in the room that would hold a countless number of people the very next day. On the evening of the private viewing, I began sitting out Joshua's things. I placed them where I felt as though they belonged, but Mr. Walker politely reassured me that his staff would take care of Joshua's items, and that I should spend some time with Joshua. Evidently, I was avoiding spending time with Joshua due to fear of my reactions. Looking back, I did a lot better than I would have ever imagine possible, but I do know that **with God NOTHING is impossible.**

Prior to these moments I was consciously thinking, but I only did that which I knew that I needed to do, which was being as present in the moment as I possibly could. I began looking over Joshua's body. I lifted his stiff hand to place a darker purple band from his nephews and niece on his arm, one of the first things that I noticed was that Joshua already had two hair ties which also rested peacefully on his left wrist, which were fuchsia and charcoal gray. One tie around Joshua's wrist exactly matched the shirt that I picked out and the other hair tie was charcoal gray, which matched his suit perfectly. Now, I knew the exact reason that I was urged to bury him in purple and gray.

Mr. Walker showed me the gold colored pin that gently rested on the cream lining of the cover, and he politely asked me if I wanted the pin for myself. I do not recall if I answered him, because I was again caught by surprise; yet, I witnessed another confirmation. You see, the gold pin was in the form of a dove, which became another part of the funeral process and another confirmation. Upon ordering the family spread, we selected to ascend a dove at the cemetery.

The floral designer was adamant that two doves were to be sent to the heavens together as protective measures from the sparrows. I buckled up, and stood my grounds on this one. To me, sending two doves to the heavens represented that two of my children's spirits were with God, but I could not send two doves. The beautiful floral designer seemed to fear that the lonely dove would be injured, but I told her these words, "His eye is on the sparrow and I know that he watches me," and I left the situation of the floral designer in God's care. It was an extremely exhausting day.

The public viewing was next to get through, and at this point, we were taking one half of a second at a time. We had not gotten to one minute at a time. There was not an impression that time would change. Actually, time remained the same, but how we got through time did eventually change.

Our family's tradition was to take a family photo every year whenever we gathered together, which is normally at least once a year when Corrinna and Joe could get home. Already, we decided that we would all wear purple and gray at the funeral, but we had two more days added to be dressed in the same color.

Color coordination was extremely important to me because it was our tradition. We all agreed on the color pink for the viewing, and that probably was because we all had something pink. We chose a cream shade for the burial. I wore the gown that I wore at Maria's wedding. I made it clear that black was not to be worn. The white shade matched the cover of the coffin.

Since the burial, I have thrown the gown away. Although the memory of wearing this particular gown at Maria and Joe's wedding carried sentimental value, wearing it the last time was a painful reminder. Additionally, I believe that I threw away the pink outfit that I wore to the viewing, and it was one of my favorite dresses too. Unfortunately, flowers were never a favorite.

I requested that in lieu of flowers that contribution be made to the football and basketball boosters' club. To my knowledge, this money was not going to serve Joshua or our family any purpose, but rather for those who continued to actively participate in these sports. The lavender bow, which matched the roses, attached to the extended family spread/floral arrangement had the words that said it all, "We love you." However, they were not the only flowers present. Obviously, my requests were not honored. I am hopeful that people did not take the time to read Joshua's obituary, which was printed in at least three local newspapers, and was made available online. Ironically, Joshua had come home from the hospital in a limo, but we were driven to and from each destination where we were honoring Joshua's life.

The limo picked up our family up from Maria and Manuel's house on the evening of the public viewing, which was held on Good Friday. Mr. Walker, who was the supervisor and chauffer, on this date, quietly warned me that there was an enormous amount of floral arrangements, despite my requests. Again, I displayed no anger, but I accepted the flowers the best that I could with a grateful broken heart. The first thing that I noticed was the smell of flowers, a lot of flowers; I assume this is how some people wanted to show their love for our family. Please recall that the smell of flowers reminds me of death, not life.

The funeral director showed us where we would be standing. At most of the viewings I attended, the family sat on the first row, and people walked by and greeted them after they have viewed the body. I was overwhelmed by the number of people that greeted me that day. It felt as though I hugged at least one thousand people that Friday evening alone. Only three disturbing things occurred at Joshua's viewing. Ray was absent. Rita's cell phone went off right in front of the coffin, and the other disturbing thing that occurred is not even worth writing about.

Joshua's dad's absence did not seem to be a matter of concern for others than our immediate family members. We did not speak about it until later. I cannot tell you the number of people that Joshua's life touched or vice versa. It began during the grief counseling at school on Monday, with the scroll of writings on the wall, and then the candlelight vigil; now, Good Friday, my arms were flooded with hundreds of hundreds of hugs.

I cannot say it enough, I am so proud to be the mother of all three of my children, but I am especially proud to be the mother of Joshua Wayne-Anthony Brown. Truly, he was an amazing son who was loved by more people than I could have ever imagined. Although his body is not present, I know that Joshua will never be forgotten! I was pleasantly surprised to see a few of my youth league team players, Joshua's teammates, at his viewing. After six or seven years of no interactions more evidence erupted that an impact was made. One male's comments, I will never forget. He hugged me and said, "You must be a hell of a woman." I was shocked to say the least.

During the viewing, many people stopped and wrote their fond memories of Joshua and I took the time to read each one. I will never forget what his best friend, Mark wrote as his favorite memory, "Just seeing him." Eventually, I read each memory, and I am *still* amazed at the responses. Other condolences were written online. Many of Joshua's teachers and friends of the family wrote beautiful comments which I appreciated very much. I cannot tell you that I read them immediately. Eventually, I read each one of them.

Many of Joshua's friends labored through love, very hard, and much of the night to put together a powerful PowerPoint presentation of Joshua's life, which was extremely powerful. It shared many people who played an iatrical part of Joshua's life; yes, Ray's face was among many other people's faces. *Still*, I watch the PowerPoint with love, honor, and pride.

Although Joshua and I were attending a local church during his last days on earth, we did not have an "official" church home. I was considered "a member," but my name is placed on a Heavenly role. I had no idea where the funeral was going to be held, especially upon Mr. Walker's announcement of how largely he estimated that Joshua's funeral would be. I did not have to ask for anything, including a church. Joe and Manuel really stood up, even though at this time they were both under the age of thirty.

They were always the "men" in Joshua's life, but during this week, they became the true MEN in Joshua's life. They did whatever needed to be done, from shining my shoes to ironing my clothing, from getting CD's and power points to the church, making certain that everything was properly set up and placed in motion, assigning the seats to Ray and his family, and they stood right by their wives' sides, exactly as they should. In addition, the girls kept busily handling other things as well. My family is not perfect, but we are a family!

For as much as I desired to have my son in-laws as Joshua's pallbearers, I knew that they would have done that as well, if I only asked. I believed and *still* believe that they should not leave their wives' sides. However, prior to the laying Joshua's body to rest, Manuel and Joe both manhandled Joshua's final remains as they gently carried his sturdy, durable coffin from the funeral parlor to the Hurst and from the Hurst to the ground. Mark grew into a fine man during Joshua's death, and I am unsure that he turned eighteen until June.

I did not believe that I could handle watching my favorite male cousins carry out my son's body. Therefore, I listed them as Honorary Pallbearers. I do believe that we all knew that it would be all over if any of us lost it during the actual services. I am sure that we all knew this too well, and we remained strong for each other. We shed many tears, but not necessarily publicly. At times, when we were alone, our only language at times only was tears and hugs. We all knew too well what needed to be done, and we were determined to do it to the dignity and honor of God, as the family of Joshua Wayne-Anthony Brown.

There is nothing wrong with anyone crying at funerals. I know this to be true because I cried at my share of funerals, but I did not want others' sympathy because of my tears. I accepted others' sympathy while sharing in their sympathy because they too have a loss. I recognize that although I may have the biggest loss, the fact of the matter is that Joshua was not only my loss.

I thank God for His strength during this time because when you are crying, you cannot see things clearly because the tears get in the way. Grief is another factor in one's vision being distorted. Therefore, I really was unable to see. Although faces are not vivid, I had the ability to see without a doubt how many people really loved Joshua and what "that boy" meant to so many people.

In planning Joshua's funeral, we gave one hundred percent in an attempt to accommodate everyone's request, especially when it came to parents' requests for the sake of their children concerning the viewing or no viewing of Joshua's body. Some parents desired that their children be in attendance, but only if Joshua's body would not be viewed. We honored this request by closing Joshua's coffin during the funeral, with a simple request for everyone to exit the church immediately and greet the family at the high school, at the repast. Some of you did not honor the family's request and that was extremely difficult for me to accept.

As a family in mourning, we made decisions that truly were to be respected. You have no idea what caused us to make these decisions. One thing that we would not settle for was leaving Joshua's body in the hallway while we were in the church. That just was not happening! We are a family, and our fleshly bodies were going to be in the same place for one last time together, and that was the end of the discussion. Even during his body's last minutes on this earth, I was of a protective nature which I am unashamed. Mr. Walker and our family talked for quite some time to come up with a plan as to how to convenience others, and the only way to do this properly was to keep everything on a timely schedule.

My cousin, aka my baby brother, Todd also stood up and was counted during our bereavement. He was very as quiet as he generally is, but his presence was SO profound! Even though a very polite announcement was made to exit the church immediately and to greet the family at the repast for the sake of time, this did not happen. *Still* some people refused to follow instructions and gather to greet the family despite the announcement. Again, I became annoyed because there was a valid reason to request this and I felt that it was pure selfishness to ignore the funeral director's directives.

It was never my intent to be rude and I am not apologizing, but Mr. Walker and I already agreed that if I stopped to greet one person that meant that I would need to greet everyone. Mr. Walker and the hosting church both individually and collectively were more than generous while working with us. We were freely given the church for a time period during this busy Easter season, and it was only respectful to get out of there in a decent time frame. Dear ones, please respect the family's requests, and know that decisions that are appropriately made for whatever the family is dealing with.

My daughters and I remained awakened until two Saturday morning, which was the actual date of the funeral. We were designing and redesigning the program for the funeral, which was to be at Staples the next morning in order to be at the church for the funeral by 11AM. The funeral director did not handle this task, and therefore we had another assignment. We were very fatigued, beyond exhaustion, but we did not want to purposely omit any known family members or have misspellings or misprints. Our endeavor was to positively dot all I's and cross every T.

As weary as we were, I am *still* shocked that we did as well as we did, but it only happened with prayer and by the grace of God.

The funeral was held Saturday at 11AM, and the obituaries were ready. Manuel and Joe made sure that the obituaries were made available when the first guest signed in at the church. Minister Sharon offered the Pastor Paul's services, and we met with him one morning prior to the services. I did not have any idea that in our conversations that God spoke the topic of the eulogy sermon, "What is in a name," which was taken from the book of Joshua.

During the eulogy, Pastor Paul spoke about many things concerning Joshua; for example: that he tore down walls, that Joshua was a prophet, a warrior, and a leader, and Pastor Paul explained how it would be possible to see Joshua again. Can I tell you, that I say amen to Pastor Paul's sermon again and again, even on this day?

Certainly, upon massive amounts of reflections, my son lived out his name in much more deeper ways than I could possibly explain to you! Pastor Paul was very mindful of the teens during the service and he reminded all of us in his altar call that if we texted Joshua saying "ttyl" which he broke down for me to understand represented the phrase: talk to you later. In addition, he reminded us all that we would indeed talk to Joshua later if we accepted Jesus Christ as our personal Savior.

Pastor Paul gave an altar call for anyone who wanted to give their life to God, and he asked anyone who was interested in responding to the call to lift their hands. He collectively prayed with each who responded to the call, and then instructed each individual to find a Bible teaching church. There was not one time that this man of God promoted *his* church, which made it all the better. Perhaps that was because he knew whom the church really belongs. I cannot say it enough, the man of God PREACHED!

It was not until the last hours of Friday night, that I knew the scriptures that would be read in our hearing on Saturday afternoon. Most of the service was done in decency and order. I did not preselect the scriptures, and I did not choose the routine funeral scriptures. Instead, I selected two family ministers that I believed lived their lives according to God's word, and I asked them to pray about the scriptures that God would be read at Joshua's funeral, and they did just so.

We have many preachers in our family, but these two ministers were the only two who God brought to my mind during the planning of Joshua's funeral. God knew that I only wanted those who are walking what they are talking! One minister, my cousin, Minister Danny, was traveling from Virginia, and he called us while in route to inform us of the scripture that God gave to him, which was from the New Testament, John 12:23-26. The other minister, Pastor Grace, was local, and God gave her a scripture from the Old Testament, I Samuel 12:20-23. Please read these scriptures at your convenience!

The funeral began with a pianist playing the piano, while the PowerPoint of highlights of Joshua's life radiated on the screen above. The pianist was pregnant, and she is a dear friend of Maria, who willingly accepted the challenge of playing the piano without charge.

My daughters, I, and others were in the pastor's office with Pastor Paul, and we were lead in prayer. After which, Mr. Walker politely announced to the audience to rise as the family of Joshua Wayne-Anthony Brown entered therein. As I walked to my seat in between my daughters, I was stunned to see Joshua's dad and some of his relatives on their feet, as the announcement was made.

My daughters, their husbands, and I began the processional. We walked in unison. We tightly clutched each other's hands. After being seated, Twin friends of the family sang, "His Eye is on the Sparrow." The gentleman who sang the National Anthem at Joshua's basketball games sang, "Amazing Grace." Minister Sharon and a member of the praise and worship team sang, "We Have Come This Far by Faith," which was the most profound song of the service; certainly, it was only by faith that we came this far. I could not prevent my eyes from beaming or the smile on my face as they sang the true words of this song.

However, I admit that I did not beam or smile during the entire service. Another trigger of anger belted me while the funeral was in process. A few things disturbed me, and my daughters recognized the written anger as it was obviously expressed on my face. Thank God that I was seated in the front of the church with my head facing front.

Another thing that angered me was the promotion of a church, which was neither done by the church which blessed us to freely use their facility nor Pastor Paul. My cousin who drove over 500 miles walked up to the podium and only read the scripture. Pastor Grace made sure that everything ran smoothly; even when the audio went awry, she made sure that it was corrected, but not once did either of them overstep any boundaries, and they are my relatives.

Please allow me to share the thing that amazed me concerning the pastors who willingly supplied us with their huge church. They provided our family with their services of ushering during the funeral. This quiet display of humbleness spoke volumes, and I am sure **that the angels have recorded this blessed event.**

Not only did they gracefully donate their humungous church without any charge, they willingly gave their services, their office space, and they never said one word. Pardon me, there is an exception they said, "You are welcome." They asked, "Do you need anything else?" Wow, they truly have a powerful testimony without saying one word.

Circumspectly, I selected the pallbearers, as one of Joshua and my final conversations during the last two weeks of his life consisted of those Joshua believed to be his truest and best friends. Without question, Mark was Joshua's main best friend, who wisely led the pallbearers. No human other than their parents' non-consent, could have prevented me from having at least these five friends as pallbearers to carry my son's body out of the church. Joshua trusted them, and so did I. There is no way on this earth that anyone that I did not trust could carry my son's body, as I would have been a nervous wreck!

Mark meekly requested that the pallbearers wear white tuxedos and red ties, which represented Joshua's favorite color. Graciously, I honored this request, and please allow me to add that they looked angelic. I did not have a choice except to silence one person due to one male's erratic episodes of behavior. My sanity or his silence, there was only one choice in that matter, but I did have a choice in who would speak.

Joshua loved to hear Pastor Paul preach! One Sunday, I told Joshua that we needed to leave early one Sunday morning because I had to go to work. Joshua questioned, why mom; why do we have to leave? As God would have it, we did not exit church early that particularly Sunday; rather, the services ended prior to the time I needed to leave for work. Nonetheless, I knew prior to Minister Sharon's offering of Pastor Paul's services that he was chosen by God to preach my son's funeral.

Prior to the ceremonies, our family met with Pastor Paul one time. Shortly after Joshua's exodus, I spoke with him briefly after a church service. Even Pastor Paul respected our privacy during bereavement and did not overcrowd us. Two cars loaded with my extended; yet, immediate family members arrived in Pennsylvania from Martinsville, VA. They brought the turnip greens, pickles, Easter baskets, cards, and condolences. My very own extended family did not come to visit me. They confessed that they wanted to make certain that I was okay, which is another reason that they traveled the distance.

Later, my extended family expressed to me that they did not want me to feel as though I needed to entertain/take care of them. They only saw and hugged me at the viewing and funeral. Although I really wanted to see them, God knows just how much I appreciate their love and respect for me and all that I had to deal with.

Many cousins and Aunt Kathy traveled many hours, but they recognized that my plate was extremely full, but they also recognized the fact remained that I did not have an appetite.

The irony of this situation is that I telephoned Virginia to make my request known that I desired that my cousin, Danny read a scripture at Joshua's funeral. I summoned for Danny because he lives the word of God, just as he teaches. My aunt and many other cousins traveled the distance; yet, they gave me the room to grieve.

Gratefully, I appreciate everything that everyone did and continues to do for our family with a completely broken heart, but the most appreciative moments prior to Joshua's funeral were those that I had with the hundreds of cards. I knew that someone thought of our family and the words in the cards were perfectly written. Some cards allowed me to respond with tears, a scream, a shout, or just a silent moment if that is what I so desired.

Please, allow me to remind each of us that a funeral is not a place to look for a husband! I could not believe the words that my ears heard, but I have no reason to lie to you. The apple does not fall far from the tree. If a grieving person wants your presence, they will find a way to get in touch with you, as our home was open for people for a brief visit. However, there was not any time for foolishness, counseling, or taking care of others.

Pastor Paul met with us at Maria's residence to prepare for the funeral. Maria was bothered by some of the things that she heard or that she did not hear the pastor say. After he left, she asked me, "Has he ever done a funeral before?" My reply to her was this, "I do not know, but does it matter if he stumbles, even falls, or whether this is his first time, especially if over 200 people give their life to God?" Maria did not respond, and that was most appropriate at that time.

Pastor Paul had a previous engagement on Good Friday, and he was unable to attend the viewing. Pastor Grace stepped right in. I stood by Joshua's head with my daughters beside me. When I was not embracing others, I was staring intently at Joshua's face. My mother, Aunt Loraine and Cousin Grace stood by Joshua's feet. Know that Joshua was surrounded by lots of love!

Although this was Pastor Paul's first funeral, he gave an altar call at Joshua's funeral. A few Sundays later, he reported to the congregation that over 200 people raised their hands to give their lives to God, who is so good! I was hurting and angry, and I encountered all type of feelings, what could I say about what I just witnessed?

A Florida resident/friend of Corrinna, Lynne, reminded me that some revivals do not account for that many people's lives saved. I cannot say what any of those people are doing with their lives, as that is not my concern. I know for a fact that when you dedicate your life to God it is His, and that He is in full control. Previously, I told Joshua that one day he would lead many, but I did not know it would be through his life and his death that over 200 people would give their lives to God. Who knows how many other people accepted God into their heart without raising their hands or by Joshua's last words, "Oh Lord?"

It may sound strange for anyone to say that a funeral was beautiful, but as Joshua's mother, I can tell you that his funeral was beautiful. There were plenty of times that I could not keep from smiling. I did not try to control it. There was a pleasant and warm aroma which did not consist of flowers; rather, a strong aroma that God was in that place. I do not know how many people were in attendance, but I can tell you that the humongous church was packed. There were many powerful things that happened.

After Joshua's friends and associates spoke, Mr. Jefferies addressed the students. The principal, Mr. Jefferies spoke to the audience, and he read Luke's words. Everyone was designated two minutes. A few of Mr. Jefferies spoken words were that I was the bravest woman that he ever met. I have a secret to disclose concerning those remarks. I always told Joshua when he was most afraid that he should act bravely until he became brave. I only acted as I commanded Joshua to do.

The seven pallbearers and three of Joshua's dearest female friends spoke briefly about their affiliations with Joshua. Then, our family spoke to the audience. Although I could not control what others said, I trusted those whom I allowed to speak, and I offered this position to each immediate family member the opportunity. My brother in-law was the first to speak from our family, and he spoke on behalf of Debra and my nephews, as Debra was unable to speak. My mom and step-father each said a few words. Manuel and Maria walked on the stage together, followed by Corrinna and Joe.

I did not have a notion of what my daughters were going to say. We did not share our notes, but I totally trusted their judgments. Corrinna recited a beautiful poem, which she personally wrote. Maria spoke her heartfelt words and confirmation approached when I spoke what was prepared the night prior. The words that she and I both spoke at different times were, "Whatever I could not do for Joshua, my daughters did."

Maria's voice cracked while she said a few words about her little brother and her children's uncle. Manuel and Joe did exceptionally well during all three events, and I am very proud to have them as my sons; they are not just my son in-laws. Corrinna did very well during the services after getting through the process of selections for the funeral. I did not even think about asking Ray if he wanted to say anything. He did not ask anything about the funeral other than seating arrangements. Unfortunately, none of Ray's other family members kept a relationship with Joshua to my knowledge.

Concerning Joshua, the absolute truth was confirmed, as I never positioned myself to ask Ray for anything. In the entire thirteen years that Ray and I were divorced, I only telephoned him one time to simply ask him to sign a check which was in both of our names listed as payees.

About ten years ago, I wanted to purchase Joshua a suit for Easter Sunday. This was the Saturday that Shirley cursed me out, and I made a conscientious vow that I would never ask Ray for anything for Joshua. Nine years later, around the same time frame is the first time this woman ever said these words to me, "I am sorry."

All that I asked Ray for was his "famous autograph" on a check that both of our names appeared. Fortunately, the check did not include the word "and." This meant that I did not need Ray's signature. We had just moved, and my finances were limited. I was trying to avoid going to a second hand shop to purchase his son a pair of gray pants. I only wanted to provide my son with a brand new suit for Easter Sunday. How redundant is this?

Once it was made clear that I would speak at Joshua's funeral I prayed hard about the words. The reality is that I did not want any young adult or adult to have to sit under any confusing words that I heard during my daddy's funeral. Somehow, I believed that the teens would be able to specifically hear me and that if any words that God did not want heard that my words from God would overshadow any mistruths about the God that I served! My message to everyone from the notice of Joshua's death was a reminder to celebrate Joshua's seventeen years of life that **God** gave to us. I learned the truth from the words of John at chapter 10 verse 10 *that it is Satan that comes to steal, kill, rob and destroy*, it is not God!

Pastor Grace reminded me that most of the time, the family sits quietly and receives words from others, but I did not want anyone to walk away with the burdens that I carried from the words that were spoken at Daddy's funeral, at the age of eleven.

Mary Kay stated that she heard that I preached a service and gave an altar call during Joshua's funeral, but I do not believe that I preached a sermon to anyone. I just talked about a special gift from God and that we should be mindful to thank God for the seventeen years **that God gave** to us through the gift of Joshua's life. Admittedly, I shared the mistakes that I made concerning my daddy's death in listening to the wrong messages, and I begged everyone in attendance not to make the same mistakes that I made. Pastor Paul preached unlike I ever heard him preach before.

The name Wayne has many different meanings in my life. It is very interesting to me that I cannot tell you how many countless people were in attendance at Joshua's funeral, and I can only give you names of those whom only God specifically allowed me to see during the time while I was speaking. In the rear of the church, standing against the wall, I noticed a familiar friendly face of someone that I fell in love about twenty seven years ago.

Yes, his fictitious name is **Wayne**. I felt my mouth move, but I am unsure if anyone heard these words that I quietly mouthed, "I knew that you would be here," and then I found my place in what I wrote and continued to speak to the audience. I did not want anyone to walk away from Joshua's funeral blaming God for Joshua's death. You see, God did not kill my son. I despise when I hear church folks say, "God will kill you," because some people do not have the accurate knowledge. God did not need an angel. Besides, we had one here on earth. Also, I stood solidly on my confession without the realization of what it was that I just ended with, and I said these words, "Today, I can say that I trust God!

After the crowd was dismissed, we had another viewing for extended family, which was very appropriate considering that Joshua's dad did not come to the private family or public viewing. Please recall that Ray and Shirley were present while the arrangements for the Joshua's viewings, funeral, and burial were planned. Some of Ray's relatives are *still* my relatives.

After the final public viewing for the extended family, there was a repast held at the school cafeteria. To my knowledge, none of Ray's family attended either. As mentioned throughout these writings, Ray is a "legend" in a large city, but not once was the focus of our son's funeral.

I did not know how we were going to prepare food for the repast or where we would serve anything to eat because we limited funds and we needed to be out of the church by a certain time. The funeral director never heard the usage of the term repast, but this is where some type of food/desert is served after a funeral. However, others took charge of this matter for our family.

Four members of the boosters' club came to our home earlier in the week to ask what we would like to serve at Joshua's repast. I did not know what selections to make. I did not have an appetite for a very long time. The new president of the Boosters' club, Juanita, insisted that we serve whatever our hearts desired. I asked Maria to appropriately choose the menu.

She chose Joshua's favorite meal, which included chicken, macaroni salad and so many other varieties of foods and drinks. I would never believe that hundreds of people would share my son's favorite meal, and especially without him. Later, I was informed that various companies donated food and drinks.

Yet, another confirmation came. During this brief meeting, I asked my friend Juanita about a picture that she took of Joshua. Juanita did not have knowledge that we needed to choose a photograph for the funeral program which would include the obituary. As God would have it, Juanita had previously wrapped two silver frames with the exact photos of Joshua, and inside these gifts had the photo of Joshua that I was asking her about during the brief meeting. Certainly, you will be able to see the smile that many students, faculty, and people spoke about. You may just say, "That boy," but with a smile!

I did not open the "gift," which included these framed photos until Juanita, Marissa, and Alisha left our home. I grasped for air once again, as God continued to confirm what and how we needed to handle each task set before us; but next, we needed to get through the funeral. The confirmation of which photograph that would be used for the funeral services program just arrived, as if Juanita was reading my mind.

Saturday morning came and the funeral was scheduled to begin at 11Am. Early that morning, I walked outside and took notice that snow flurries were falling from the sky in mid-March. I looked up and began to pray these words,

"Please, God let this snow stop."

I was praying because of the amount of people that would be traveling to Joshua's services and the distance. I was concerned because of the amount of inexperienced, and hurting teen drivers that I assumed would be on the road. In just a little while, the sun finally appeared, and the weather cooperated beautifully. Regardless as to the conditions of the roads, I knew that the full twenty four hours of the day would continue, no matter what, and so did Joshua's funeral.

The senior high school was very generous to us, as they opened up their cafeteria doors to us and hundreds of people on a Saturday afternoon during Spring break without supplying us with a bill. I believe that they may have paid overtime for the janitors.

Although I had many different types of pains, my numbness kept hunger pains at a minimum. Food was not on my mind, stomach, or heart. I did not attend the repast, but the rest of our immediate family attended. My taste buds were just as unconceivable as the awful taste of death. After the funeral, my only desire was to be alone with my thoughts, pains, and moments; besides, I became worn and terribly exhausted. Plenty of extra food was sent home for our family. Later, I learned that the firefighters of our community were fed as well. Wow, what a blessing on the eve of Easter. The next day became Easter Sunday, which was very difficult for me, but Easter Sunday was being celebrated as normal.

For those who the Easter bunny visited, Joshua's death did not stop you. For those you who wore brand new Easter bonnets, Joshua's death did not stop you. For those who sold Easter flowers Joshua's death did not infringe upon the sales. Even for those who do not celebrate Easter at all, that Sunday still came. I realize again, that the life was not going to stop even if I wanted it to. In addition, Church was in session as usual.

Easter morning, I spoke with Aunt Louise and she asked me if I planned to attend church. I answered, "Yes." Without mentioning another word, Aunt Louise said, "I will meet you at the church." Once again, she sat quietly with me, but that was all that I really needed or wanted. Indeed, God knew exactly what I needed even before the asking was necessary.

Someone, but not just anyone; Aunt Louise right there sitting next to me. I did not need anyone telling me anything or asking any questions. Certainly, I did not want anyone patting me or crying for me, or anyone depending on me for their lack of strength.

At times there were people who I really did not know that wanted to preach at me every time that they saw me, which created unspoken miles of distance. I really did not want to hear much during this time, except from the *still* quiet voice of God. If I had a question, I asked spiritual mother who knows the word!

I was listening for the directions that God was quietly whispering in my ear, which did not come from preaching on the streets. When I was able to listen to preaching, I attended church, but hearing sermons from the book of Joshua were terribly uncomfortable.

Night fell again and again, but the morning did come, and the time did come to lay my son's body to rest at his final resting place. Joshua's burial was held on Easter Monday morning. I took Mr. Walker's recommendation, and Joshua's burial was listed as private. It was schedule for 10Am on that regrettable Monday morning. Patiently, I waited until that morning to tell most of those invited. This only included those who I believed that I could trust.

Aunt Louise informed me that she had a previously schedule chemotherapy appointment and that she would not be present at Joshua's burial. Karen missed her mother's chemotherapy appointment. I wonder if Aunt Louise insisted that Karen be present at Joshua's burial. Whether or not it was a request of Aunt Louise's I appreciate Karen's presence so much, as she rarely missed a chemo appointment with her mother. In addition, I understood that others' lives continued as well, even after the limo arrived the final time.

The last time that this limousine would come for us, I decided that it would be best to be picked up from the apartment where Joshua and I lived, laughed, and loved. Everyone knew that our family was staying at Maria's home. It was weird to be picked up each time, but this time was even more difficult. My spiritual mother, Mark, Corrinna and Joe rode in the limo one last time. Maria and Manuel drove their car in the event that they needed to get back to their children. My mom, Corrinna, Maria, and I took seats in front of Joshua's casket.

My previous experiences warned me to be cautious that no one would disrespect our directives, which there was a hint of a few times, and that these last moments indeed needed to be private. Before we went to the cemetery, the limo drove us in front of the funeral parlor, and therein we entered.

I had the task of covering up my son in the cream cover which did not reveal his burgundy shoes which matched his burgundy belt. As I took my time, inch by inch, I slowly covered his legs, waist, and next his chest and arms. Then, I stopped and kissed him at least a thousand times.

Next, I slowly covered Joshua's face, as tightly as I tucked him in, one last time. Ray and members of his family were invited inside the funeral home and to help assist in lifting Joshua's coffin into the Hurst, but none of them came into the funeral parlor after Ray walked out the first time.

Pastor Paul read the scripture, Psalm 139; I will never forget where the verses are located in the Bible. I stated very similar words to Joshua just weeks ago during one of our long conversations without even realizing that I was reciting scriptures. During this particular conversation with Joshua, he was continually saying, okay preacher, and he was not being disrespectful or discourteous. I said, Joshua, I am not preaching to you, I am talking to you as your mother, but he responded saying, "Okay preacher," with that reassuring smile.

I had reminded Joshua that I dedicated his life to God when he was only two months old. God graciously allowed me to be faithful to my covenant with God that if He gave me a son, that I would dedicate him back to Him. I explained to Joshua that he had some serious decisions to make but to remember, that no matter where he went that God was there. **If he went to the mountains, God was there. If he went to the valleys, God was still there....**

I am totally confident that it was only God who laid those words on my and Pastor Paul's heart. Then, we inched our way to the cemetery Mr. Walker's assistant drove slowly behind the Hurst which carried Joshua's body. It probably was the longest ride that I have ever taken, even though the distance did not include many miles.

Uncertainty continues to be present when I calculate which ride was longer, the road going to the cemetery or the road coming home. Before we left the cemetery to return to my bare apartment, my daughters and I laid our lavender roses on Joshua's coffin, which were the only roses that I desired to have lowered into the ground with his casket; only roses for a rose!

During the burial ceremony, I handed out fourteen purple roses that were pulled out of the family spread. I will admit to you that I did not necessarily give these roses to those whom I originally had in mind, but this would be the second time that I put a rose from God's garden in the care of Shirley! Lastly, I walked down the path in the cemetery to release *one* dove into the sky, and the dove went home by himself. The dove and Joshua were safe in the arms of God.

You see, God's eyes really are on the Sparrow, and I do know without any doubt that God watches over Joshua and me. He watches over everyone, as the song that children sing is true, He has the whole world in His hands. We may not understand on this side of Jordan, but I strongly believe that we will understand by and by!

That evening, I returned to a very vacant apartment, but I was not totally alone. Once again, I felt the aloneness that my son's death brought my sorrowed heart. Grief invited itself inside my heart and apartment. This time, I really knew firsthand that others were also hurting; recall how Corrinna broke down when we had the duty of selecting the caskets.

Although I held many young teens in my arms as they sobbed during the viewing, I did not notice anyone's tears during the funeral, because my concern was that everyone would know that God did not kill my son, our friend, teammate, student, peer, cousin, nephew, grandson, and respectable young man. I get immensely angered when I hear church folks say, "God will kill you, because I do not view God that way.

Please allow me to share with you that Corrinna was so strong while we were in the process of losing the place that we once called home. Also recall that she was in the process of healing. Certainly, God blessed me with very specially made and talented gifts! Many years later Corrinna served four years in the Marine Corp. She graduated from college, and Corrinna was blessed with a job which offers her the great flexibility of working from home.

Corrinna stayed in my apartment for approximately thirty days. During that time, she basically made most of my major decisions. Joe was very kind to be so generous with his wife. Corrinna did not leave my side. She always remained very close because love knows no distance!

I did not know how I was going to pay the costs of Joshua's funeral services. The vault, the flowers, the dove, and his clothing needed to be paid for upon acquisition, and that took most of the money that was available to me at this point. Mr. Walker never once pressed me for another dime up front, and he assured me that I could take my time in paying the balance my obligation to him.

Mr. Walker kindly assured me that he would not charge me a penny of interest. In addition, he told me to take as long as I needed to pay these expenses. I did not hear from the insurance company, but I recognized upon receipt of the coroner's report via the telephone that payment would be denied.

Joshua's classmates and friends raised money from the t-shirts and selling of his CD. I already handed that check over to Mr. Walker. Sometimes I got angry thinking that these young teens were doing a grown man's job, but that was my anger speaking. The teens were showing their love.

About one week later, I received a phone call from my spiritual mother with an offer of a check to be made out to the funeral parlor. Her church only included five members, but the size of the donation was much larger than anyone would expect. I handed that check over as well. *Still*, I did not know how I would pay the balance.

Joshua's child support was aborted immediately, even though I am uncertain that I received all money due to me for the month of March, and I only had one very part-time job during this time of my life.

Upon my physician erroneously reporting that I either had a tumor or a cyst on my spine, I terminated my job as VITA coordinator, and I only maintained my part-time job as a paraprofessional tutor at a local college. *Still, I* continued my studies at a private college.

Whatever monies that I earned, I saved every penny to help pay the balance. My bill sizably diminished, but I did not know how the balance of the funeral would be paid in full. Rather than fret, I continually petitioned God.

A Special Gift

During the Philadelphia Eagles' basketball game verses the teachers at the high school, a moment of silence was offered as Joshua's basketball jersey number flashed on the screen. The Philadelphia Eagles gave Mark two tickets for the Dallas Cowboys verses the Eagles-Dallas game which was to be rallied off as a fund raiser. Mark won the tickets and he and his mother went to the game.

We were all truly blessed. Also, I praised and thanked God for any amount that I received, after thanking anyone who blessed us. I truly believe that if we praise God in the small things, that the blessing pours down from heaven bigger and bigger. My special prayer is and will continue to be that God will abundantly bless those who blessed our family, and I received confirmation that this is happening today!

I never vacillated to look Mr. Walker directly in the eyes and reassure him that every penny would be paid. Somehow he trusted me at my word, even though this was the first time I ever met this wonderful, kind, and polite gentleman who sponsored summer league basketball team that Joshua played in 2007. Within two months to the date of Joshua's funeral, I made a presentation to Mr. Walker.

By May 15th, 2008, the total balance from Joshua's funeral was zero. It was exactly two months from Joshua's date of death. William, the wonderful male who produced Joshua and his family, planned another fund raiser which also assisted in the costs of the funeral. That check was immediately endorsed and signed over to Mr. Walker. Will Jr., sold CDs as well.

Looking back at how God blessed us during this time, I recalled a conversation that Joshua and I had prior to his exodus. He looked at me with one tear coming down his face, and he said, "Mom, you always told me to be good to people, because it always comes back." Recently, I heard a sermon about giving to people. **Joel Osteen** stated that you may not receive it back when you expect it, but when you need it the most, it will come back. I am a living testimony that **Joel Osteen's** words from God are so true! The Bible says it this way, at Luke 6:38, **Give and it shall be given unto you.**

I did not have the means to provide this funeral for my son, and Ray did not offer one damaged red cent, but my heavenly Father provided more than enough to pay for Joshua's funeral. I did not have $10,000 for Joshua's total last rights expenses, which could have easily tallied nearly $20,000; thank you Mr. Walker!

I can testify in agreement with the songwriter who states that **my father is rich; all of the cattle on the hills and even the hills belong to Him!** Everything that we have belongs to God, even our precious children and our time is borrowed from God! Joshua's funeral charges were paid in cash in its entirety, five scholarships were given, and a stone is placed on my son's grave. God is so good, and He is so worthy to be praised. Just because you do not see your blessings; please do not discount that they are there.

Although I realized it was God's goodness that Joshua's funeral services are paid for, I witnessed over 200 people give their lives to God, and I handed five people, which included Luke, $200.00 scholarships. *Still*, even though I shared many blessings that came to our family, I cannot express the manifestation as to how my heart was ripped into shreds. If you have ever felt that a circle of pain that literally around your heart, then you will know the beginning of my pain. It is much more painful that RSD as I described earlier in these writings.

I did not go to counseling at first. Previously, it did not work. I did not think that it would work. Perhaps I did not have the right counselor. Maybe I was unwilling/unable/not ready to do the necessary work. In my opinion, counseling takes a good counselor and real work if you want real results. The one that worked for you may not work for me, but I had a really good counselor who did not pull any punches with me, and for that I am so grateful!

Instead of attempting counseling immediately, I found myself right back at school and work; even though I am sure that I looked and felt like a zombie and felt like one too. I have pictures to prove how much exhaustion took over my life. I look at pictures, and I think, WOW! Maybe Victoria said something correctly. She stated that I looked as though I died, and her statement became evident in photographs others took in May 2008. A huge part of me died on March 15, 2008.

After burying Joshua, I kept my normal schedule; although, it was not because I knew that which I was doing. Many days I cannot tell you how I drove from point A to B. All I know for certain is that I did follow a schedule. God guided my driving, and I graciously accepted his offered footsteps from one place to the next. He is carrying me through every day as he continually lifts me higher.

Often, I think back to the day after Joshua's funeral, and how I rushed right back to school. It was a way to get away from people that I did not want to be bothered by. I recall prior to going onto campus for classes, looking at the pizza; generally, I purchased a salad or something to eat daily. *Still*, I did not desire to eat or even enter the campus. I barely ate since I received the telephone call, and if I did eat it was because my mother reminded me that I needed to eat. I was wise enough to drink a nutritious drink, but even when I ate it was so little that it really did not matter.

Before my son died, I was a very active and an enthusiastic student. Always, I lifted my hand, as I was a well prepared student who was ready and willingly to answer most questions or to ask a question. Upon my return, the day that Spring break ended, one professor asked me, "Are you on strike?" At first I did not reply. He asked, "What did you do over Spring Break?" Then, I replied, "I buried my son." The whole class became profoundly silent, just as if death was in the air. A number two pencil could have fallen, and everyone would have noticed the emptiness of that loud statement.

Looking back, I do not think that the professor heard me correctly, because he just stood there. His facial expression gave evidence that he pondered what it was that I just said. I excused myself and went to the ladies' room where I found more tissues to wipe my eyes. As I shared with you previously, my son wrote a song for me, which is entitled *"Wipe Your Eyes,"* and I have been following his instructions since his song was produced in August 2007. Many of my tears are from tears of pain, but I cannot deny that some of my tears are tears of joy from Joshua's life.

Days prior to going on campus to attend class, I would sit in my car and listen to Joshua's songs over and over again. I can never thank Will or his father, William, enough for the gifts the CD brought to my life. I desperately wanted to see Joshua and touch him again more upon hearing his voice. Actually, I am unsure if the song was the true reason, but the pain felt the same each day. At times, I *still* have those selfish moments, but I know that I will see Joshua again. I know and understand that neither his body nor his mind will ever experience any type of pain or rejection again. Joshua will no longer wipe any of his tears.

I sat in my car and I cried until it felt as though I did not have any more tears, but to my surprise there were more where the others came from. I must admit that hearing Joshua's voice also helped me make progress on many hard days. It has brought some healing into my life, even though; *still*, I miss him, and I am reminded of him in everything that I see or do. My one and only sister, Debra lost her first born son. She warned me at the time of Joshua's death, that it never goes away. I trust her words. I chose to recall that **Jesus took the sting of death away.**

Now, I really realize the importance of having the hope in Jesus Christ. Without that hope, I would not know without a doubt that I will see my son again. However, it is only natural to want to see Joshua every day that I awaken. I realize that is not going to happen here on this earth, and that realization, at times, is overwhelming. There is not one day that passes that I do not look at Joshua's pictures.

Two photographed basketball buttons proudly hang on the roof of my car. They travel wherever I venture in my vehicle. Also, I am he proud owner of a wonderful photo of Joshua that the Booster's club presented to me, as they did likewise in 2009 for the senior basketball players. For this, I am so grateful! The pictures of Joshua that Juanita gifted and framed for me, Maria, and Corrinna sits by my bedside and in the girls' living room. Clearly, there is a picture everywhere I go, but there is always a picture in my mind and in my heart of my one and only son!

One lady who lost her son informed me that she eventually took her son's picture down because seeing his face was too painful. I prayed that I would not reach that date. As of yet, I have not. Sometimes when I run across a picture that I did not see before or in a while, a tear, or tears gently fall.

Some days the intensity of missing Joshua is so grueling that I beg God to take the pain, or I have asked Him the question, will it ever go away? It has only been twenty months that my son is gone, but I can tell you that I continue to have days where there is extreme intense pain. It is just that I no longer beg God to take the pain away. Rather, I ask for His help in embracing each feeling as it comes, and I no longer fight the pain.

At one point, my family physician was required to perform an EKG and a complete urinal study because of the results from the blood pressure monitor, which ran so high that I thought about exiting from college. My professors did not treat me any differently than any other student. This is in reference to the amount of work and their expectations.

You see, life really does not stop.

After my blood pressure escalated, I was offered to turn in assignments at my own pace. I am sure that I could have taken extra time off from school but that was not my desire. I am unsure this would lessen that amount of work that I would have to make up. I do recall entertaining the idea of taking an incomplete for the semester when my blood pressure skyrocketed to 210/100, but one professor, Professor Lucinda Whip, challenged me and stated, "Over my dead body."

For the fact that Professor Lucinda dared to choose those words without regard to the fact that my son just died, my ears stood straight up like a Doberman pincher's ears which was sharply snipped. If that image is not vivid enough, think of any dog's tail that senses alarm. Please note, that I became extremely tensed and alarmed.

Once I calmed down and was able to breathe again, the ability to recognize that she may have only had my best interest at heart came into view. Lucinda probably surmised that if I did not have anything to do that I would die, and if this was her assumption, she surmised correctly. There were many days that I wanted to sleep all day, or keep my head under the covers, but the intensity of the physical and mental pain assured me that I was alive, and I was reassured that one day I too would die. Also, I knew that when I did wake up that my only choice was to live each day as it came.

Overall, my experience of returning to college was very helpful, and I am reminded that school was somewhat of a healthy outlet for Daddy's death as well. Without a schedule, I am unsure what I would have done. I continue to suffer with physical pain daily, with an underlying sleep disorder; therefore, staying in bed is not a good option. I would suffer more internally and externally.

Lying *still* continues to amplify the pain in my body, and this creates magnification of the pain that is in my heart and mind. On the other hand, being *still* and listening for God's voice is so peaceful and calming. I recall too that **an idle mind is the devil's workshop.**

After Corrinna returned to her home and her husband in Florida at the end of April, I thought that more of me would die at this time, but I did continue to live. Prior to Corrinna's departure, she had packed me and my apartment and moved me into Manuel and Maria's home. Realistically, I really did not want to move, and I did not want to stay. I really did not have much of a choice. I was financially, emotionally, and physically bankrupt, even though my credit score continues to reach a perfected level.

I worked very hard after I filed bankruptcy, was injured, and lost my house in 1998. Some of the first words that I shared at Joshua's funeral were that it was not an accident that we moved to this community. I did not believe that ten years prior in 1998. I was extremely depressed, and I felt like a failure while moving my family in the middle of the night, as though I was guilty of something.

Faulty guilt is a heavy burden to carry, especially when some things simply are not your fault because they are out of your control. It really is that simple. You see, Ray and my divorce already forced me into bankruptcy. All twenty credit cards which were maximized during our "marriage" were in my name, as he did not have any credit or very limited credit. Therefore, those credit cards became solely my responsibility after the convenient "relationship" ended.

At this time, I was not in any medical condition to accept permanent employment. However, if I knew that this curve ball was heading towards another disaster; I could have improved my batting average or moved myself out of the way to prevent the walk. Many great lessons were scored and tallied in the midst of this game, I learned to become more self-sufficient, and I believe it was the beginning of trusting God.

Trusting God does not eliminate our feelings, it just is confidence that God is in control. I was blind sighted, believing that we were medically insured. When I discovered the truth about this issue, there was not much that I could do in my own strength. I went to court and fought for the coverage and even that was not in my own strength, but **faith is the key that unlocked the door. Without faith, it is impossible to please God.**

There was an absorbent amount of times **that mountains were spoken to and moved** from my life. I did not give credence to the fact **that I have faith as a grain of a mustard seed.** The honorable judge became furious with Ray while he was in contempt of court for dropping the medical insurance. After winning the court case I petitioned for leniency, and I asked the judge not force Ray behind bars. I did not believe that this experience would be beneficial to any of us; thus, I suffered and eventually, we lost our home and many of the contents within.

We moved into the ideal community, and we faced many challenges that I never knew prior. For at least a few months we tolerated pests, but as time moved on, we moved up and it went well. I thought that I became an expert at shedding tears all of the time, as I constantly blamed myself for just being me. At this time I did not understand what I did to cause such calamities to come upon us; today, I can say it is by God's grace and mercy that we moved into this community. You see, it never was about me!

Aunt Louise listened to me cry over and over about losing my home. I did not understand why God was allowing this to happen to us at that time. Already, I learned that He has all power in His hands. I am sure that I questioned God. Now, I truly believe that I do have the answers. Would I lose my house all over again? My answer is in a heartbeat, but with an entirely different attitude. Did God take my house away? The answer is absolutely not!

However, God knows before we ask what it is that we need. He knows all things to come, and He put me in the best position and with some of the best people to enable me to handle my son's death as well as I am. God allowed me to be surrounded me by a community that genuinely loved Joshua and our family, and this became apparent in many different ways.

I may or may not be able to purchase another home in this life time. This is not a priority or a choice that I am able to make at this moment. The point that I am trying to convey is what this community gave to us is something that we could never purchase. The love, support, respect, and honor, which are all priceless blessings, demonstrate the power of God who gives us each special gifts.

Chapter 12

I never gave thought that about the "flowers" that I call buttercups. I would never imagine that they would have much significance or become so beautiful to me or that they would reflect the brightness that shines. Many times, I placed them under Joshua's chin to shine. When I see these "flowers," often referred to as weeds, I think of how Joshua picked them as a small boy. He brought them to home with that bright smile on his face. Decoratively, I placed them in a paper cup full of water.

Often, I think about Joshua standing by a gate as a real little boy, while I observed him maturing into a fine young man. I reflect on Joshua when I see Fixodent, and I laugh very loudly. You'll have to ask his best friend Mark about that one! I reflect on Joshua when I see almost anything, as I had seventeen years of raising him, and most of his life I was at home with him alone.

Trees also remind me of Joshua. One is planted in the natural forest in his honor. Leaves remind me of Joshua. Family Services has a leaf in memory of Joshua Wayne-Anthony Brown proudly displayed in the main office.

Twenty one years ago, I was crying because I was injured, and I felt that my life ended. Today, I am grateful to God that I was injured because I am unsure if I would have taken the opportunity to be home with Joshua. I am sure that I would not have wanted it any other way. God granted me the desires of my heart without my realization that is what it was **He does know exactly what we need even before we ask.**

When I was injured, I cried and I begged God for remedy, but I learned to accept what life brings and allow God to help me to deal with whatever needs to be dealt with, including the death of my son, which I can say that God has brought me from a mighty long way since March 15, 2008.

After completing the last semester of my junior year at college, I flew to Florida, where Corrinna and Joe resided. Strongly, I felt the need to get away, because everyone within a wide radius of our community seemed to know my situation. It did not matter if I walked into Wal-Mart to pick up an item. A stranger found it appropriate to ask me personal questions, and I only went to pick up an item. The problem was that I did not have boundaries at this time of my life.

I understand that people may not have meant any harm, but there were enough triggers of pain in reminders of everything. Walking into Wal-Mart has its own reminders. I did not anticipate someone, a stranger, would stop me to talk about the death of my son. Would you believe that it *still* happens whenever I wear Joshua's t-shirt? *Still*, I believe that some people are just being plain nosey.

Some people were very rude and inconsiderate, but I do believe that in general that most persons meant well. Also, I learned that most citizens do not know what to say when a mother loses a child. Please allow me to say this that there really were no words that comforted me in the beginning.

Someone, but not just anyone, quietly sitting with me and just listening is the best that I did receive, but that too needed to be a request. The best initial therapy that I received prior to counseling was reading the words from the many cards that I received. I was so appreciative of the hundreds of cards that I made an attempt to send everyone that gave me a card a thank you note in response.

The beauty of the cards was in the words. If at any moment I did not want to read the card, I was unconcerned if anyone was offended. I could put it aside until later. If the words of the card made me cry, I did not have the worry how I would make someone feel if they saw me cry. The person was not there. I was only in the company of the card, myself, and God.

In addition, I sincerely, respected, and appreciated the prayers of righteous people. The Bible states at James 5:16 states that **the prayer of the righteous availeth much.** Although I could not directly hear the words of these prayers, I felt the power of these prayers daily. Although I felt God's presence during this time, I continued to learn to deal with many mixed feelings.

Some people suggested that God put me in a fog while getting through the first stages of my son's death. Perhaps that was true, but fog is most prevalent at night. Reality settled in after all the funeral process ended, the phones stopped ringing, and people stopped coming around. My first day of my son's death, nights began to be days and nights *still* were nights. However, the darkest days and nights did not come until later.

There is what I describe as a rawness of the death. When I first experienced the loss of my son, it took all that I had to absorb the shock of the loss. I believe that even if you are expecting someone to die, it is *still* a shock. No one can say specifically what day or hour someone is going to take their last breath. I do not believe that anyone can prepare themselves for a shock. There just is no way to brace one's self for what lies ahead. It is only the beginning when you realize that your loved one is gone from your presence.

It is my belief that even if you have a doctor's best estimate of the day and time or a forewarning for God that *still* there is no preparation concerning how you feel or what feelings will come. Feelings are not something designed by humans, they just happen, which is knowledge that I needed to get comfortable with. Attempts of controlling your own feelings and especially someone else's feelings, I believe are virtually impossible. My best advice is to learn to accept the feelings as they come and be responsible for your responses to your feelings.

Some people go through different stages of grief at different times. I was very angry and anxious in my first stage of grief.

Everything and everyone was getting on my nerves, and I know for sure that it was not everyone else. I felt the need to get away in an effort to deal with my feelings and to become acquainted with these new feelings that I am learning to live with.

Somehow, I thought that going to Florida was going to remove the anger and some of the emotions, but changing states does not change one's state of mind. I figured out rather quickly that a different state, where a lot of people did not know about my son's death was healthy for a bit. However, it did not take away all that I needed to manage.

Mornings in Florida were not much different than nights in my home town, unless I was in the company of family. When night fell, while others were silently sleeping, the pain was the same, and my pillows located in either side of the equator could write about six books each. The floor was introduced to my knees or I met the floor relatively quickly. Many times, I could not accept the softness that my soaked pillow offered.

I cried out to God with my face buried in my flooded pillow which was soaked with sadness. It felt as though the levies broke the window panes which lead to my soul. The stubborn cloud, which remained in my view, obeyed the roaring winds, thunder and lightning and all types of electrifying shocks that the storms brought into my world. I did not have a choice concerning refusal of allowing the sun any hope of shinning. Included in these raging storms or tornadoes, were whirlwinds of feelings. I did not have any idea of which way I needed to go or where I really wanted to be. I was worse than my favorite character, Dorothy, in the movie, *The Wizard of Oz*; at least she wanted to go home.

Already, I had met my own Wizard of Oz, and I was not very fond of him or his nonsense; thus, I depended on God. Nonetheless, I did not have any real place to call home, but I needed to go back to Pennsylvania because there were more things that I needed my attention. I begged God for the courage to order a stone for Joshua's grave, and I also prayed for a brain with a mindset to create criteria for Joshua's memorial scholarship. In addition, I needed my heart to desire completion of my Bachelor's Degree in accounting. In all honesty, I did not want to do anything, but I knew that being stagnant would not help my situation at all. My mother taught me this at an early stage in life, but it was not until later that I could appreciate how she viewed this world.

I managed to laugh now and then, being around my son in-law, Joe, made it absolutely impossible not to laugh. Upon my arrival to Florida, one of the very first phone calls that I made was to Ray. I asked him how he was doing. Upon Ray's answer, I hurriedly found the need to terminate any further conversation, as the call was much too painful to handle.

Today, I am grateful that I dealt with Ray and Doug prior to Joshua's death, because I am unsure if I could properly conclude those two conversations. My son in-laws were enraged that Ray did not offer one expression of grief for me, but I was concerned about him. It was the last time that I spoke to Ray, but I speak with his daughter, my stepdaughter and friend, Pastor Renee.

I continuously encouraged her to engage in a relationship with her father, Ray. Some people may think that this is a strangely bizarre request, but in all sincerity, this was not as much for Ray's benefit as it was for Renee's gain during her process of healing.

Unfortunately, Ray was not majorly involved in his children's lives as most normal parents, but I knew first hand that at least two children, Joshua and Renee were hurting from his disassociations. I believe that if the wound is left untreated, that the one hurting will eventually rot, and that all "relationships" will be tainted. I do believe that God is a healer to the nth degree and a restorer, but be reminded that **God gives us free will.** Today, I am grateful to report that Renee and Ray do have some type of father/daughter relationship. Unfortunately, I cannot report the same concerning Ray's other daughter, Shannon.

Shortly after Joshua died, his half-sister, Shannon died. I believe that she was forty years old. I was not afforded the opportunity to meet Shannon in the eleven years that I suffered in silence with Ray labeled as my husband. However, I cannot deny that I did know that she existed and departed.

Soon after Joshua died, Corrinna had my phone number changed. I only gave it to people that I believed that I could trust, which was a minimal number. With the multitude of pain that I felt and much time to deal with it in Florida, God brought to the forefront people whom I may have offended.

I placed a call to anyone who God brought to my attention that I may have caused any pain, and I made restitution. Whether the pain was intentional or unintentional was not the issue, and I begged their pardon for any pain that I caused them. Although this was not my first, but hopefully, it was the last apology to my mother, as she was one of the first on my list. God also revealed to me those people who needed to exit my life because of the unnecessary pain they were causing me. Slowly, but surely, I needed to shake them off.

My pain was incredibly strong, and I did not want anyone to feel even an ounce of what I was feeling, whether or not they caused me pain was definitely irrelevant at this point and time, and *still* it is extraneous. Yet, those who continued to cause me pain, it became time to let them go. There was only room for the pain from my son's death, which was extraordinarily overwhelming. God is still identifying those who I need to let go that I may continue to heal. In addition, He has provided TRUE friends that mean me well!

I spent a lot of time with Corrinna and Joe, and they kept me very close to them; under their wings. They watched me closely, whenever I was not having my pillow times of pain. Corrinna always seemed to believe that it would be wise for me to have a male to go through the process of grief. I believe that this may have been okay if I was already in a healthy relationship, but when one is vulnerable, I no longer believe that a relationship is wise.

My wounds were attaching to other wounds rather than pure hearts. When one allows this wound attachment to happen, one may discover too late who or what you got yourself involved with. I have definite issues concerning boundaries with my children but I am working on it daily. During the grief of Joshua at times, we switched roles.

A male named Lewis, continually came to the house to visit my son in-law. At first, I was uninterested in him, but the more that he came around I began to like him too. In between my tears and pain, I could not identify what it was that I liked about him, but I recognized that he reminded me of Joshua. This was not because of his looks, as my son was handsome; rather, it was because of his actions. A grown man acted like a seventeen year old boy. This incident signaled to me that I was in need of great help.

I thank God that I could recognize that I was latching onto someone for all of the wrong reasons, and it was then that I decided to return to Maria and Manuel's home. Besides, I needed to handle my business.

Upon my return to PA, God granted me the courage to order the stone that now marks Joshua's grave. Joshua's stone has an engraved picture of a dove in the middle of these writings, We Love You JBrizz, Joshua Wayne-Anthony Brown. His date of birth, Nov. 13, 1990 and date of death, Mar. 15, 2008 are also inscribed on the stone. In honor of his retired jerseys a basketball emblem with the #31 and a football emblem with the #14 are also engraved on the bottom of the stone.

Although I was unaware of an actual ceremony for the retirement of Joshua's football number, the number 14 was retired. I am the proud owner of his white sports jerseys. One day, I hope to have both of his jerseys framed and displayed in my own home. At first, momentarily, I considered another selfish moment. In that moment, I wanted to have these words *I love my son* inscribed on his stone, but it did not take me long to come to the realization that Joshua is not only my son. He is a brother, nephew, friend, student, grandson, an uncle, great uncle, cousin, artist, and a basketball, baseball, and football player among other things to other people. Joshua's Rap name was *Bad News Brizz*, but his friends shortened it by using his first initial and had called him JBRIZZ. As one of Joshua's closest friends stated at the funeral, "He was not bad news at all!"

My first revisit to the grave occurred after receiving the call that the stone was placed on Joshua's grave. I asked Mark to drive me to the graveyard in Joshua's old car, which I gave to Mark after Joshua's death. Strongly, I believed that Mark is the person who Joshua would have wanted to have his car, as Mark was a part of our family since him and Joshua were very young and he spent much time in Joshua's car.

This was the first experience of crying with anyone other than my daughters and their husbands, but Mark is family. It amazed on me that I did not afford myself the opportunity to cry with anyone else other than my children and grandchildren. Although I shed tears, this was a different soft cry.

There were other things that were bothering me, which included where I wanted to reside. The attempt to attach to a thirty nine year old male who reminded me of my son and the fact that I did not cry with anyone other than my daughters, son in-laws, grandchildren and only once with Mark prompted me to realize that I was dealing incorrectly with Joshua's death. Soon thereafter, I made an appointment for counseling after nine months of trying to get through by myself; ironically, this is as long as Joshua was in my womb.

Cleaning out Joshua's room was one of the most difficult challenges after his funeral. As I sifted through a special box where he kept several personal things, I found a prayer that Joshua wrote to God. As I carefully read each of his papers, I found several prayer requests that Joshua had written. One writing in particular Joshua was a written prayer that I would get out of this city and get out of the struggle. Your children may be praying for you too!

I had serious conflicts about leaving Maria and my grandchildren, but conflicts of not being near Corrinna were present too. One of the first things that I needed to figure out was how to continue with my life without Joshua next to me, and where I would ultimately reside. However, I continued to keep Joshua's words in my mind as I attempted to gather my own thoughts, and I began to deal with unnecessary pains of life, as Joshua's death was a necessary pain to deal with.

I prayed prior to selecting a therapist, as I knew that I was limited due to my insurance's network. Therefore, I was limited in my selection, which resulted as a good thing, because I did not know what it was that I needed. I recognized that I was in dire need of assistance. I was walking around in a daze, trying to get through an even more shredded life. No longer did I know if I was coming or going or what I wanted from life or even if I wanted life at all.

If you ask did I contemplate suicide, the answer is no. I did not contemplate suicide, as that was unsuccessful in my past; already, I had full knowledge that there was a possibility that a suicide attempt may not work and that one has to deal with yet another issue if you do live. I am unsure that I entertained suicide as a viable option. I cannot even explain to you if I was able to think clearly. However, once I awakened I knew that I needed to face another day and the challenges that it brings.

Nonetheless, I walked into my scheduled appointment, but I did not know the work that awaited me as I stepped foot in the door. Many people stated that going to counseling took courage. At this point, I am unsure if I saw it as courage, but rather a necessity. I instilled so much into my children that I lost myself along the way. Now, I needed to find my way without having children who depended on me.

At the first appointment, I regurgitated most of my life story during the first session. Surprisingly, the psychologist asked me if I thought that we could work together. That was not a concern of mine, as I bared most of my life story within the allotted 50 minute appointment. I barely heard the sound of the counselor's voice.

I am unsure if this is the moment that I realized the next thing that I am going to write, but when life breaks your heart open, and it probably will, my experienced advice to you is to deal with EVERYTHING in it so that you may properly heal. After vomiting most of the bad occurrences/horrific experiences of my life, my therapist, Dr. Johnson, gently asked me, "What brings you here today?" I replied, "My son died." Dr. Johnson offered his condolences that day and the process already began. Then, we waited until next week to meet again. While in the wait, I cannot tell you the amount of thoughts that went through my mind. I had so many harder issues to deal with than my senior year as an accounting major, which was very challenging.

I did not know what just began, but what I did know for sure was that there was an extra ordinary amount of work cut out for me. I had the challenge to address every true and false self-allegation that I brought before this man, many of which were full of embarrassment, pain, resentment, shame, guilt, and sorrow. My son's death sentenced me to do some serious work and time.

The homework was the worst. It was mentally exhausting and intense. Dr. Johnson did not give me any written assignments. The week was extraordinarily long as I revisited the grief of Daddy's death. I made numerous connections with Joshua's death. I recognized and faced the empty faces. I heard the sounds of the phone ringing continually. In addition, I made many associations, including the connection of having school as an outlet, smoking, and even though I was around people, I dealt with my grief alone. One huge difference in my grief now and twenty eight years earlier is that I know who God is, and that **I can do all things through Christ who strengthens me.**

I acknowledged that I continually missed Daddy throughout my life. While attending others' funerals I cried hysterically. *Still,*

I was in mourning over Daddy's death. I was reliving dad's funeral at others' funeral, but I never knew how to articulate these words without people telling me to move on. I did not know how to move on or what I was to be moving on from. My dad's death is a part of my life.

I rest with the certainty that this is abnormal when you have not totally dealt with the grief of a loved one you have lost. I was stuck in grief from my daddy's death. Without any doubt, I did not properly heal. I do believe that children and adults who have an experience with grief will eventually revisit unfinished grief, unless they properly heal.

It was very strange to me that many other funerals that I attended: cousins, uncles, aunts, and friends that I cried with such agony, but during my son's candlelight vigil, viewings, funeral, and burial, I did not shed a single tear during any of his services. The agony was a mixture of feelings, the loss of another loved one without resolving the death of my daddy. After deeply thinking about it, this terribly baffled my mind but what I realized is that I was able to identify that this was my son's funeral. It was not an instant replay of Daddy's funeral, because my son's death became dearest to my heart.

Without any doubt and shame, I believe that my entire extended family expected me to be laid out on the floor, kicking, hollering, and screaming, because I was so emotional at all other funerals that we attended. God definitely had His powerful hand on my life, and all praise, glory, and honor go directly to Him. Without Him, I am nothing. He gave me His strength, because in my own strength, there is NO WAY that I would have made it!

Also, I realized later, that another reason for my tears during the other funerals was because of the many sorrows that appeared to be a result of losing Daddy at such an early age, such as being raped, abused, and assaulted by various people in the bodies of men and at times women.

Still, I was very vulnerable, and I had a lot of work to do.

At the time of my son's death, I was able to identify that I was no longer that eleven year old little girl. This is odd because I knew that I had unresolved issues from my dad's death since I was a little girl. I did not know how to become unstuck, as the glue trapped me until God set me free. He is putting the pieces of my puzzling life back together. After the death of my son, I was able to recognize that I am truly a strong woman; yet, as soft as a real lady.

Joshua told the cyber-world on "my space," that I was the strongest woman in the world. I thought, how dare he tell the world this about me? I felt that I had to live up to what Joshua spoke over my life. This is one example of there being power in the tongue which can be used to speak life and death. Also, I recognized who would defend me at this point of my journey, if I just allowed God to do just that, but I could not just allow anyone to do anything to me and remain totally silent ever again. In addition, I subconsciously reminded myself that I was not going to allow just anyone too close to me because I knew how vulnerable I was at this time of my life, just like my mother.

My favorite Aunt Louise, who departed her life six months later after my son's death, confidently expressed these words to me: "Sweetie, you are going to be alright." May God rest her soul; I believe this major player in my life spoke life into my life again.

Now, I understand how it was that my mother did not cry at Daddy's funeral. I completely understood the stabs of pain that may have entered her heart. I comprehended that even though a tear needed to fall that she may instead ingested only the salt from the tears inside. I know that is what I did. I wanted to make sure that everyone else was okay. This apple did not fall far from her tree!

Be careful that when you prevent your tears from falling from your eyes that you are not drowning your heart with salt. It is an awful experience, this I know all too well. I did not want others to worry about me. I am sure that some people did not understand my actions or reactions, Alisha openly offended me when she stated, "I just don't understand, what is it the drugs?" I refused to take any antidepressants, but that painful remark definitely sparked several nerves. The bottom line is that some people just do not understand **the peace that surpasses all understanding**, which only come from the **Prince of Peace.**

You can have it too!

Realistically, upon hearing these words, in the flesh I desired to express some of the anger that I did not transmit on her. Alisha did not know what I was feeling or how I was dealing. She was clueless while I was not in her company, and I only saw her on this date. However, I felt compelled to honor my son's life and not act in an undignified fashion by keeping from slapping anyone because that is not a good a Christian representation.

No matter what storm we go through, I do not believe that we should allow anyone to dim our light. I am not speaking about crying at this point. Rather, I am speaking about choosing whether or not to react to my anger, despite her inconsiderate choice of words.

There were many times when I felt rage and wanted to speak my mind. Instead, I chose what I believe was the wiser route, pray and then speak, but only if necessary. Some ignorance is not necessary to address, but remember that thinking is unclear during grief. Somehow, I realized that I no longer represented myself as a person, but I represented my son's mother and a child of the Most High that I am.

Friends, you have no idea of the burden that you bring to others who are in the midst of their own grief, especially if you were not close prior to this death. Besides, I had many bigger things to deal with other than the ignorance of people. The bereaving family has a HUGE loss and so much mental, physical, financial and spiritual labor ahead of them. You may be putting others at the defensive position of guard, which creates oppositions to watch how one moves. The family already realizes that others are hurting. So, I added more salt added to my wounds, and I did not want to walk around with this baggage. Hindsight gives a clearer vision, and I believe that my and my mother's pillows would probably share familiar stories about the tears that no one else saw. May I share that my mother and my process of grief are *still* very different.

Now, I totally understand and respect that everyone grieves differently, even if you share the same loss. Two sisters can lose their father, but their method of grieving can be entirely different, but no one's way of grieving is better than anyone else's method. Grieving is very personal, and it is not for anyone else to judge.

As I continued counseling with Dr. Johnson, it was not my son's death that was regularly addressed, but rather many of the events that occurred within my wilderness journeys. Some experiences, I had never shared in an effort to seek resolution.

When Dr. Johnson noticed a smile or tears, he politely asked me what was I feeling, and a few times, I was so absorbed in missing Joshua that I did not have much to say. Some days, I managed to smile as I thought about Joshua too. However, I admitted that I did miss Joshua and when a smile crossed my face; generally, I was thinking about Joshua too.

Many times, my tears fell because of how terribly I missed Joshua. Finally, I cried in the presence of someone else and shared how much I missed him. However, more issues came to surface or resurfaced since Joshua's death and some of the nonsense issues brought tears to surface as well, as my healing began.

The days seemed much longer than twenty four hours while I dealt with every ounce of pain that ever entered my life that was unmotivated by love. I realized that for such a long time that I learned to be silent about a lot of things that happened to me, which was unhealthy.

I learned to respect Dr. Johnson's notion that keeping a secret is poison. Although one's lips are silently stiffened, anger oozes out in everything that one does. Eventually, the anger turns on you, which is what most professional counselors seem to label as depression. I never unveiled the secrets of my first or third brutal rape shortly after Daddy died, and it was eating me up alive. The first male who raped me threatened that he would kill my family, and I was too naïve and afraid to trust differently.

I "believed" that I was protecting my loved ones or either I was living in denial. While in fact, we were killing each other because no one knew what in this world was wrong with me. I was not conscientious that I was angry because I loved them enough to try to protect them. Perhaps it was faulty guilt that I took some blame for being raped.

The male who raped me may have continued to live a life of anger, but so did we. However, we did not have to, but fear, shame, guilt, confusion, and humiliation trapped me inside of a secret.

Counseling uncovered and discovered so many things in my life, which I believe resulted because I was willing to do the necessary work. You see, there was no room left for nonsense garbage that was brought to my table to eat or distorted types of pain. My first adult encounter with pain that really mattered occurred when my son died!

Dr. Johnson did not say much in the beginning. It did not take me long to realize that he listened very well. He allowed me to verbalize my experiences in a safe setting, but the challenges became prevalent once my foot stepped into the real world. I could chose not to think about the confessions that I made and the profound statements that he interjected, but I chose to evaluate and participate in my healing.

One of the most profound things that Dr. Johnson said to me was, "You carried your son for nine months in your womb and now you will carry him in your heart for the rest of your life." It did not dawn on me until counseling almost concluded how profound these words were, and they gave new meaning to me concerning Joshua residing in my heart for the rest of my life.

I realize that I will miss my son for the rest of my life. The pain is a part of the process of death, but I see the relevance of my heart being happy because that is where I will carry Joshua for the rest of my life.

By the conclusion of counseling, I honored the truth that I did not finish grieving Daddy's death and that I lost myself in grief of his death and the miseries from old man life. In all actually miseries grew from many unhealthy carnally minded people. I take ownership of my part as well. A secret that someone else was carrying for years which greatly concerned and affected my life was revealed on the last day of counseling too. God promises that **He will not keep His children in darkness.**

Certainly, I thank Dr. Johnson for his wisdom, but God is the one who unveiled many things while in Dr. Johnson's presence. God is so faithful and worthy to be praised. I asked Dr. Johnson, "Do you think that these things are a mere coincidence?" He had replied, "No." My comment was that is what I call GOD!

As I shared some of the toughest challenges that I faced growing up, Dr. Johnson insisted that some things simply were not my fault; finally, I could receive those words. I am only responsible for my own actions and reactions. I am not responsible for what others say or do.

While my mind worked overtime, I realized that if I was perfect, which would be Jesus, that I would have never caused anyone any pain. I am imperfect even though I have spent a majority of my life trying to be a perfectionist, which is another amount of wasted time! In addition, I noted that an attempt to be perfect only magnifies one's mistakes because it is one of the biggest mistakes any of us can make.

I shared with Dr. Johnson that I even apologized to God for being myself. Dr. Johnson's response was extremely powerful, and his clever counseling skills made me examine what it was that I verbalized. He did not consider himself a religious man. Well, "not like you," were his exact words. I explained to him that I was offended because being religious has nothing to do with trusting God and knowing that He is in full control, which I believe encompasses spirituality. We smiled.

Still, I do not always make the best decisions. I will continue to make mistakes. However, it is not because I am blatantly doing wrong. Sometimes we are not in the best frame of mind to choose wisely, but I learned that it is best to learn from that unwise decision. My continued prayer is that God will have mercy and continue His favor on my life. I pray that He will not allow me to make the same mistake over and over again.

I learned that I did backward flips to be forgiving to others, as I really am not one to hold grudges. Although, it takes time and effort on the other person's part to trust after being hurt. I no longer believe that trusting someone really has anything to do with forgiving someone. Trust is earned, while forgiveness is given.

According to Dr. Johnson, and I believe this to be so true, kindness to some people is not saying a word, while to others it means talking every day. At first, it took me a minute to get that one, but I learned to set boundaries. You may not be able to clearly define them in my writings. However, they are included, as I did not disclose to you half of the horrific events that occurred in my lifetime. Only God knows my entire life story. Dr. Johnson knows a lot more than I have shared with you.

By the end of the nights I could begin to see some days and I began to heal even more. Continually, I miss my son and I *still* cry, but I allow myself to smile when I think of the many happy moments because of his life. A huge difference began at Joshua's funeral, as my words, I felt compelled to live up to. I believe that the claim that I trusted God spoke life into my life, as we know that **there is power and death in the tongue.** I believe that God is making my confession a reality! Do I still become afraid? Yes, at times I do, and I continue to boldly speak the words, **God did not give me the spirit of fear, but of love and of a sound mind.**

Although I want to be honest with God and tell Him how I feel, I need to stand on the word of God, because my feelings do change, but **His word does not return void, and it will never change**! That is LOVE!

I already told the audience in attendance at my son's funeral that I trusted God. Did crying mean that I did not trust God? No, it simply meant that I was saddened. I feared the day of my son's jersey retirement ceremony because I did not know how I would react. That evening came, and I chose to drive to the school alone because I did not need to be confined to anyone else's expectations. If I wanted to leave I did not have to answer to anyone or ask anyone to take me home. I did not have any idea as to how I would handle the beginning or the ending of the event and I needed my space. I sat outside where the t-shirts were being sold to avoid going into the gymnasium, and when I felt overcrowded, I went to my automobile and then I returned to the table.

I had not been to the gym since the last time my son played against the same exact team last basketball season. I stayed out of the gymnasium as long as I could; finally, I went into the forsaken gymnasium where I took a seat in the packed gymnasium, which became so empty without Joshua. There was standing room only.

The retirement ceremony was held during half time and to watch as others play stimulated missing my son even more. Seeing Joshua's name *still* spelled out on the score board gripped my heart time after time, as it was a painful period of time. While sitting outside, I heard the team warm up to

Joshua's hit song, *"I Don't Know about You, but I Am Fresh."* I got a glimpse of the team's warm-ups which proudly displayed his basketball number 31, with his initials, JB.

I recalled the saddening of my heart as I watched Joshua, approximately two years ago, slip on the black wristband with the number 45, which represented the death of another young teen. So, I compared my sadness at that time, and I assumed how sorry others must have already felt for our family. My feelings were all over the court, just as my son once was.

I remember the hard swallow that I took when half time approached prior to walking across the solid gymnasium floor. However, my friend, Juanita, eased some of my fears as she took my hand and gently guided me to the other side of the court where the ceremony began.

Mr. Jefferies spoke first, and next Joshua's coach said some words that were muffled. Then, the team captain, Champ, who was one of Joshua's closest friends and pallbearer, spoke about Joshua's huge heart and their friendship. Then, I said, "Thank you for sharing in the life and death of my son, Joshua Wayne-Anthony Brown."

I think that another stripe of reality sank deep within my heart during the retirement ceremony, almost one year later. Rather than give a moment of silence to remember Joshua's life, the principal requested that we applaud his life. My request at the funeral became a reality, as we celebrated the seventeen years of life that God granted Joshua Wayne-Anthony Brown.

At that moment, I was stunned, but I was very happy. My son's life received a standing ovation from hundreds of people as his retired basketball jersey was unveiled. I did not have any other desire than to capture every moment and record it all in my memory forever. Once again, I became the proudest woman on this earth to be the mother of Joshua Wayne-Anthony Brown.

Right after Joshua's jersey was unveiled, the emptiness was vivid again, and I exited the gymnasium. I have not returned to that part of the school as of yet. *Still*, there were many more days and nights that I needed to face.

Chapter 13

Many wondered how I would handle my son's birthday. In all honesty, I pondered this question myself. The anxiety of the approaching of Joshua's birthday was actually worse than the day itself. The first thing that I did the evening prior to Joshua's birthday was to pray that God would prevent anyone who had any evil in their heart against me from contacting me. God answered my prayer. I will not detail who did or those who did not contact me on Joshua's birthday. I know beyond a reasonable doubt that God answered my prayer. There was not one time that I felt the need or desire to reject any calls, ignore any texts, or emails on that day.

One of my girlfriends, Marissa set up a Mass at her church in Joshua's honor. I had never attended a Catholic Mass, but it was excellent planning on her part. I thank God for the experience, which began at 6:30 AM.

Maria and I arrived on time. I wore my sweatshirt which displays Joshua's name, date of birth, and date of death, a pair of jeans, and my sneakers. Normally, I would have dressed up to attend anyone's church, but I went with how I felt on this date.

It was a nice surprise to see some of Joshua's friends at the Mass, especially this early in the morning. My day started out in a very bright fashion, but I was poorly dressed for the occasion. After the Mass, we went to breakfast, but I *still* did not have much of an appetite. I wanted to personally get to know the pain that I became acquainted with.

I forewarned my professors that this day might be difficult for me and that I was unsure if I would be at school on this date. After breakfast, I went home and got my calculator and books; then, I headed to school. I sat in my car as I listened to Joshua's CD. This was the first time that I recalled smiling as I listened to *"Wipe Your Eyes."* Then, I went into the classroom, and school ended around 2PM. I went to the cemetery that day as well.

Joshua's date of birth was very unique; often, I found myself reminiscing on Joshua's delivery. It was as if I relived every minute on the day that he was born just eighteen years ago, and I can tell you verbatim most of what happened at very specific times on his date of birth. I smiled more than I cried, as I warmly recalled the joy that I felt from this little boy's life.

I recalled, after midnight, that the doctor told me to go back to bed because my contractions felt only prickly. I remembered my girlfriend, Dara, coming over and timing the twinges of pain. I redialed the doctor to tell them that the contractions, although not strong, were barely a minute apart. Ray came home from the radio station, while his boss filled in for him. Off to the hospital the girls, Ray, and I traveled.

I remembered the reminders of the painful bumps in the road that a new life was about to begin. In addition, I remembered arriving at the hospital and handing the girls over to the care of my mother at the emergency room. I was wheeled to the elevator as they took me to the delivery room. I could feel that the time came for the doctor to tell me to push. I visualized the female doctor's surprised face after only having to push twice. Joshua came flying out like a football into her arms. I gloated in the feeling of having my answered prayer, from God Almighty, born at 3:52 AM on that Tuesday morning.

I recalled the proud feeling that Joshua was the only boy in the nursery on that day. He weighed in at 7lbs. and 6oz, and measured 20inches long. I evoked that I had very little if any pains on the day of his birth. Throughout Joshua's life there was no need for numbing or stitches. What a blessed day to remember! This day, is the date that I became convinced that the labor process is a predetermination for the pains that our children cause us during their time on earth. In addition, I believe that the stress one is under during the pregnancy has a lot to do with the child's demeanor after he or she is born.

Although Ray and I were unhappily married, while carrying Joshua, I was one of the happiest, fattest, hungriest, and prettiest women in this world, despite my problems and issues with Ray. Although when I got tired, I was grumpy, but to get over it, I just went to sleep as soon as possible. Joshua was by far my easiest child to deliver into this world, and his life caused me the least amount of pain as well. Joshua's birthday became the beginning of turning my mourning into joy, but at that time I did not realize that was what was happening.

I asked Dr. Johnson if he thought that I was crazy for the manner in which I handled Joshua's birthday. He replied, "No, Who said that? Actually, it is remarkable." I trusted that he would be honest with me; yes, I hesitated to tell anyone about my day for fear of condemnation, and thinking that people would not understand or judge me.

Another profound thing that I have learned through this process is that much of my journey may be understood by anyone, and that it is not for others to understand. Many mothers and fathers lose children, but I believe that even our processes of grief are inimitable. God has designed each of us as unique individuals who handle matters differently.

After Easter, Mother's Day was the first holiday that I faced without Joshua. On this day, tears inundated my face, my clothing, and my shoes, as I carefully watched children kissing their mothers, and I heard the words Happy Mother's Day.

After I attended church, I did not give or collect any gifts, but I went directly to my room and that is where I tearfully remained. I wished that the day would hurry up and end, but it *still* included twenty four hours. There were still one thousand, four hundred, and forty longs minutes. Even selecting a greeting card was a challenge that took me a long time to master.

Certainly, I did not want to ruin Maria's day. I wanted her to enjoy that day with her husband and children, but I can tell you that I was awfully sad. I think that I may have given Maria some money, and called it a day. I was painfully, yet, pleasantly reminded of the last Mother's Day that Joshua and I spent together. I asked him not to spend any money on me for that day, as Joshua loved to spend money. I am grateful that he disobeyed me on that date. I have the most precious card that he picked out for me. It details just how much he loved and appreciated me. He signed it, your one and only son, Joshua, which he will always be! Certainly, holidays already were different.

I will not detail my entire first Thanksgiving Day holiday for you, but I flew to Florida to spend time with Corrinna and Joe. Then, we drove to Texas from Florida with Corrinna and Joe. This is when I stated that I would love to live here. Thanksgiving used to be one of my most favored holidays. Much of my joy came from the family experiences and watching as Joshua ate was such a reward! Corrinna and Joe came home on last Thanksgiving, and it was during this time of thanks that we took our last family photo. We wore red and black.

Corrinna and Joe were rarely able to attend Joshua's games due to their military obligations, but during this season 2007, Corrinna and Joe were able to come to Hoop it up night, and they watch Joshua gloat in his blue and white warm-ups and jersey as his name was announced. Joe reminded me that they were home at one time when Joshua was younger while he played during the little league that I coached. Joshua was so happy and proud to have his entire family present at Hoop it up night. We all received t-shirts at that event. When Corrinna and Joe came home, everyone stopped their plans. All of my children went to see *This Christmas* together, which was a very difficult movie for me to watch, but I have gotten better.

A Special Gift

Chris Brown reminds me so much of Joshua in that movie and in other ways. The next holiday would be Christmas, but it was not very merry. Joshua mentioned that Ray told him that Chris Brown stole his job. That was one of the funniest jokes that I ever heard Joshua share that Ray said.

On Christmas day, I experienced a double whammy. This was my first Christmas without my son and the day that my best friend departed her life on this earth. I cannot tell you that I did anything special. I did not. Again, I did have some painful pillow time. I believe that I was at Maria and Manuel's home. I could not stomach going to my mother's house, and I spent the entire day in my room at my daughter's home; again, I was just waiting for the day to end. Mom sent me a plate of food, but I cannot remember if I ate.

However, I reminisced about last Christmas, as I waited for Joshua to return home from his scheduled visit with Ray. It was Joshua's last Christmas Day on this earth, but the irony of this day was that his mommy and dad were under the same roof with him at least for an hour. I went to my mom's house, and I asked Ray to drop Joshua off there.

Joshua called me to announce that Ray wanted to stop in, and Ray did just so. This event did not occur since Joshua was at least four years old. In addition, as Joshua and I were shopping, I showed him a white pair of slippers and asked him if he wanted me to purchase them for Shirley, and he said okay. I purchased Joshua and Ray the same exact sweater for a gift from Joshua too. I always made sure that Joshua had a gift for Ray, but this was the first year that I recall purchasing a gift for Shirley. I gave Joshua every material thing that he wanted and much more; including his first vehicle. I will never forget his expression of joy as he exclaimed, "Thank you mommy! You got me everything that I wanted!"

I considered purchasing a brand new Toyota Corolla Sport and Joshua wanted me to buy it with all of his heart. However, the problem was not my credit. If I purchased that vehicle, I knew that I could not afford to purchase Joshua his car, which was more important than any vehicle to "make me or Joshua look good." Purchasing Joshua a car made me feel good on the inside, and I am so glad that God granted me the ability to do so. I settled for my 1999 Nissan ALTIMA, and I *still* have it today. It gets me from point A to point B, and I am grateful.

Joshua received a TV, a digital camera, clothing, money and his car for Christmas. Yes, Joshua was a bit spoiled, but when people would make that remark I defended myself by stating Joshua is loved, which is so true! The greater gift is in the memory of the joy that Joshua had on his last Christmas Day. Amirah's TV blew out, and now she has her Uncle Josh's TV.

We cannot take any material thing with us when we depart from earth, but I do have that memory that Ray, Joshua, and I were under the same roof of my mom's home on Christmas Day and the joy that Joshua exclaimed! How was it, except by the grace of God that this day would provide us with a miracle on the last Christmas Day that Ray and I had with our son? It only lasted approximately thirty to sixty minutes, but the Bible tells us **in all things give praise and thanksgiving**.

I was not anxious about the approach of Valentine's Day. To my surprise, grief hit me really hard on that day. I thought about Joshua. The last Valentine's Day that he lived, we had so much fun while we laughed and joked about picking out small gifts for Joshua's many female friends who might give him something on that day. I cried terribly when I saw the little red bears that resembled the ones that he collected and put in my basket. I thought of the flowers and candy that Joshua tried and succeeded to get me to pay for while we laughed with such joy that evening.

Joshua was such a character, to know him was to absolutely love him. The boy loved life, and he had fun in most everything that he did. He found a way to smile, through our most difficult ordeals. Admittedly, many of his friends admittedly envied our relationship and so did some adults. We played around in a heartbeat, but Joshua also knew and respected when I was so serious.

It would be misleading to you if I would say that I did not anticipate the anniversary of my son's death. I dreaded facing March 15, 2009, and it no longer had anything to do with the date that I "married" Doug twenty nine years ago.

People other than Corrinna were insisting that I needed a romantic relationship. Yes, people thought that a man would help me get through this experience. I believed the exact opposite. This was a time in my life that I needed to heal before I even considered a relationship with anyone except God and my children.

First of all, the task of healing was not designed for a male to handle. Furthermore, I was not bumping into real men along my journey. An ex co-worker of mine stated these words, "Joshua had to die so that you can love again." I became irate, but I did not retaliate by force. Well, not immediately or so that she could see the force behind me bumping my head in the wall. Instead, I lashed out in my own way by getting involved in a past relationship with Richard, but I did not realize that is what I was doing until it was done. Soon, I discovered this was a pattern that I needed to break.

I wanted to "prove" to my highly opinionated co-worker and others that their words were untrue, but I did not use my words. I already knew that the past relationship with Richard did not work. I did not believe that anything changed about the male. Richard was selfish and constantly lied. I am of the opinion that he is *still* selfish and continues in his lies upon my revisit, but he agreed to escort me to the cemetery on that dreadful day, the anniversary of my son's death.

Intentionally, I procrastinated until almost dusk, before going to the cemetery. I figured that others would go earlier that day, and I did not want to be at the cemetery while others would be there. Upon my arrival, it became evident that many had come to visit Joshua's grave.

I determined earlier that I did not desire to take flowers to the cemetery, because flowers always were a way for Ray to avoid saying I am sorry. Besides, flowers were such a memory that death was in the air. So, with those thoughts, I decided to take balloons because whenever I made an error, I used my words to say I am sorry. I made corrections of my actions as a form of not repeating the behavior in an effort of true repentance. This did not always happen overnight, but God knows the effort that I put forward, and He blessed my efforts tremendously.

Instead, I purchased three red and silver balloons that spelled out these three words, I love you. Why three balloons? Well, one was for each of my daughters and one from me. Neither of my daughters has returned to the cemetery, which is their personal choice. I neither condemn nor condone, as each person has the right to grieve in the mannerism that fits them. My daughter recently told me that her children want to see their Uncle Josh's rock.

Once again, my professor, Mrs. Lucinda Whip, highly offended me when she laughed at me. I told her that I took balloons to the graveyard, and she stated they are just going to fly away; again, the way that I handle things may never be understood by anyone. As long as God is pleased with my behaviors that is all that matters to me. Unbeknownst to Mrs. Whip, I purchased a red weight so that the balloons would stand proudly. They stood pompously for a reasonably lengthy time. Once the balloons deflated, they did not fly away.

Richard, an old associate, rode with to the cemetery with me. Yes, I drove, as he did not have transportation. I was a bit perturbed because he did not have enough respect to attend my son's funeral. So, why did he go with me? His claim was that he needed closure, again at my expenses. On the way from the cemetery, I played Joshua's CD. Richard exclaimed that he was impressed because not many teenagers mastered the ability to get a CD produced. When he remarked that it did not sound like

Josh's voice, the space that was between us became much larger at that moment.

It was over before it really begun. There was nothing except distance between us, and I needed my own space in completeness. I had enough along time ago. Once again, I did not want a relationship, as I knew that I needed to work through this grief and heal before I could even think of anything as such. Richard did not cause me much grief because my focus was Joshua. Rather than trying to "prove" to my coworker that I did not need a relationship at this time of my life, I should have known that I needed to live with myself.

Eventually, I told the co-worker some of the things that were on my heart in a nice email, and she has not spoken to me since. For that I am grateful, because sometimes kindness is NOT saying a word. Besides, some people think that only what they say is the only things that matter, but I am of the opinion that opinions change.

There were days that I knew that I was at school, but I did not know how I got there, which book we were using, if I was in the right class, or what my name was, as my concentration became horrible. I had shared these things with Mrs. Whip. My feeling at that time was that she was berating me.

Often, Mrs. Whip told me that Joshua is making this or that happen. I disagree with that, as I give all praise and honor to God for every good thing that happens to me. My cousin Grace advised me that she believes that Joshua and my dad are having a ball in heaven at my expense and I can appreciate those remarks.

After being humiliated in front of my classmates, Mrs. Whip instructed me to see her after class so that she could continue whooping me. I stood there waiting for the belt as tears slowly came down my face. I was saddened that people could be so cruel for no apparent reason. She said these words to me, "Joshua is not resting because of the way that you are acting!"

I took in a deep breath, and I prayed as I tasted each tear that slowly traveled down my face to my throat. They tasted and appeared awfully salty. No other professor spoke to me in these mannerisms; with mercy applied; perhaps she did have my best interests at heart. Before I could get out of the building, I was dialing my cell phone.

Almost immediately, I telephoned my mother. My voice continued cracking, and my mom was boiling concerning the process Mrs. Whip strived to "motivate me or break me" from the grief of my son. Dr. Johnson questioned if Mrs. Whip had it in for me. I ranted and raved for several days until my composure came back together. The Bible tells us at Colossians 4:5-6 **that we should be wise in the way that we act…and to let our conversations be always full of grace, seasoned with salt, so that we will know how to answer!** Finally, the day came to peacefully knock on her office door to address the comments that she disrespectfully allowed to come forth without thinking.

In a very respectfully manner, I softly reminded her of the words that she spoke to me, and I politely said, "I do not believe that you spoke correctly. I did tell you that Joshua wanted me to be happy; right now, I am unhappy.

Chapter 14

Loved ones please choose your words carefully when you are dealing with someone in grief. If I did not have love for my God, myself, Joshua, and Mrs. Whip, many ugly things could have resulted on that date; mainly her rating as a professor/advisor and her superiors could have become involved. Unfortunately, many people use guilt tactics to motivate their pupils, inside and outside of the churches and schoolyards. I lived and experienced this most of my days after the death of my daddy. Perhaps God was preparing me for this day all along.

I am unsure that God is happy with this type of motivation. Someone recently told me that manipulation of the scriptures is a form of witchcraft. Please do not quote me on that. It is not something that I personally read or researched, but if you are interested do the research.

Personally, I do not believe that these tactics are successful by any measure. I entertained the idea of withdrawing from school on that day. However, that would be a defeat for me in the long run.

I was already unmotivated by Joshua's death, and I became less motivated to attend class, but it was something to take up my time. I became livid, and I abhorred her class, as my anger was not only in my heart. It was present in my pocket, until it was resolved. The reality is that I was absent; although, I barely missed a class while she taught, until my anger was properly dealt with, but God did prevail. He saw me through this occasion and many others. I am sure that God knew that I was dealing with enough, and I thank Him for fighting this battle too! He always wins! I was very unhappy with the recommendation of my advisor to do an internship or anything that she offered after selection of her words. However, my advisor, Mr. Brandt, from another College submitted my name to a CPA firm, and I received the offer of an internship on the spot. I am grateful that I was obedient.

I did fairly well the days preceding the anniversary date of my son's death until I decided to attend my aunt's sister's funeral. My Aunt Bea was very significant to me during my adolescent years. Aunt Bea attended Joshua's funeral, and I wanted to show my face for her. Her sister's funeral was being held on a Saturday, and I was scheduled to work. The funeral was held at the exact funeral parlor my dad's viewing was held at in PA. Wow, that's healing to be able to walk into that place.

I appropriately dressed for work and the funeral. I made an attempt to go to work immediately after the funeral, but upon reaching my desk, I felt pain in both my body and my heart, and it must have been written all over my face. Gently, I was encouraged to go home, and I did just so. I returned to work on that following Tuesday. No one said an ill word about my experiences. The internship ended after tax season, but graduation day was finally approaching in May.

Graduation day approached, and I knew that my son would have been extremely proud of me, but that did not take the pain away. I was unexcited about graduation day, because the reason that I believed that I entered college was absent. Joshua and I were planning to graduate in 2009.

The way that I missed Joshua on this date is unexplainable, but I was able to recall a different graduation day. Today, I am grateful that I was attending college. God knows what is best for us, and He knows what He is doing. As surely, I did not! Attending college was not a personal goal that I set for myself. I know for a fact that God set this in motion a long time ago. I began attending again college in 2004 after my endeavors at Villanova and Ursinus Colleges were halted while injuries were an issue. Additionally, I was certified in computer programming through Penn State.

Originally, I believed that the purpose for my entrance back into the college world was to demonstrate to Joshua that there really was a different way. I believed this was more effective than yelling at him about his grades. Absolutely, being an example worked as Joshua and I both put forth efforts. I did not consider what career path I would choose. I was positioning myself to get into a field that I might pay for Joshua's college education. Being a mom, a wife, and overall good person were my only goals in life, as I was already saved by the grace of God.

Prior to receiving my Degree, I was encouraged to submit an application to a private and extremely expensive college. Within what appeared to be a few days, I received a letter stating that I was accepted and that I was offered a large scholarship amount. I did not tour the campus prior to my first day of class. By graduation, *still*, I did not know the campus very well. I am convinced that I needed to be at this particular college to meet Pastor Paul who would perform Joshua's eulogy. Perhaps there are more reasons for this endeavor, as God has not entirely shown me what He has in store for me.

On May 24, 2009, I graduated with all types of honors, including Summa Cum Laude. I give all praise and honor to God. I did not know how I got to the scheduled classes after my son died, and I owe many special thanks to Grace who prayed me through almost every test while dealing with Joshua's death.

Two years ago on a previous graduation day, I was actually happy and proud at my previous graduation because Joshua, Maria, Manuel, Aunt Louise, my mother, Amirah and Tony were present upon receiving my degree and accolades. Micah was in his mommy's womb. During this cold and dreary graduation day, someone whistled when my name and accolades were announced. I am assured with all of my heart that it was Joshua's whistle, even though I never questioned him, and he never admitted that to me.

In addition, to my joy at this particular graduation, I also felt very proud for one of the first times in my life, but I felt sad because Aunt Louise was receiving chemotherapy treatments. It was a cold, rainy, and long evening for her, and the event was held outside. Yet, she did not complain. However, I am grateful that Aunt Louise was able to witness the receipt of my degree. Aunt Louise spoke these words to me, "I never saw anyone turn their life around as you have."

Although Maria, Manuel, and my three grandchildren were present when I received my Bachelor's Degree of Science, I was missing someone who is very special. A few tears fell during the ceremonies; again, I had my pillow time that evening. Joshua's absence was extremely prevalent and painful even though fourteen months passed, which equals a rose for each month. So, does time really heal all wounds? How long is time?

I only attended Baccalaureate Services because it was mandatory, but I ended up being very grateful for the experience. The topic that the speaker awesomely spoken. The sermon entitled "What is meant for you; is meant for you." The speaker spoke so much life into my spirit that day. I know that God designed this speaker to be there way before I knew that I would be attending this service. The sermon made so much sense, and more things began to click for me. The speaker made an absolute point to remind us that if something is meant for you, no one can take it from you, because it is yours. I believe these words to be true, and the preacher's remarks made the day a bit easier to get through.

I am reminded of my high school graduation, and during that day, nothing seemed to encourage me. As you can see my healing was beginning. My high school graduation was an extremely sad day for me, and I am sure that this reverts back to Daddy's absence and some unfortunate experiences prior to my High School graduation. I found no joy on that day, absolutely none.

Most classmates and their family appeared to be happy as they tossed their hats with gladness. For me, graduation from high school was one of the saddest days since my daddy died. I missed Daddy terribly, and I was in so much other internal pain. *Still*, I cry at the sound of Pomp and Circumstances, but I love the song that the choir sang on that day, which was, "**You Will Never Walk Alone.**" Was God telling me something through that song on that day?

In 1978, I did not know where I was heading in life.

Mom paid my application fee, and I was accepted at West Mansfield State University. Mom was quite upset that she sent in the money, and that I did not choose this route. I did not articulate to my mother that I was too frightened of life because of my many negative experiences. I was afraid of beginning this new adventure. I was captured by fears, secrets, depression, anxieties, low self-esteem, and grief.

Even to this date, I never shared this information with my mom, but I was so afraid to attend school because I was always afraid of both failure and success, which are both important aspects of life. Yes, admittedly, I was afraid of life. Instead of embracing life, I was desperate for love. Thus, I reproduced what I was afraid of, life, which I reproduced through a child. I wanted love more than anything in life. Daddy taught me its value and healing power at a very early age, but I did not feel it in its completeness by a human since my father's death.

I missed the warmness that produced wonderful feelings which shinned from my daddy's face lighting up whenever I stepped one foot into his presence or when I acted in a silly manner. Life as a youth taught me at such young ages that love does not cost a thing. However, as I got older, I learned that providing the things that children need and giving them what we desire them to have is an entirely different story.

During my children's lives, I wanted my children to know that material things come and go, but love lasts a long time. I purchased each of my daughters diamond rings so that they would not have their minds blown by the size of any ring, but rather have their breath taken away because of someone's amount of love and respect for them. See, there were methods to my madness, if you qualify my methods as such.

By all means, to raise a child is not inexpensive, but love has no costs or limits; although, boundaries must be set and respected. Birthing my daughters at such a young age, I did not realize the responsibility that comes with having children, but I took on that responsibility by doing the best that I could with all of my heart. I did not know what I was doing, but I didn't fail because of trying to learn. I attempted to give them everything that I received. The things that I should not have received, I tried to avoid duplicating. At times, I was successful; other times, I failed.

I was much more mature when Joshua was born. I was twenty nine years old. By this age, I had three children, two of which were preteens. I am forever grateful for Joshua's life, and I can state that today I celebrate the seventeen years of life that **God** granted of Joshua's life, and I praise **God** for knowing who He is in my life. I celebrate **LOVE**. Although I can tell you these things today, there are certain things that I had to deal with during the process of grief.

During the grief process, one thing that I know for sure there is an inability to concentrate. Some days were not as bad as others, but for the most part, concentration took extra effort and the inability to focus remained. It took extra effort for a long time. This is why I give all praise and honor to God for graduating with honors and many awards.

Often, I telephoned Grace for prayer because on some days if someone asked me what was two plus five, I would have said six, and that would be my final answer. Testing brilliant in math did not suffice during this time. The other problem was that my job title was a college paraprofessional tutor. The subjects that I tutored were: algebra, statistics, economics, Spanish, various accounting levels, and other subjects. My very patient employer understood, and they lowered the number of classes that I tutored during some of this time. My brain felt clogged. I just couldn't think clearly.

In the stages of grief, there was a period of time that I am sure that I was unable to operate at full capacity due the shock of my son's death. In its entirety, I felt as if I was going through the motions, as if I remained in a dream. Somehow, at the same time, I knew that it was so real.

After going to Florida from May until August 2008, I thought that time would take some of the pain, anxiety, depression, shock, and all the other feelings away. I thought that being away from the area where Joshua's death occurred would take me away from the memories of all that just happened, but it did not. As I began facing the reality that I was heading back to deal more with my son's death, and finding my life without him, I began having panic attacks.

Panicking was not new to me it just arrived in a very different form. If my children fell down on the court, or in any way were injured, there was no way that anyone could keep me off of the court. Immediately off to a hospital or doctor's office we went, while I demanded proper attention and treatment. If I am crazy for that, so be it! Strongly, I believe that we must be our and our children's advocate when it comes to health, education, safety, and other related issues.

When Joshua played football, I panicked and prayed prior to every game. I always enjoyed watching football, as I was a Dallas Cowboys fan but when my children were involved in any sport, I was their number one fan. Although I was proud to see my son on the field in his blue and white uniform, wearing number 14, no one knows the fear that gripped my heart each time he played in the game. Of course, I was extremely excited when he scored. It was more than I could bear at times because he shined. When he went across the goal line there was a double amount of joy. Joshua scored, and he escaped my fear of being injured. Panicking was very different while going through grief.

I thought for sure that I was going to lose my mind in the midst of at least one of those panic attacks. During this time, I also knew that the doctors stated that Aunt Louise did not have much time left on this earth either. I read several books on grief, and even though one book in particular specified that panic attacks can be a part of grief, I was unequipped to handle them. Some days, one panic attack came right behind the other; until, I finally got off the plane, which is when anger lifted its ugly head. Obviously, it had not been resolved correctly.

Who asked for the dreadful task of burying their child, having a marker put on his grave, and setting the criteria for a scholarship? I did not ask to bury my son, but I realize that God entrusted me with this task. I did not want to be back in the area. That was not the true reason for the anger. My thinking at the time was that I made the mistake of coming back to the area, but that was not the case. As a matter of fact, I did not have a desire to be anywhere. Actually, I was angry because I did not want to deal with the death of my son.

Anger is one of the violent stages of the grief. The problem is that you have no idea how broad or minuet the triggers will be. Once I was able to identify the triggers, I could deal with the emotions that followed as I learned to walk my way through grief. Many of my days and nights were filled with prayers begging/bargaining/demanding that God take the pain away. Any words that I thought would work were spoken. I just believed that I wanted it to go somewhere but I did not know where, but first I needed to do the work.

Very respectfully, my Spanish professor invited me to entertain if I really desired the pain to go away. I pondered that question because if the pain was erased, did that mean that I would lose memories of my son? There was so much conflict within that question. At that time, I did not know the answer to that question.

Certainly, I never want my son's memories to go away, but did that mean that I had to be in pain all of the time? I was too new to the real process of grief to be able to sort out the answer to that question at that time, but I will share with you what I eventually learned. The death of my son is the most painful memory of my mind and heart, but I no longer dwell on that moment. I am unsure that I ever dwelled on that moment, but the massive pain of my heart comes from missing Joshua. I am positive that I will miss him forever; no matter how long forever is defined on this earth.

In the beginning, all that I could think about was how much I missed Joshua. I begged those in attendance at my son's funeral to celebrate the seventeen years of life that God gave to us, but I was unable to conquer missing Joshua enough to be able to hold onto the smile even when I was able to reflect on a positive or funny moment from his life. At various stages, I found myself angry when someone else said anything funny about Joshua. They were not stating that Joshua's death was funny. Joshua's death does not take away the fact that Joshua's life had some hilarious moments, because he was such a character.

It was not until I addressed this confusing issue in counseling that I was able to get past some of the confusion that losing a child brings. Perhaps, guilt may be a better choice of words than confusion. Was I feeling guilty because I smiled since my son died? I believe that the short answer to that question is yes. With this in mind, I became certain that guilt really is a part of my grief process as well, regardless as to the form that it chooses to present itself.

I asked Dr. Johnson how I was supposed to be happy at any time since I lost my son. His respectful and profound response was that he supposed that many parents who have lost children battle with this question. This is one of the many questions that he left to my answer; perhaps, he did not have this experience himself, and I pray that he never will.

What I learned is that as the pleasant memories of Joshua's life come back into view, I never wanted to lose these memories either. I began to hold onto them as long as I could as I attempted to push away the pain of missing Joshua. I learned the tough way that I was battling myself while I unsuccessfully attempted to force my feelings away and keep other feelings present. Eventually, I learned to accept and actually feel whatever it is that I am feeling at that moment and to accept where I am in grief. This is huge for me, because at the same time, I am learning how to accept myself.

I continue to dream about Joshua, but the dream cycle has changed as well. In the early stages of grief, I dreamed that Joshua was hiding. When I saw his face, I became extremely excited, and I asked him where have you been? Also, I asked him who was lying in his coffin. I realize now that God was showing me that I did not fully accepted Joshua's death, which some people label as denial. I did not want to believe that I was in the stage of denial; perhaps, that is why these dreams occurred, but I do believe that denial is a very common stage of grief.

I eye witnessed the trauma unit work on my son for what seemed like hours. I clinched the last clothing that he played ball in: the black t-shirt, the white shirt underneath the black t-shirt, and the black shorts that were cut off of his body. I have the sneakers that he was wearing on the black top court when he collapsed.

I knew that Joshua's death was real in my heart and mind. Selectively, I picked out the purple and gray clothing for the undertaker to dress my baby. Maria, Corrinna, and I selected the coffin, the emblem, the flowers, the dove, and the cemetery plot, and I knew too well that my daughters and I tarried all night while we wrote, proofread, and rewrote Joshua's obituary.

I recalled the warm feeling of hugging what appeared to be 1000 people just at his viewing, but it *still* seemed like a dream, even though I knew that it was too REAL! No one stated this to me, but I believe that you can know that a death is real but the denial part may be denying your feelings to meet the reality.

My belief is that you are not dealing with reality until you accept what has happened as your reality of life.

I knew that we were at the church, funeral parlor, and the graveyard, but I felt like I was watching the whole experience, as if I was there but not really there. As much as I wanted to be there for my son is as much as I did not want to be there at all. I know without a doubt that God offered me footprints, and He was carrying me through this entire experience. I willingly fell into His loving arms which would carry me through my son's death, and I knew that I was decreed safe too, while He hid me under His wings of love. Even though it was hard to accept, my heart ached unlike ever before in my life.

Although God carried me through this entire experience, I thank God for Dr. Johnson and his wisdom and very capable professionalism, diligence and due care. It is very interesting looking back at another counseling session. I complained to Dr. Johnson about the circle of pain around my heart. I did not believe that it was an envisioned mental circle of pain, because if I literally touched any spot on my chest that this circle encompassed, I could physically feel the severe intensity of this real pain. It is worse than RSD, and Reflex Sympathetic Dystrophy hurts like heck, especially if the spot is touched. Dr. Johnson's reply to me was, "This is how you know that it is real." Did he realize without commenting that I was in the stage of denial at that point of grief? I do not know that answer. His very tactful dispositions did not expose the word denial to me, even if that is what he diagnosed.

During one of the sessions, Dr. Johnson asked me to tell him about Joshua's funeral. My answer described every minor and major detail from the beginning to the end. He asked me if I felt like a spectator, and he left me to ponder that question too. I guess that is what I am describing above when I state that I knew that the candlelight vigil, grief counseling at schools, cleaning out Joshua's locker, reviewing the writings on the walls, viewings, funeral, and burial all occurred, but I could not grasp that all of this really happened to my son, me, or our family.

I do not believe that total reality hit me until my heart, mind, body, and soul could all deal with this horrific tragedy. When it hit me, it was worse than any of the eight car accidents, many surgeries, and any of the physical, mental, financial, spiritual, or sexual abuses combined that I ever suffered at anyone's hands or words.

This was the first time of my life that I knew without a doubt that I did not do anything that caused this tragedy to happen to me. If anything, I was the overprotective mother, and the one who would take the blows to avoid my children feeling any pain. I would not wish this experience on my worst enemy. I could not imagine anyone else wishing this on me. I shared with you that I fully realize that God has all power, and that He allows things to happen. There were times that I did ask God why? Not, why me, but why Joshua? This was the same question that Manuel initially posed. Others continually expressed their uninvited opinions to me.

My same highly opinionated co-worker sarcastically replied, "Oh Joshua was just too perfect for this earth!" Again, I was extremely livid; yes, she is the same one who demanded that I needed to date, and she said Joshua had to die so that I could love, but I remained silent again. It's a good thing that God is not a man. **God cannot lie! He will not lie.** Certainly, we believed that Joshua was in a somewhat of a perfectly healthy condition, and whatever knowledgeable condition that was imperfect, he had medications, but no one is perfect. I assume that I spoke too highly of Joshua for her hearing prior to his death.

Neither the doctors nor I knew of Joshua's heart condition. If Joshua sneezed too many times, generally, he had a scheduled and completed doctor's visit. As a matter of fact, the doctor informed me that Joshua only needed a physical every two years; not every year. The physician's words never cured me from getting Joshua a physical every year. I am very grateful that Joshua did not suffer as a sickly child and that he did have a fulfilled life.

I questioned, did I do everything possible for my son? Upon learning from the coroner's office that there are no symptoms for Joshua's condition, which was fatal; the final answer is yes. The only way that Joshua's condition could have been discovered was through a sonogram, which no physician noticed any symptoms that required this test. Even if they did a sonogram, according to the coroner, the only treatment for Joshua's particular heart disease was a heart transplant. There is medication that can extend one's life, but Joshua's heart disease was fatal.

The short version of Joshua's heart condition is congenital Hypertrophic Cardio Myopathy. This disease can be an inherent condition. At Joshua's time of death, I was unaware of anyone in our family dying from this heart particular disease; later, I learned that at least one of my favorite uncles did have an enlarged heart, which did not result in his death. Instead, cancer made him a victim. In addition, my maternal grandfather died due to some type of heart condition at the age of approximately forty years old.

Next, I questioned if it was better to not know about Joshua's condition or to be acquainted with Joshua's condition? It is my belief that the hard answer to this question is yes. I think that it was better to not know. I trust that answer because God is in control! The coroner's office explained to me that the *only* treatment available for Joshua was a heart transplant. It was stated that there are medications which can possibly slow down the process of death. However, the coroner reminded me that the particular disease that Joshua suffered from is fatal, and that most children die *very* early their youth. Joshua already outlived the odds of almost living to the age of eighteen.

Yes, I am counting my blessings!

Now, if I knew for sure that Joshua could have had a heart transplant and lived a full life; certainly, without reservations, the answer to the above answer would be no. However, I do not know that information for certain. What I do know for sure is that I was already an overprotective mother and that Joshua was only seventeen, but he lived a fuller life than many of us who are much older.

When Joshua first begun riding a bike, I hated the thought of him scraping his knees, and that goes for my daughters as well. I did my best to protect my children from the injuries of life, even though I felt like a failure.

Taking things personally was my nature of guilt.

When my daughter was raped and cut, I felt guilt, but I realize that these things were not because I failed to protect her. There are many things that occur in life that are totally out of our control and are simply not our fault. I was always anxious until my children came through our door. I became especially anxious once they began driving. Being injured from several car accidents magnified this fear.

I worried excessively that my children had proper nutrients. It was rare to allow Joshua to have caffeine. Later, I read that caffeine was not good for his condition. We did not eat many chocolates either, which is another thing that was unhealthy for Joshua's condition. If I knew that Joshua had HCM, I somehow believe that our relationship would have been severely impaired because if he would have walked too quickly, I would have yelled, "Slow down!" You see, Joshua, as well as my daughters, became upset with me several times because of my overprotective nature without any knowledge of Joshua's fatal condition.

The coroner's office confirmed that most children with Joshua's heart condition generally die very early in their youth. While I was visiting in Florida, I met a woman at the salon who shared with me that her baby sister had HCM as well, but her sister died at the age of two, and she was on medication to prolong her life. This woman oddly gazed at me when she realized that I was unaware of my son's condition and without medication to prolong his life, Joshua lived to be seventeen. He would have turned eighteen in less than eight months if he had lived.

If anyone knew of my son's condition, Joshua would not have been able to play any sports. Being a part of a team was a **huge part** of Joshua's life, whether he received playing time was not the vital issue, as being on the team and being treated with respect was of utmost importance. Joshua knew the real game of life, being a part of a team. He knew the truth. There is no "I' in team and respect.

I had serious problems with the mannerism in which I felt that Joshua and other teammates were being treated during his junior year. It seemed as though the coach played favorites. Considering that Joshua was a junior, he received a decent amount of playing time. It is possible that I was overreacting because of how harshly I felt treated because of my attempts to warn the Boosters' Board members that something was terribly wrong concerning suspicion of the missing money. However, I also know for a fact, that I am not the only parent who felt this way.

I asked to meet with the basketball coach after Joshua died, but God did not manifest that appointment. Something of much more importance came up. However, the coach responded to me that my son will always have a special place in his heart, but I do not believe that Joshua knew this, which I believe is the most important issue.

I watched my son hate to go to practice and play basketball, and it ached my heart to see the love for the game lost on the court, but he continued to practice to make himself worthy of this coach's respect. I do not believe that any coach can ever state that Joshua ever disrespected them, regardless as to the matter in which they reacted to Joshua. In one of the coaches "speeches," after Joshua died, the coach stated that he wished that he had 15 more Joshua's but they were only words to my ears.

Joshua's ninth grade coach, Mr. Burns, was the best. He treated all of the players individually and collectively. Believe me, Mr. Burns had a passion for winning, but it was evident that people were more important than winning. Joshua played center during ninth grade, and let me add, that boy jumped as if springs were attached to his legs when he had the joy of the game.

Joshua was not the tallest player on the team.

When I coached, I had one particularly favorite player who happened to be my son. A few others were very talented, but I never blatantly disrespected any of my players, even those without any talent at all. It is not all about winning, which I believe is a pride issue. I never yanked any of the team members out of the game as if they were trash. Everyone is someone's child, and I encouraged them to the upmost. I showed them the errors of their ways. Yes, I yelled, jumped, screamed, and loved every second of it, but I did it with any ounce of disrespect to my players.

From an early age, it was obvious to me and many others that Joshua loved life, and he lived every minute as if it was his last one. To say that brings so many feelings, smiles, pride, tears, and realization that he lived his last minute doing one of the things that he loved while attempting to improve his basketball game during a pickup game of basketball on black top court.

Joshua did so many things that a lot of people who live to be 90 or 100 have never experienced. I have a picture of Joshua with Billy King at a 76er's game. Joshua enjoyed many behind the scenes passes. Joshua attended concerts and plays. He was my star of the high school talent show. He sang in the choir and played the drums, and he was the champion of Madden.

Joshua met many celebrities, and he traveled a large portion of the United States. He ice-skated, roller-skated, rollerbladed, bowled, golfed, jet skied, snowboarding, danced, and he had a CD produced. Joshua learned the art of modeling, and he was a creative artist. There are many more that I cannot even name. More importantly he gave and received so much love! The reporter, Tammy did an editorial which she entitled, "Only the Good Die Young," in which she summed it up when she said that Joshua was already a shining star.

Joshua also drove a Mercedes and an Infiniti. Joshua asked me to purchase him a BMW, but he understood that I could not afford that. Within his rights, Joshua decided to turn his black Grand Am Pontiac into his own BMW, as in his mind it was a BMW! Joshua lived a full life even though he died at the age of seventeen.

Joshua had everything that any other child had, and he was so rich in love that it is incredible. He was an incredibly and beautifully spirited young man; a wonderful son, and he gifted so many lives just because he had such special gifts from God. He embraced self-respect, respect for women, and living life to the fullest. Joshua was taught to open doors for ladies and to treat them as if they were of value. He states in his song, "You taught me how to treat a wife," but most importantly he dedicated his life to God. I thank God that I know that I will see Joshua again.

Another question that I taunted myself with was did I say, I love you, before I hung up the phone during our last call? My children and I rarely hang up the phone without stating those three words. I learned the importance of telling someone that you love them at the time of Daddy's death.

Also, I believe the Bible's warning when it states **not to let the sun go down on your wrath**. In the confusion of grief, it is still hard to recall our exact last words of that phone call. Generally, we hang up the phone with the words I love you or love you. However, I think that the last words via phone were talk to you later. My children and I made it a point, no matter how mad we were any evening, prior to going to bed, we always said, "Good night; I love you. Sweet dreams," which was properly placed on Joshua's home going program. This tradition is carried on by my oldest daughter and her family.

Please allow me to share with you of an important event that implemented these traditions. Around the age of ten, I thought that I became a big girl, and I wanted to go to Virginia to spend a week or two with my cousin, Mattie, and my parents agreed.

Daddy and my Uncle David drove me to Aunt Vanessa's home, which at that time took approximately eight to nine hours. When Daddy's black pickup truck pulled off, I knew that Daddy and I were in trouble. Immediately, I became violently ill; yes, homesick, to put it mildly.

Telephoning the operator to place collect calls home was my only refuge, but these massive amount of calls only made mom angrier. Cell phones were not placed on the market during this time. Besides, my daddy was not nearby or near home. I began eating raw cucumbers. As a child, I believed that would make me even sicker. Of course, I needed to have a bellyache. Oh, my heart ached as soon as my Daddy pulled off. I cried, called, and cried and called home more. Continually, I induced my mother's anger. About nine hours later, which seemed to take an eternity, Daddy answered the phone.

Politely, Daddy asked me to allow him get some much needed rest, and he assured me that he would be back for me as soon as he rested up to get back on route 81 heading south. He did just so! My Daddy traveled for at least thirty two hours in a two day time period to make sure that I felt loved, safe, and protected.

I became the laughing stock of our extended family for many years, but more importantly some really good lessons resulted out of this experience. Yes, undoubtedly, Daddy spoiled me rotten, which I may have confessed in the very beginning. I really am Daddy's little girl. More importantly, this is when and how I began the examination of the true meaning of real love. After a few days passed, while we were at home, I sat crouched up on the landing of our stairs, as I wept lightly. Daddy had ears like an eagle, and he detected my soft cry. He knew that something was wrong with me. After he called my name, which was Sweetie; I do not recall Daddy ever calling me by my real name, he requested that I come downstairs to his green recliner chair. I sat in his lap with my arms around his neck as he asked me why I was crying. Loudly, I burst into more tears as I hugged his neck, and I said,

"Daddy, you really do love me." I recall his smile with a big grin and his words, "Of course I do."

I had this golden opportunity to tell Daddy how much I loved him. I thanked him for traveling the distance for me. I took full advantage of that opportunity, and I am so glad that I did! This is what I learned about love at a very young age, that love knows no distance! I am and will continue to be forever grateful to have the ability to revisit this experience since my Daddy died. It was not because he turned around and picked me up, but that I know, without a doubt that I told Daddy that I loved him, and it was with sincere meaning.

The reason for the enormous amount of pain of Daddy's death is first and foremost the loss of the love from any man on this earth, and no man's love has been quite like his since. No male has ever loved me like Daddy until I conceived my son, Joshua Wayne-Anthony Brown.

I asked myself the question while trying to recall every sound and word of my son's voice the last time that we spoke to each other on the cell phone, but I know without a doubt that there were an infinite number of times that I told Joshua and more importantly showed my son that I loved him unconditionally. As a matter of fact, I continually tell him every day!

Also, I do know that I told Joshua over and over again how proud I am to be his mother. I did not wait until the reporter came to interview me upon his death to say any of those words, and with that I can **lift my head until the hills from wince cometh my help!** Without any question, I knew that Joshua heard me in the hospital room as I prayed with him, questioned him, and whispered the sweet words…I love you buddy. Most people called Joshua, Josh, but I usually referred to him as Joshua or buddy, because he lived both of those names!

As I journey through grief, some moments of thoughts are rather amazing. I recall a conversation with my dear friend Juanita. I did not realize that Joshua entered my room. I was expressing to Juanita how blessed and proud I felt to be chosen as the mother of Joshua. I would be lying if I would state that Joshua never made me angry or did things that I did not approve. I have shared some of his mistakes with you. I would not dare tell anyone that my child was perfect while on earth; after all, that would make him God, but I will tell anyone that he was perfectly made for my life, just as his sisters are too.

Joshua was more protective, gentle, caring, respectful, and loving; perhaps, this was because of his gender. I learned and was taught so much about love in raising all three of my children. A child can be a great teacher if you allow them to be. Okay, so I was naïve, but I used to think that love is a feeling, but I know today that is just simply untrue. Feelings do change, but **love does not change**, as love continues even if the person does not. I recognized that a portion of my problem was that the fear of the love conditioned my heart to discontinue in a healthy relationship with any man that I loved or loved me because of the possibility of abandonment of that person through death.

Along with that is the fact that I did not totally heal and abusers with the sick scent sensed that about me. I ran right into the traps. However, on the flip side of that is the fact that it is not easy to really love an abuser, you just learn to tolerate them. It did not take much to consider whether I would love my children. This love for me was instinctual.

I wanted children; although, there were many rough times that love continued because it is real. I never imagined that I would bury any of them. I always believed that my children would bury me, because that is what we call the "natural" process of life. Now, I know for sure that it really is better to love and loose than to never love at all.

Definitely, Joshua was a warrior, and God used his life to bring so much peace into my life that I can smile when I say or write these words. As I mentioned earlier, Joshua expressed that I needed to be strong enough to let him go. It would be impossible to be strong enough to let my son go in my own strength. Who would think that any mother could ever be happy and relax after her son died?

During intense grief, I used to think how Joshua dared tell me that the desires of his heart were for me to be happy and relax. I never dreamed of this possibility, but once I claimed at Joshua's funeral that I trusted God completely; God took the reins and began to teach me how to do just so!

Do I stumble along the way? Yes, at times I do. However, in each stumble, I ask God what He is teaching me, and I try to learn. I am not always successful, but as I told Joshua, when you make a mistake, do not just lie in it, but pick yourself up and try again. My mother taught me that the only thing that beats a failure is a try.

You see, **I really can do all things through Christ who has strengthened me**, as stated in Philippians 4:13. Joshua's life prepared me how to begin to trust God and his death showed me the miracle and beauty in trusting God implicitly! Strongly, I believe that the process began prior to his death because Doug, my daughters' father/first husband, telephoned me and asked me to forgive his financially obligation of child support debt.

I did not answer Doug immediately; rather, I told him that I needed to pray about the matter, and I did just so. When Doug telephoned me, the amount of large accumulated debt was in excess of $36,000, which meant he did not pay much during the girls' life time. Maria and Corrinna were 28 and 27 years old when I received this phone call. I prayed a lot, and I finally received some answers.

This court ordered child support resulted because I was out of work due to the life threatening ectopic pregnancy episode, which I strongly believe that Doug's ill behavior created. Once the child support order was placed, I was grateful when I received a few dollars, and angry when I did not, which was the majority of the time.

Eventually, I became accustomed to not receiving any money from Doug. Realistically, our daughters were just as much Doug's responsibility as they were mine. I did not have a lot of extras, as I spent everything that I had on my children, and they never hungered or thirsted. Many nights, I longer knew hunger pains because after a while, they lost their affect.

Doug moved to Bermuda, as he was the one who was on the run. Upon one of his visits to the United States, the police confiscated his passport. Being out of the country, he did not file his taxes within the United States, even though he *still* remained a citizen. Doug's access into the United States was voided unless he paid his arrearages and child support obligations.

Doug attempted to sell me a sob story that his sister was extremely ill and that he needed to take care of her. I knew better than that, as Doug is from a family of nine or ten and the rest of the siblings are in the United States, but that was not the issue. I laugh now, but I did not laugh then. Doug actually left his daughter with his sister before he moved into the United States. I have reasons to believe this move was not for his sister's betterment.

I also knew that the educational system in Bermuda is not as highly promoted as that of the United States. Doug's children by his new wife deserved a good education; and perhaps, my daughters and he would finally have some type of relationship. Well it was a thought. As I prayed about this decision I asked myself a few questions, was it the money that I truly wanted? The answer to that question was no. I needed to let go of the fear that once held me hostage, which is a heck of a ransom. Keeping Doug out of my space, even though I did not have control over the operations of domestic relations, became a safety zone for me.

Was I *still* afraid of him? The answer became no. I am no longer the little frightened girl that he treated horribly. Doug is remarried. Even if he was not, he and I would never sing a duet or be a duo again, and so I inquired my mind the true worry of allowing him to be free of this monetary debt. Then

I recalled the scripture which states at Matthew 6:15, that **in order to be forgiven we must forgive.** Did that mean that I had to let go of his financial responsibility in order to be forgiving? Absolutely not! However, the only way to get Doug to accept any responsibility for his careless actions was this monetary situation. Finally, as instructed, Doug called me back in one month, and all that I really wanted from him or the ex-pastor, Saul, for that matter, was acknowledgment of their actions.

I believe that was the first step towards true forgiveness for me of all of Doug's transgressions. After several talks, Doug finally acknowledged some of his wrongdoings, and I released the debt, literally and figuratively. He is back in the United States for over a year. I have more to share with you in my next writings. Maria and Corrinna are grown, and we made it without his emotional, physical, financial, and spiritual support, which all were ill. I asked one thing in return from Doug, which is for him not to make contact with me again.

Some of you may think that is acting in an unforgiving manner, but I offer this to statement to you that Dr. Johnson shared with me. Sometime, kindness is not saying a word. My mother always phrased it this way; if you do not have anything good to say, then do not say anything at all. Could I have used this money? Absolutely is this answer. Was there any law or other way that Doug was able to bail out of this debt? No, absolutely not, there was any other way for Doug to be released from this debt except to pay it in full. Am I free? Totally free is the correct answer to that question. Is he free? I do not know that is between him and God is the only answer that I can offer. I am grateful that I am free.

During 2007, prior to Ray's illness, I was occasioned to telephone Joshua's dad at work. Finally, almost nine years later, the opportunity was presented to explain to Ray the conditions that we lost our home when he cancelled our health insurance policies. He thought, as many did, that I left our home due to fear while I was on the school board. In addition, I explained the manipulation methods by which people tried to get me off of the school board. The main threat was to attempt to have Joshua taken away from me, and our security alarm going off nightly. I shared with Ray that the physician reported the first suspicions and concerns of child abuse and that I followed through as any good mother would. Communication was an ineffective tool with Ray and me from the beginning.

I made a conscience decision to apologize again to Ray for the pain that I caused him. Whether or not Ray caused me pain first was not the true issue. Many times when we are in pain, we retaliate without really thinking about what we are doing until later, if at all. However, we are not responsible for others' behavior, but we are responsible for our own behaviors. I believe that the stage was set for me to begin to deal with the pain that my son's death was about to bring. I seriously doubt that I would've been able to speak with Doug or Ray about any of our issues after Joshua's death. That is just my thinking, because **with God all things are possible.**

As I began the painful journey of grief, I became aware of my reactions to people. Even though I had an excuse to be angry, I did not want to make the same mistakes that I just openly repented for doing. I am not sorry that I was careful in dealing with other people and that I did not react in anger, because it would have opened up more fresh wounds.

In addition, I did not want to turn my pain inwardly and become severely depressed either. When people said negative things to me, even though I felt like lashing out, most of the time, I was able to just pray and talk to my earthly and spiritual mother, or counselor, and later I addressed the issue in a different frame of mind.

Once I truly identified who my Father is and that I am His child, I have awareness that if anyone intentionally offends me that my Father will take care of the situation, and if their intentions are ill; then, they need to identify the roots that their words/actions stem from, as that is not my problem. For the first time in my life, I became selfish enough to deal with my own problems and trust everyone else to deal with their own set of problems, which I label as the beginning of setting boundaries.

There was one occasion when I negatively responded to Alisha out of anger that initially was triggered by the question, what is it the drugs? This incident occurred at Maria's home. In addition, on this same date, Alisha was making derogatory comments about the hospital which just kept my son alive that I may be able to speak and pray with him. I was injected twice with rage. My toes curled up, and before I could even give it a thought, I slammed my fists on the table, and I dared her to say another negative thing about that hospital which just kept working on my baby.

Upon my return from Florida, it may not be of a surprise to you, but Alisha was one of the first persons that I visited and offered an apology. Alisha never apologized for her comments and perhaps that was because she did not have any ill intentions of saying something that would offend me; regardless, she did thank me for my apology. I wanted to apologize for my angry reaction, and this is how my healing process has gone. Besides, I want my little light to shine. Later, I received a card from her which spoke volumes, as she noted my quieted sprit.

Although I allow my feelings to come and go at their own rate of return, I no longer avoid my feelings; rather, I try to control what I can control, which are my reactions, especially when they are not going to be pretty. I assure you as long as there is life, some ugly things will show up, but it is up to us to control which side God shows us as blemishes. I long to be in a place that I can just laugh at the ignorance of people, but I guess that would be in a perfect world, because ignorance is neither pretty nor funny.

One of the healthiest conscientious decisions that I made during my life was to deal with everything that was in my heart from early childhood. Some state that people carry their baggage into next relationships. I offer this statement; you do not have to if you deal with your baggage before you enter into a relationship. I believe the baggage is oneself. If you know and love who you are and heal prior to moving forward into any relationship, I believe that a relationship can be healthy. Establish your first true relationship with God, and then someone else can join you in a healthy relationship.

Chapter 15

As painful as it is, I am examining everything that becomes a thought as thoroughly as possible. Once I understand, I lay it to rest with a prayer of thanksgiving and a smile, which becomes easier to do upon feeling the warmness of God smiling on me for the hard work that I am continually doing. As I lay each of these events to rest, my life becomes easier to deal with. As my issues of life became easier to deal with, I realize that my son's death will always be a part of my life. When I changed my residence to Texas, I did not have a choice except to leave Dr. Johnson's care, but God is always with me as **He promised never to leave me or forsake me.**

Some people think that going to counseling is a sign of weakness, but I totally disagree with that statement. Some Christians don't believe in counseling, but I offer this to you, not one time did my counselor disrespect my beliefs. If anything, I think that at times he may have admired my beliefs. Another profound question that Dr. Johnson asked me was, "Did you name him Joshua so that your walls would come down?" My answer was, "I never gave any thought to that question." I did a lot of hard work since my son died, and Joshua tore down a lot of my walls, as preached in Pastor Paul's sermon during Joshua's funeral. As I learned to accept Joshua's death, I am also learning to accept my reality of life, which is the fact that life is hard, but God is *still* good. God never promised us sunny skies every day, but remember that we need rain for most things to grow properly. Besides, who wants to be a cactus? I don't. Do you?

As a matter of fact the word of God tells us that **we will have trials and tribulations, but be of good courage and He will strengthen our hearts.** Courage is defined by many people, but my definition of courage is as stated in the Bible, **to trust in God with all of my whole heart and lean not to my own understanding.**

I am learning to live this scripture and so can you. One of my favorite scriptures is Isaiah 40:31. It is a promise that I keep dear to my heart, and it reads, **those who wait upon the Lord, shall renew their strength; they shall mount their wings like eagles; they shall run and not be weary; they shall walk and not faint! Wait, I say, wait on the Lord!**

As **I walk through the valley of the shadow of death, I shall fear no evil.** As much as I shared with you, there is so much more that you do not know. As I claim these scriptures over my life, they are becoming my testimony. Slowly, I begin to take each moment as they come. I made progress from one half second at a time to a second and a time, but I continued to make progress to one minute at a time. Now, I take one day at a time, but attempting to stay in the present moment can be challenging, yet so rewarding. While I am still growing, I am learning so many valuable lessons.

I learned that **it is not good to worry about tomorrow. If the next day comes, it has its own anxieties.** Rather, I now attempt to live in the present moment as I recount the times that Joshua and others' lives took my breath away. I continue to dance as if no one is watching, even if gospel music is playing.

Each day I put one foot in front of the other, praying ***not to faint or to be led into temptation**;* now, I take only one step at a time but I *still* do not find it effortlessly to anticipate what is in front of me. **Prayer is the key, but faith unlocks the doors** of fear. It took me almost seventeen months to get where I am today, which *calculates* to one month for each year that Joshua lived on this earth. I have so much more to learn and to do.

I do believe that God is continually growing me into the woman of God that I am meant to be. It was only upon writing these words that I found so much joy in my life, and I am learning to live, as I truly believe that these writings are just a portion of what God has in store for me. I am holding Him to His words that **He will give me double recompense.**

I cannot disclose to you all of the things that were stolen from me, borrowed and unreturned because I just do not know the face value amounts. I will not share with you all of the things that I have gone through. I will not share all of my loses with you, but I get joy in knowing that God's word at Hebrew 4:12 is so true, because **His word is alive and it exerts power and it cuts sharper than any two edged sword.**

God does not mind if we read His Word, keep it, and speak it into our own lives either! According to His words, I have a lot to look forward to, and I am fully trusting in Him, because I do know that **God is faithful**. He is already restoring and pouring down blessing in my life so abundantly that I cannot praise Him enough.

I mentioned earlier how important cards were to me at the time of my son's death. I believe that I mentioned that I wrote out thank you cards to many because of the comfort from the hundreds of hundreds of sympathy cards that we received. I read the cards again, and eventually, I had the privilege to personally thank the special woman who mailed one particular card to me. Theresa and I recognize the God appointment. Today, I call Theresa, my spiritual grandmother, because of the warmness in her heart. Do you recall the special person who gave me the book with Jeremiah 29:11 on the first page? She sent me a sympathy card right after Joshua died.

This particular sympathy card came along with an invitation to share my grief. It took me over a year to respond and get to a meeting. Hesitantly, I responded to the invitation. At the time that I received this card and invite, I knew that I was not ready to share my story or to hear others' stories about their experiences with grief.

I believe that it was July 2009 when I read the sympathy cards again, and it was then that God gave me the courage and desire to share about Joshua's death, and my story of grief. The group met on a regularly scheduled evening. Finally after praying, I attended and shared my story the first night, and I was able to listen to others attentively. The meetings were extremely powerful and rewarding. Respectfully, we shared our feelings of fear, sadness, guilt, and whatever we were dealing with during the weeks.

We examined the scriptures and watched videos from some who experienced grief of various forms. On the last evening of the final chapter of the book, as God would have it, that was the last time that I was able to attend the meetings as well, as I knew that I would soon be on my way to Texas, but I will always be a part Theresa's heart; this I am fully assured.

On that last evening, I learned that I was in a healthy stage of grief, as we viewed a video about Heaven. Tears flooded my face while I smiled at the same time, and that is how I knew that I was in a healthy stage of grief. I am unsure of what that means about tomorrow. I do not know what God has in store for me. When I think about how Joshua lived each day as if it were his last, I say, "Wow." Joshua was a very respectful young man, but he had a good time regardless as to where he went.

I recall a time when we were invited to a rather sophisticated wedding, and it seemed that others were frowning upon Joshua and me while we danced, as he clowned around with me on the dance floor. I felt the stare of people, but we danced as if no one was watching. I am reminded of the song, "*I Hope That You Dance,*" which I dedicate to both of my daughters. Now, I thank God that I listened to their dedicated song, as I can always recall that dance, as it was Joshua and my last dance together, at least in this life.

I failed to mention the enormous amount of newspaper coverage that my son's life and death received. There was an article in at least three local newspapers, besides Joshua's obituary. The reporters did a fine job. I only identified one problem from all three newspapers that I read reporting Joshua's death. I am unsure where the misinformation originated, but I sat quietly as I read each of the newspapers.

The newspapers reported that my son collapsed at a specified Community Park, which was the same park that the candlelight vigil was held. The bizarre part was when Joshua telephoned me, he requested to play ball at a different park. Joshua knew too well the rule that he needed to let me know if he went anywhere other than that which we discussed. It was one of the rules that he was not particularly fond of, but I knew that I could trust my son to do as I asked of him. I did not believe that Joshua collapsed at the reported Community Park. I did not have written proof. Juke, who was at this particular event stated, "This is not where it happened," and I just smiled.

My son and his whereabouts were confirmed when the ambulance bill arrived via mail. The bill was addressed to me. After opening and reviewing it, I forwarded the bill to the responsible party, who is Ray. The bill stated that the ambulance picked Joshua up at the playground that he requested to play basketball and from this place he was transferred to the hospital.

No one has reported the facts that I am about to disclose to you in the newspaper article or otherwise, because these were my first private moments at my vacated apartment previously known as home. Joshua had emptied the full dishwasher. The dryer was full of a white load of Joshua's dried clothing, and the washer was full of a clean load of his dark clothing. Joshua's room and the apartment were very tidy, and he had left a CD lens cleaner on the living room table.

The significance of the lens cleaner is that I asked Joshua to find this CD cleaner a few weeks ago, and I told him that I was in no rush. I was amazed that Joshua did all of the things that I asked of him before a final farewell just a few hours later. I taught Joshua to play as hard as he wanted once his responsibilities were completed. I can say, "Well done my son." I was afforded the opportunity to pray and talk with Joshua prior to his death and ask God to please say the same. It is my prayer that my Father will say well done to me as well.

In August 2009, Pastor Paul preached a sermon he entitled, Fill your horn with oil and go; it was then that I knew that it was time to go. It was determined that I would travel to Houston, Texas to see if that would be my permanent residence. God ordained the trip. This I know for sure, as the weather was picture perfected, and my 1999 vehicle did not cause me any problems or pain at all.

I asked Carrie to travel with me as she was unable to work during this time; thus, I had company. Although I did all of the driving, thankfully, no one tried to run us off the road called life this time. I was off to a new life. Although I did not know what God has in store for my life, I do know that He holds my life within His very capable hands.

It became obvious to me that God perfectly mapped out the trip just for me because I had to face every fear of the roadway. I believe that God will take us out of our comfort zone. Previously, I reported my fear of bridges. Magnificently, God brought me across so many huge bridges with no way out, except to drive over them. Being in more than seven different car accidents caused me unspeakable fears in the car, but God brilliantly allowed me to deal with each of these fears as well.

Recall that Gunnery Ellis took me over a bridge when I visited Corrinna in California, and I will never forgot that I never quivered because we talked the entire way over the bridge. I was not thinking about what Ellis was really doing at that time, as he knew that this was one of my fears. I think that the comfortableness that I felt with Ellis allowed for no fears on that day. So, each time I went over a bridge I thought about the man that I met named Ellis who God allowed into my life at crucial times of my life, and I smiled as I thought about the goodness of God, and that maybe Ellis was meant to be a bridge himself during very difficult times.

It only took two days to travel to Texas, and I thought that I would have arrived full of joy. The day that I arrived here, I became so sad that I did not know what to do, and that lasted for several weeks. Again, I began to question why. Surely, I previously asked God about Texas, but I think the real deal was that I knew that the time came to face the reality that I had the task of searching for my life without Joshua. Before, school and work kept me quite busy and distracted, but counseling kept me focused.

Last November, while I visited with Corrinna and Joe, we had driven from Florida to Texas. I mentioned that I would love to live here, and God made it happen minutes away from where I stated those words. While I was at home finishing school, Joe received an email that stated that they did not need his services in Florida. So, Joe put in a package to relocate to a different area. Corrinna and Joe did not know where they would be heading, but Texas was on the top of his list. As God would have it, Joe received orders to relocate, and they moved right around the corner from where I made my request known. God is awesome! Texas is known as the Bible belt.

The drive here was beautifully and wonderfully prepared by God alone. Carrie and I arrived safely without any car problems, even though my 1999 Nissan, ALTIMA is ten years old, but I *still* was unsure what God was doing in my life. I unpacked my laptop, printer, and my clothing little by little. Some items continually remain in my trunk. *Still*, I did not make Texas my permanent residence; therefore, I had the option to settle back in PA. I scheduled a flight to return home on October 11, and I ***thought*** that it would be then that I would make a firm decision.

After my arrival to Texas, I began writing and I became extremely frustrated as I attempted to write these words to you. I became so frustrated that I slammed down my laptop and just went inside my car and sat. As I angrily pouted, I also listened while I politely folding my arms. God reminded me of the scripture that He gave to me at the basketball court and that He confirmed this many times.

The time came that I knew for sure without doubt or concern this is how God was instructing me to begin these writings. I wrote most of these words within three days. Confession time; tweaking this book took much more time than seventy hours. It became perfectly clear, just as the weather was on the drive here, how I was supposed to begin these writings that God birthed into my spirit, and thus this message begins with Jeremiah states: **"For I know the plans that I have for you to prosper you and to do you no harm and to give you the future that you desire."**

Within three days, the deal was sealed, and the words flowed unlike ever before. After I finished writing, I laid it to rest, until it was time to begin the tweaking and editing process, which *still* may not be perfect. In the meantime, as I lay on my bed, in my spirit I heard the name, Joel Osteen. I went downstairs and told Corrinna that somehow Joel Osteen is to be a part of this project. Corrinna replied, "You and that book." I humbly tucked my head, but not in shame, and returned back to my room without any more thought about the situation. On October 4, 2009, Corrinna and I planned to visit Lakewood Church, but as God would have it our plans were not manifested. I am fully aware that it was not His appointed time.

In all honesty, I would not have taken the initiative to visit Lakewood Church alone because of the distance, and at that time I became easily intimidated by the new freeways, belts, and highways of Texas without being equipped with a GPS at this time, but I have one now! Nonetheless, another part of the reason that we did not make the scheduled trip to Joel Osteen's church because I could not gain my composure on that day from the joy that filled my heart.

You see, Corrinna and her husband were trying to have a baby for years. They have been married for eight years and no child was brought forth. In September, they visited a fertility specialist for a consultation visit, and before they could return they became pregnant. Sounds like another miracle child, just like Joshua! For the first time since my son died, my heart was pierced with joy, as I cried and prayed that entire day. I guess you could say that I had church at home.

I understand why we did not go to Lakewood Church on that date, as it was not God's appointed time. I also understood that Texas would be my home, and why Pastor Paul's message, *"Fill Your Horn with Oil and Go"* saturated my heart in a manner which would cause me to pack up and leave everything that I finally knew, including my mother!

A few weeks later, Corrinna came into my room with an invite to attend Joyce Meyer's conference. I did not know that Joyce Meyer was here in Texas and that she was giving a free convention at Lakewood Church. *My plans* included attending an all-night prayer service, but I agreed to accept Corrinna's invitation to attend the conference, as *God* had other plans.

After receiving the invitation into my spirit, I thought, WOW, I get to see Joyce Meyer at Joel Osteen's church, but there was much more of a blessing in store for me! Pastor Joel was away at a book signing, but I did get to hear the powerful teaching of Joyce Meyer who spoke on subjects that God chose for the hearing of my daughter's and my ears. The Bible says **those whom have ears let them hear**, and we certainly heard much that we both needed, and we digested!

Previously, I dreamed that scriptures appeared on a wall, and I could read them clearly. I did not have a clue as to what God was showing me in this dream, and this resulted in a consultation with a pastor. He said, "this is your gift, the gift of prophesy." I accepted that answer in part at that time, but, there is more to the story. While Corrinna and I attended the Joyce Meyer Women's Convention, at least a seven fold blessing had unfolded. Oh God is so faithful!

I did not know the subject matter that Joyce Meyer would be preaching, but she taught about spiritual birth, while relating it to the natural birthing process. *Still,* tears overwhelmed my eyes, but on this evening, tears of joy flooded down my face, as the goodness of God unfolded right in front of my being.

There I sat with my daughter, who is pregnant with child; my granddaughter. Yes, according to the ultrasound, she is a girl, who has already defied all of the laws of nature. She already had powerful words spoken over her life. In addition, Joyce Meyer was preaching about the birth of what God put in one's spirit as well. Joyce Meyers did not directly tell me that there was a book inside me, but through her words, the Holy Spirit ministered to me concerning one of the jobs that God has for me to do by the method of these writings.

My friend, Mary Kay, prompted this question, had I planned this experience in advance? My response to Mary Kay was that only God could have planned this event because it was perfectly designed. As Corrinna and I were eventually able to crowd through to get on the escalator, I looked up. Literally, without warning, I screamed! My dream came true right in front of my eyes as *I saw the words written on the walls of the Lakewood Church...*"**For I know the plans that I have for you, to prosper you and do you no harm and to give you the future that you desire, Jeremiah 29:11.**"

My piercing scream startled my daughter and she inquired, "What happened?" She seemed to think that I was either injured or frightened. I smiled as I stuttered, "Look on the wall!" She did not totally understand what I was saying because I did not share with Corrinna that this is how God instructed me to begin these writings.

Although Corrinna heard the testimony concerning the confirmation of the scripture at Jeremiah 29:11, I did not share my dream with her concerning the writings on the wall. However, when I shared this portion of my testimony with my oldest daughter Maria, she replied via email, "Relax mom, **all things work for the good of those who love God and are called for His purpose. Romans 8:28**." I shouted again, because as I mentioned previously, neither of my daughters have read these words; therefore, neither of them were privy to the information contained within. However they are to receive the two of the first printed copies!

My mother kindly reminds me that I came out feet first, and I believe that I was running from *life*. *Still*, I may have the tendency to do things "backwards." I was a breech baby, but regardless as to how I have done things, I am proud of my successes and have learned, and I am continually learning from my failures. I became a mother, and I believe that I did a pretty good job.

I did not attend college right out of high school, but I now hold two degrees in Accounting of which I graduated in the top percentages of my classes, just as in High School. An eventual goal is to attend graduate school and obtain a Master's Degree in Theology or Psychology, along with classes in Philosophy, that I may eventually become the director and founder who will assist in the healing of teens with ill heart conditions because of circumstances beyond their control and hold women ministry seminars.

Eventually, I plan to open my own shelter for children called *The Healing H.E.A.R.T*. An additional goal of mine is to open my own Accounting firm specializing in taxes to provide proficient tax accounting to the underprivileged. Most importantly, I know who my Father is, and that I am His child. No one on this earth can take that away from me. God gave me this gift and I have graciously accepted all of His special gifts, and I say, "Thank you!"

Chapter 16

Parents/Guardians please take your children to your place of worship. Please spare them and yourself by not sending them to the sanctuary. Your children may have questions that only you can answer. If for some reason you cannot take them to the sanctuary, make sure that what they are learning is fruitful. Better yet, may I suggest that you learn so that you will be able to teach your children the ways of God? Then, you and your children will know when you notice when/if things are incorrectly spoken. The scripture states **that Satan desires to sift us as wheat.** What better ages to begin his tactics than the ages of a child?

Clergy, if you do not know the answer, sometimes the best answer is I do not know. If you are ashamed of that answer, you can suggest that you will do some research in the Word and reply later. It really is okay to say, I don't know, but we can remind anyone that **God is love.**

Today, I am able to share with you that a religious ritual, such as attending church every Sunday does not give certification that one has accepted Jesus Christ as their personal savior. A person who does not attend religious services may in fact have a personal relationship with God. However, the Bible does tell us in Hebrews **not to forsake the assembling of ourselves together.** This day, as I did yesterday, I pray that God has ministered to Uncle David who shared that mistruth with me and convict him of the truth concerning salvation, which is a free gift upon acceptance of Jesus Christ as one's PERSONAL savior.

Perhaps you have lost a loved one, and you may not have any idea if your loved one asked God into his/her life. The reality is that you may not know because accepting God into one's heart is a personal experience. However, I guarantee that once you have an encounter with God and you really begin to understand the love that God has for all of us, and that **He does not desire that any would perish, but have everlasting life**, you will recognize that we all have the same opportunity.

Remember, just because you are not a witness to an event, your presence is insignificant for this measure of faith. Final judgment is in God's hands. It is not in our hands. Meanwhile, make sure that your relationship with God does not disappear while attempting to figure out someone else's final destination.

Daily invitations are given to accept Jesus as our personal savior and these invitations are not only given at places of worship. Regardless as to how things appear, you too can learn to trust God in all things and in all ways. I do know that **a seed can be planted, watered by someone else, and then God gives the increase! God is a God of love** and know that God is always working things out all of the time that we may or may not have knowledge about. The Bible reminds us that *God never sleeps or slumbers*, and He is always available to each of us.

You can trust that which you need to know that God will reveal at His appointed time! Surely, you have heard that **God is married to the backslider**. It is not the place of worship that saves people; **Jesus saves**. The House of God is supposed to be a place to worship God; not man. The body of the believers may judge you, but that is *their* issue, but **in Christ there is no condemnation**. Please remember that statement, but trust me on this one, to the utmost **Jesus saves. In due seasons, you shall reap your rewards**.

My daddy's death increased my search for a true understanding about God. I studied many religions, but my counselor reminded me that studying religions only teaches you about people, but when you study God through His Word and have **faith**, *which* **is the key to unlock the door**, you will know Him! Earlier in my childhood, it may have helped if I read and comprehended the Bible for myself. Eventually, I spent a lot of time searching for answers and building a relationship with God, and I was rewarded with getting to know Him better. *Still*, I am learning. In order to accept life, we must accept death.

It is because of Satan that death has even entered into our lives. Remember the **wages of sin are death, but the gift of God is eternal life.** How does one continue to have a relationship with someone you believe took away your loved one?

I caution you, because accepting death does not eliminate the grief process. I believe if one does not properly grieve, a person may become stuck in denial, guilt, anger, depression or any other stage of grief and one may want to seek some assistance. Yes, **Jesus did take the sting out of death**, because he gave us a hope of seeing our loved one again, but there are stages of grief that I believe are natural because with death, feelings do come. I suggest that you entertain them and allow for them that you may properly heal. I am of the opinion that putting the blame on God, ourselves, and anyone else only creates a destructive path. These are only my beliefs from my personal experiences. I believe that we have to take responsibility for our actions and allow what Belongs to others; allow them to shoulder their own issues.

Another thing that I learned is that for some people death is a release. I do not understand this notion but, I believe that grief is an extremely important aspect of death. However, if you see death as a relief, one may get trapped inside of guilt! If you find yourself stuck, admit it, and please get some help.

Unless, the rapture comes, no one is leaving the earth alive. The way that the rapture was preached in my hearing sounded awfully confusing too, but this subject is another book in itself. Some religions teach that there is no such thing as the rapture as other religions explain it. I believe that God's spirit is already here and that when our loved ones die that their spirit is caught up with God's spirit.

I did not go deeper than this to gain more understanding, but these are my beliefs today. The Bible tells us that **we will be changed from mortal to immortality in the twinkling of an eye, and to be absent from the body is to be present with God.** Regardless as to what we believe, one must do the work that grief requires.

Perhaps, I may have benefited from being taught more about God than about Hell, because according to the Bible once you **accept the Lord Jesus Christ as your personal savior, by believing that he died and He rose from the dead; though shall be saved! God sent His son, Jesus, into this dying world that we might have life more abundantly** is so freeing to my mind. I pray that you too can be freed. There is no need for shackles on our feet!

Some religions have us so bound that it is absolutely crazy; especially when I think of **God sending His son that we might have life and have it more abundantly.** Some folks are trying to work their way into heaven, but that is impossible! Some of us are striving for earthly perfection, which is also impossible. Some are trying to please man, which is not glorification for God. However, **faith without works is dead.** Put your faith to work by trusting God.

Some religious groups will not allow you in their faith if you do certain things. I believe that it is God, who cleans/sanctifies, not we ourselves. After all, it is about His righteousness, not ours. I know that He is the only one who deserves all of the praise for continually stripping off the old me. Remember, He is Jehovah Mekoddishkem-The Lord who sanctifies me.

Salvation is a gift, you cannot earn it. You cannot work for it, because it is a gift from the Most High God. No! My friends, working will not get you in the door! Albeit, remember that the Bible states *that* **if you have done it unto the least of mine, you have done it unto me.** In my thinking, it would be wise to be kind to God's children.

As a child, I neither could totally understand what the total sacrifice of the life of Jesus meant concerning forgiveness of sins, nor could I comprehend how valuable my faith would become. Even as a child I was so grateful that **God sent His only begotten son to this earth, who died a horrific death, and I believed that He rose from the dead with all power in His hands.** I heard a testimony of a woman who dreamed that her friend did not make it into heaven. According to this woman, her friend did not do enough work to get in the door. I was so upset because she was ministering to people through the testimony of her dream, and some people may not have realized that **salvation is a gift! God's gift of eternal life is absolutely free!!!!!!!!!!!!** Won't you accept the gift of eternal life today?

I pray that neither you nor your children will ever encounter a rape experience. However, if you do, please know that God can clean up this mess that you are not responsible for, and **He will make a table in the presence of your enemies. He will feed you until you want no more and quench your thirst like never before. God is able to do all things except fail!** Know that you too can overcome, but I would caution you from getting locked into fear. For the fortunate ones who have escaped this torment, know that a lot of garbage is eaten and the table that it is spread upon is dirty, nasty, and horribly disgusting. There is nothing fruitful during these unpleasant meals.

Teenagers and adult friends, attempting to place culpability on any other person than the responsible party is totally irresponsible, even if the alleged guilty party is you. Pushing responsibility onto someone else does not change what happened. As a matter of fact, it only locks you in walls and confines you into being angry at the wrong person for incorrect reasons. Meanwhile, forgiveness for the blamed person is impossible. They did not do anything to require repentance or forgiveness. This is a method by which many get stuck with nowhere to turn, run, or hide.

I believe it is important to forgive the rapist, as he/she is ill. Please know that the rapist had/has the right to petition God for forgiveness. I believe that he/she can be forgiven by God if he/she truly repents, whether he or she is incarcerated is not the issue. Meanwhile, if he/she repents, the rapist becomes free while you rot in your own jail cell, but you do have choices in the matter. The two choices are forgive or do not forgive. I believe that another situation which results in being incarcerated behind bars of hating oneself is blaming God for every occurrence in our lives that goes wrong, remember; **in Him they found no fault.**

Many people discount young pregnant teens as having ruined lives, but did you know that Mary conceived Jesus around the age of 15, perhaps even younger? I have just recently learned this information from my new leader, Pastor Weather. He informed the congregation about the age of Mary, as I never gave her age any thought. I was surprised to say the least.

By no means am I condoning teenage pregnancy, but I am merely stating that we are not to judge any man, woman, boy, or girl. We do not know what God is doing in anyone's life. After all, **Jesus was Mary's baby.** Besides, how dare we play God ourselves? The Bible clearly identifies **that man looks on the outward appearance, but God looks on the heart.** You and I, my friend, have no idea what anyone has gone through, is going through, or will go through. Perhaps it really is best to be kinder than necessary, and kindness can sometimes be not saying anything at all.

When I see mothers who doll themselves up with the most expensive things and beside them stand their children who look like ragdolls, this is very disturbing to me. I am unsure if that is judging or just an explanation of my major pet peeve. You can decide that for yourself, but I have asked God to help me with this issue. It is none of my business, but it irks me to no end. I agree with the statement that children are our future.

Jesus asked His father, **Must I drink of this cup."** Then, **He willingly and freely laid down His life. No man took His life, as He could have called a legion of angels to stop anything, but he willingly laid down His life that we might have a right to the eternal life.** Then, **He asked for God's mercy because they did not know what they did.** When I go through things, I think about all that Jesus went through and at times, I *still* ask must I? And if He says yes, I go through it. I believe that there are valuable lessons in everything that we go through. Besides, if my life was different, I wouldn't have the relationship that I have with Him today. *Still*, I have a lot of growing to do! I want abundant life that God offered to me while living on this earth. How about you?

Feelings really do change! Be not deceived, God already forewarned us that *there will be trials and tribulations in all of our lives.* The word also tells us that **unforeseen occurrences befall us all.** After all, when the war occurred in heaven, **Satan was kicked out of heaven, and he is considered the ruler of the earth.** God is *still* in full control and much wiser, powerful, and loving than Satan, you, or I. Sometimes, we can be our worst enemy.

God is omnipresent; whereas, Satan is not! God is much bigger that we can comprehend. If you read James 1:17, you will also see that **all good and perfect gifts come from above**. I understand that God knows what He is doing even when I don't know what He is doing. I am *still* learning many life lessons. However, I know it is all for my good! Perhaps, I would not have so much to share with you if my course ran a different path.

Friends, I plead with you, read your Bibles for yourselves, pray for understanding, and find someone called and chosen who teaches the Bible and truly directs God's sheep to Him; not unto himself. I caution you from believing every word that you hear just because it comes out of a preacher's mouth.

Pray about where God will have you planted and watch how *He* will grow you and transform your life! Matthew 22:14

reminds us, *that many are called but few are chosen.* The Bible *warns us of false prophets, calling them wolves in sheep clothing.* The Bible also warns us *that some will say that they prophesized in His name, cast out demons, and performed miraculous healings, but the end result will be God saying, I never knew you not, depart from me you workers of iniquity.* Pease allow me to add that the Bible teaches us to be as *wise as a serpent, but as innocent as a dove.*

I believe that the nature of human pride stems from the original sin of Adam. Sometimes pride causes us to operate in our flesh and not in God. Being human, we all make mistakes; some are intentional while others are unintentional. The Bible reminds us that *we prophesize in part.* Just because someone states something to us that does not mean it is so. It is not up to us to judge who is chosen or not, but what our job entails is detailed at I Timothy 2:15, *study to show thyself approved unto GOD, a workman, rightfully dividing the word of God. Oh, and please do not forget to try the spirits to see whether they are of God.*

If God speaks something into my spirit that someone else prophesized to me, I am willing and ready to be in total agreement. At times, I have to examine from whence a prophetic word came from. If God did not speak these words to me, I place it on the shelf. While I was deep in grief of my son, some prophesies were spoken to me that made me very angry because I did not understand.

Pastor Grace confirmed these words to me unless God Himself directly speaks to my spirit, she advised me to "put the words of each prophesy on the shelf." This is extremely significant, because when you put something on the shelf, it collects dust. If the prophesy is not manifested or confirmed then you will know that it was of man. It was not God. *Purely dust.*

I believe that anyone with the gift of prophesy needs to be careful not to get caught up in the gift or themselves. Some use their own words because at that particular time, they may not recognize the real Power behind having the gift of prophecy. Some religions teach against prophesy, but **the Bible declares that young and old men will have visions and prophesize.**

I believe "prophecy" can be used as a tool to control or to show one's powers. Remember **in all of our ways we are to acknowledge Him and He will direct our paths.** My concern is that if the gift is abused, then babies may be turned off to the prophet or prophetess. Even more dangerously, a Christian baby who is only *drinking milk* may not understand and may be turned off to God. They may have to search in hard places as I did, while God is patiently standing right there. **He will never leave us nor forsake us.** Remember that *we prophesize in part.*

However, I do realize that God is *still* in full control and once anyone dedicates their life to Him. The final say belongs to God. The word teaches us that **no devil can pluck them out of His hands;** no matter where they go, see Psalms 139. My advice to anyone with the gift is to remain on their face, and be *still* while seeking God for His *instructions. I Corinthians Chapter 13 remind us that **even if we have the gift of prophecy and not love that it has no meaning.***

Men have a serious responsibility to God concerning their families. I learned that God first deals with the head of the house, also known as men. Husbands, do you know that if you don't treat your wife right, your prayers are hindered?

Women are to be submissive to their husbands, and I would urge women who have a God fearing husband to do just so, because it is written. My belief is that your blessings can only be enhanced if you hearken to the words of God. If your husband is operating under the authority of God; please ask yourself this question, how can you go wrong by being submissive?

Husband derives from the word house band which is the band that keeps the house together. Men, it may behoove you to choose your wives carefully, as the Bible tells us **that *it would be better for a man to sleep on the roof than to be in the house with*** *a contentious wife.* **Sleeping on a roof at night can be very** cold or hot with very little protection outside. I can only imagine the discomfort of sleeping on the roof. It must be awful to live with a contentious wife.

Ladies, if your husband is not a God fearing man, you too are to follow God's words. Perhaps you did not allow God to do the choosing, and you might have to live with the consequences of your decisions. Please do not hold yourself hostage if you have made a poor choice. However, recall that we each have to see Jesus for ourselves. When you die you will not be able to blame anyone else.

People can be married for a life time and they may never really know that person. So, is timing the true issue at hand? Today, I am unsure if timing is the concern because I think that the bigger issue is to love and trust God, love and trust you which involves being healed, and then have the ability to love and trust the other person, which involves the other person being healed, regardless as to the time period. In order to know if you really love study **I Corinthians 13:4-8.**

I dedicated my life to God over and over, again, and again, but my past created a lack of self-esteem. It was just too simple for me to believe that God accepted me as His child the moment that I accepted him into my heart. Certainly, today, I recognize that all this time, God had my life in His hands, and He is reconstructing my life which I gave to Him, regardless to my lack of self-esteem.

Jeremiah1:5, **before God formed me in my mother's womb, He knew and approved of me. Before I was born He separated and set me apart, consecrating me. He appointed me a prophet to the nations.** Ephesians 4:1 compliments Jeremiah's words by telling us **even before the formation of this world that He chose us in Him and that we should be blameless in His love, and holy because of His shed blood. He winks at our ignorance** according to Acts 17:30

Jesus came that we might have life and have it more abundantly. Jesus paid the ultimate price by laying down His life that we might live. When we fail, fall short, and sin, we have the responsibility to repent and ask for forgiveness and trust not in ourselves but that God is faithful and just to **forgive us of our iniquities and cleanse us from all righteousness.** If you do not believe that **God can and will forgive** you then you doubt God at His word.

Concerning relationships, my experiences have taught me to ask these questions first? How are both of our relationships with God? This would be the first question that I would ask you too. The answers are not in what one says, but rather by what one does, because love is an action word. We will know them by the fruits that they bear. Are we **patient, kind, meek, lowly, and demonstrating the words in Galatians 5:23**?

Then, I would ask how my relationship is with myself. Do I trust myself? Then, I would ask, do I trust the other person? The final three questions I would ask are: do I respect myself, and do I respect the other person; finally, have I mended all relationships from immediate family members and healed from past experiences? How do you know what another person feels or thinks about important issues such as their beliefs, raising children, credit, morals and values, if there is a lack of sharing one's thoughts, ideas, dreams or where you will reside? Anyone can say that they love God, but what do their actions show? If you are not healed how can you really pay attention? For those of you who mentally or physically abandon your children with a short term goal of appeasing any male with this type of calibration or any other agenda; please know this, if any male mistreats your/his/anyone's children, these males are already mistreating you, and you may not recognize that you are also mistreating yourself.

The Bible reminds us that Jesus told the disciples to **suffer the little children and forbid them not to come unto me**. If Jesus has a heart for children, shouldn't we? We cannot enter the

Kingdom of God unless we **become childlike**, knowing that He is our Father!

I believe that there are processes of change, but God also gives us free will. I did not study the laws of nature, but common sense helps me to believe that change produces change may be one of the laws of nature. I realize that seasons change, and we have to adjust to these temporal changes; therefore, change produces some type of change. When it is hot, generally, we adapt by wearing less clothing or putting on an air conditioner. In addition, when it is cold, we accommodate the changes of the weather by protecting our bodies by adding more clothing, turning on the heat, and preparing our vehicles for the challenges of the weather. Not only do we as humans change, animals hibernate or fly south when it is cold, and the forms of trees change.

Additionally, I believe that when people change, others around forcibly change. I am not stating how others change, but I do think that change has an affect others' behavior, whether it is for the good or bad may depend on the changes that you make or on the other person's make-up. However, I reaffirm and decisively believe that change produces change, and if you want anyone or anything to change, that you must change. If God is in the equation, I believe that a relationship would have worked effortlessly, because that is how real love goes. I am not stating that marriage is free from work. However, slaving should not be an issue. The Bible reminds us that **in marriage there will be tribulation.** The Bible also **forewarns us not to be unequally yoked, and asks how can too walk together unless they agree.**

Recall that **God is love.** Love sacrifices. If you are on a spiritual plain that your spouse is not, how can you see things in the same light? Your eyesight/vision will be different. If both are sacrificing for each other because of the love of God in their heart, how can anyone lose?

Loved ones beware that other people know when you are suffering from low self-esteem, because it is written all over your face. Your body language speaks volumes even if you never say a word. Remember **the devil desires to shift us as wheat.** No matter what occurred in your life, whether it is rape, molestation, or abuse in any form, know that you did not cause these things to happen to you. It is not God's fault either. The persons who did these things to you projected their angry and detestable issues onto you. Until you recognize this fact that I one day faced, you will continue to live a defeated life. Deal with your issues.

The one thing I always shared with my children is that when a person does something to intentionally hurt you; do not look at the person, but look at the spirit behind the person. I did not state if they should allow themselves back in the presence of this person, as this is a personal choice. However, I believe that if you keep the image of the person in your mind that hate can possibly take over. I believe that it is best for everyone's sake to forgive, because hate is a heavy burden to carry around. If you hate and recognize the spirit of Satan and His tactics, you will be on the right side of the fence. **Being lukewarm will not be a problem, where God will vomit you up.** God **would rather for us to be hot or cold**, but rather love and trust God even the more!

Walking in the fullness of God allows you to see beyond the natural and walk by faith even more. Remember that Satan has no dominion over God's people; sometimes, I believe that we as Christians give Satan a bit too much praise. One other thing that I continually preached to my daughters is to never be a doormat for ANYONE, and it was not my desire to set that example either. It would be hypocritical to continue in the form. When you do demonstrate that you have self-esteem, do not be deceived that some will be challenged by this fact because of their own lack of self-worth. These people are not your problems either. When you recognize the self-esteem that God placed within you I believe that boundaries will be set. If others cannot respect these lines and continually cross them, you may realize that you must allow them to grow independently with the help of God. Are we crossing the lines when God allows each of us to accept His invitation at Matthew 11:28, which *God* **humbly asks us who are laboring and heavy laden to come unto Him and He will give us rest?**

Only God can give us rest for our souls. Yes, **we are to bear the burdens of one another and confess our sins to one another,** but neither you nor I can allow others to totally drain us. My experiences taught me that when a person does not have their own defined boundaries a problem results with others' set boundaries.

If someone has no boundaries, that maybe a clue that they are lacking self-respect. It is not your or my job to develop boundaries for them. The Bible clearly tells us that we must **work out our own salvation.** While no man is an island, I am a witness that **there is a friend who sticks closer than any brother, and His name is Jesus, who is our shepherd.**

All that you have to do is open the doors of your heart. Regardless as to what man thinks of you or me, **who is man that he should perish?** My God! Oh, only God has the final say all of the time! Please know, understand, and receive this into your spirit! I pray that you are already learning from my mistakes! Even though I read and heard that **my Father is rich, and that He owns the cattle on a thousand hills;** yet, I could not distinguish that I was accepted as His child. The Bible reminds us **to not be only hearers of the word, but doers of the word.**

Believing that Jesus Christ died and rose again was too simple for my complex and confused mind. Believing that was all it took to be saved. Some prominent people in my life even told me, "You are not saved." Please do not accept this statement from anyone. **God is not a man that He should tell a lie**! I realize that I did not become what other people wanted me to be or react according to their preferences. However, that did not have an impact on the fact that once I confessed **Romans 10:10,** I was saved from my sins. Tell people to please be patient with you, as God is not through with you either! We are all a work in process. None of us will be perfect until we see Jesus.

Philippians 1:6 which tells us that **He that began a good work in you will perfect that work until the day of Christ Jesus,** and the Bible clearly identifies at 3 John 1:4 that **He is able to keep us from falling** John 10:38's states that **no devil can pluck us out of His hand!** These scriptures I read or heard, but they were not completely imbedded into my spirit. I had too many maledictions which *still* needed to be contended. I used to challenge God at His word, I would say, where are you God? You promised that you would *be a* **father to the fatherless, and a mother to the motherless!!!** Where are you? I was the one who misunderstood, because He was right there in the midst of my screwed up life. **God does not leave us.** *We leave Him, or we are unable to recognize His presence in the midst of our storms. He promised that* **He would never leave us or forsake us! Low, He is with us, even until the end of the world.** *God is faithful.* At your leisure please read Romans chapter 8. Paul also reminds us in Romans *that <u>NOTHING</u> can* **separate us from the love of God; neither life nor death.** This day, I am confident and will tell you again and again, that God is so faithful!

The Bible tells us that **without faith, it is impossible to please God. God politely petitions us to come and let us reason together and although our sins may be as scarlet, He promises to make them as white as snow. He even casts them into the sea of forgetfulness!** God is so faithful, but man will fail you every time! Sometimes as people, we have the audacity to be unforgiving.

We can apologize to others with a sincere heart all day long, but we have no power to make our wrongs right. People have the right to choose to forgive us upon our petition, but once you ask for forgiveness the responsibility is placed on the other person. If they do not forgive you, then they begin to live a defeated life. Truly, God does give us freewill.

If one does not see their actions as "sinful," then an apology feels unnecessary, but that may be a result of our forefather Adam's pride or selfishness. The Bible tells us that **if you eat meat and it offends your brother, then don't eat the meat in their presence.** We are to be considerate of one another's feelings and boundaries.

According to the Word of God, **unless one forgives, one cannot be forgiven,** but it is God's job to vindicate us from our sins. Forgiveness does not free us from the consequences of our choices. However, know that hefty price of vindication of our sins has already paid by the preciously shed blood of Jesus Christ. I believe that we are actually attempting to play God when we attempt to maintain our personal forgiveness, which is why this task is such a challenge. I believe this is virtually impossible because **He is God alone!** Are you trapped in a cycle of guilt? Guilt is meant to be a red flag, not a life sentence. We must trust God at His word that **if we confess our sins that He is faithful and just to forgive us.**

This is not a ticket to do whatever we want; certainly, there are consequences for the decisions and choices that we make. Look at David. He fell in love with another man's wife, and he had the man killed. **David was a man after God's heart.** He repented and God used David mightily, but David also lived with the consequences of his decisions.

I have learned that it is not how you fall, get knocked down, or how far you tumble downhill, but once you get back on your feet you should stand! Stand on the promises of God! How can you know the promises of God? Read your Bibles, pray, and attend a Bible based place of worship that teaches the Word of God.

In life, as humans, we will continue to be full of mistakes, but we should learn from the mistakes and keep it real with God. We adopt patterns in our lives. It is important to recognize the patterns and make some changes to avoid repeated behaviors. Remember that God *even* **knows the number of hairs on our head**, which translates to me that He knows **EVERYTHING** about us anyway. So why try to hide from ourselves? We are only kidding ourselves!

When I think about how I was as a mother, wanting my children to have the best, having each need met, and providing everything that thought that they wanted, I think of the scripture that asks **what child would ask his parent for bread and his father give a stone?** Then the question is asked **how much more does our heavenly father give to his children?** God is **SO** good and when I think of His goodness, I want to scream with joy. Sometimes, I just dance, smile, and laugh because of His goodness! Know this, **surely goodness and mercy shall follow us all the days of our lives**; after all, we are God's children and that **makes us joint heirs with Jesus Christ, and more than conquerors.** It really does not get much better than that!

God is everywhere that we are and even where we are not. As a humanly parent, I wanted to be everywhere that my children were. Although, that did not work well after they became teenagers. A field trip notification was all that I needed to volunteer as a chaperone. I believed that I needed to be both of my children's parents. I attempted to fill the void of the absence even though Ray honored court order visitations. Let me say this, I could never be my children's dad, as I am not a man. I was a single parent. I am their mother.

Money is not the answer to anyone's problems. It is not here to make us happy. Money cannot perform any task. Rather, money is a trading device that we all need to survive, but it has no ability to buy or substitute for happiness or love, which are free and produce so much freedom. You can have all the money in the world and be the most miserable person on earth. I heard many people misinterpret the scripture, but it is not money that is the root of all evil, but **it is the love of money that is the root of all evil** according to the Word of God.

The Bible asks us, **what does it profit a man to gain the whole world and lose his soul?** As for me, one of my favorite songs and testimony is that I would rather have Jesus that silver and gold. Additionally, I would rather have people in my life who treat me more valuable than any treasure they can buy me. Treasure is not to be laid up on earth. Where are your treasures?

I chose to pray for prosperity because I am a child of God. I have accessibility to the richest Father in the world, but I *never want to mimic* **the prodigal son and lie down with pigs ever again in my life.** Besides, in Proverbs it tells us that **those who seek for righteousness and love will find life, prosperity, and honor.**

God's word is true and that settles it for me. How about you? I am not stating that there is anything wrong with being wealthy or prosperous, but please do not let money be your ruler or become your God in whom you love and trust. Recall too that **God is a jealous God** aka **Qanna**, and **He will not have any god before Him.** Everything on this earth, including money, belongs to God. If we just trust Him, **He will provide each and every one of our needs according to His richness.** I am a witness by many of my own experiences!

Some people take kindness as a weakness; this may be consequences for the choice of trying to be good to anyone who crosses your path. The Bible warns us **not to give that which is holy to dogs**. Recall this though. The BIBLE declares that **kindness is a fruit of the spirit**. If anyone takes advantage of you, God will handle that too!

I am not suggesting that you go around without protecting yourself or standing up for yourself, but just know that God is in full control. Even when people wrong you, **God sees and knows all**! He even knows the motives of man's heart. I am just learning to stand up for myself, as you may read in the next book. Although the law can handle some things, **vengeance belongs to the Lord**. This scripture I witnessed the evidence!

When people do you harm this is their issue, it is not yours. If you have a relationship with that person, you can talk about it and see if your feelings matter to that person and then make some decisions. If anyone does take your kindness as a weakness, you may want to reevaluate the company that you keep. Kindness is a fruit of the spirit, and it is strength. If adjustments are not being made you might want to stop, look, and listen. Remember that **God sees everything.** I have felt that some people including family members think that they have read the word stupid on my forehead, but what the mark on my forehead represents is in fact the mark of God.

A pet peeve of mine is the fact that some grandparents think that the first grandchild is extra special because he/she made them a grandmother, but I feel that is such a disservice to the other grandchildren. The other children may feel something missing in their lives just because of their birth order, which they have no control over.

Parents, your presence and your time are so important to your children, much more than your money! Please do not wait until your children are grown to attempt to participate in their lives; after all, it may be too late. Believe that a child knows whether your love is genuine.

Fathers, if you are reading these words, please take heed. Save your sons and daughters from anger that you can prevent by just giving them your time. You may be able to save yourself some guilt later on in life. I believe that we all will have time to reflect, especially, if you have not repented.

Many women and men do not want their spouses' children involved in their "new lives," but the children are the innocent victims of a divorce and have nothing to do with the new or old marriages. These are adult choices, and the children already have the burden of missing one parent, especially, if one is inactive in their child's lives.

If you are projecting your problems onto your children, more than likely, they will carry your burdens which can delay their own internal healing. They will not understand what it is that they have done. In all actuality, they did nothing, as they were born. The divorce or remarriage was not their choice, as these are supposed to be adult decisions. The children are not the problem.

Children will not have the capability to answer the question as to what they have done wrong. A result can be that they blame themselves just because they are who they are. Sound familiar? I beg you. Please, do not project your problems onto your children. No one wins, but everyone loses this game.

We are all borrowed gifts from God, but we are accountable to God for how we handle those who God has placed into our lives. People are given to us to love, respect, and treat them in a mannerism which is written within God's words, but **God gives us all free will**. Yet, it does not take away the accountability that we have to God! Please, handle your gifts with care. Yes, I reiterate that **we are merely dust**, humans which *God* **designed in His image and He does forgive our mistakes and sins if we have repented.** Just let us be careful that *we* **don't forget to entertain a stranger, as he/she just might be an angel of the Lord**. It is written in His word! You might miss a special gift.

Be careful as to whom you marry or chose to lie down with. However, if you do choose unwisely, please do not hold your gifts from God or God responsible for your actions. It is not your child's fault that you laid down with that male or female. If you were raped and decide to carry the child to term, please don't hold your children or God accountable, but remember to thank God for the gift of life.

Perhaps you believe that you were with the wrong person, but look at the blessing of who your child is because of that person and your conception. You have a unique, special gift, which is an inheritance from God. Besides, **God does not make any mistakes.** Remember, we are the ones that are human. I hope that you get this next point too. I have identified, without a doubt, that my children would not be who they are without their father's donations. I would not change any of my children or trade either one of them for anyone else's child, even at our most difficult moments.

I am of the opinion that a child does not have to suffer from a divorce or broken home, as long as the parents remain intact in that child's life. Certainly, I believe in the ordination of marriage, as this is what the Bible teaches. My step-father warned me that everyone joined together is not joined by God. Also, it is my belief that the causality of broken homes can be much greater for the children, and that they have no say and are blameless with the decision to be brought into your wonderful world of marriage; yet, so many of our children become our bell boys/girls and carry our baggage.

Firmly, I agree that the word of God is true. It states that **all good and perfect gifts come from above**. Regardless as to whom God puts in your path along your journey: an employer; a good salesman, an awesome undertaker, friend, sister, brother, boyfriend, husband, wife, or your children please recognize the gifts. I am not speaking of monetarily blessings either, because some things a.k.a people and gifts of the spirit are absolutely priceless!

You cannot take money or people with you, but you can see those who believe again even after death. There will be no more tears, sorrows, rejection, pollution, death, pain, or sufferings, and there will be no need for money there either, *because the streets are paved in gold*. Remember that **He clothes even the lilies.** He promises in His Word that **if we seek the kingdom of God and seek His righteousness that all things will be added unto us***!* Why don't you claim your blessings today?

Money is not the answer, but the true answer is God. He is **Jehovah Sabaoth-***The Lord of hosts*, and I know for a fact that **He will make your enemies your footstool**! He did it for me time and time again, and He will do it for you! Imagine this, God provided me with my most incredible blessings through two who were my enemies.

If you are a villain, my prayer is that God will deliver you! Please do not rob, hurt, or murder anyone; and note that your **tongue can be a weapon.** The Bible declares that *there* **is life and**

death in the tongue, so be mindful when you are gossiping, as you may not know the whole story. You may be killing someone internally. If you are a thief, know that you may be taking a hungry child's loaf of bread. The Bible reminds us to **do unto others as you would have them do unto you**!

My mother always reminded me that whoever wronged me that they had children too. I would think what does that have to do with anything? Everyone is someone's child! If you cannot love yourself, but you can love your loved ones, let us please treat each other the way that we would want our family members treated. How much of a better place would this world be?

The Bible says **only the pure in heart will see God**. I am unconvinced that is only when you get to heaven, because I can see the hand of God in most anything by the detection of the spiritual eyes that He is granting to me. My prayer is that the clay be lifted off of your eyes if you cannot see the hand of God on your life.

When I see parents who treat their children/step children as if they are Cinderella or slaves, this angers me to no end. Yet, we as a Black/African American culture continue to harp on the fact that we were forced into bondage beginning in Africa. I read in history books that we sold our own brethren to the white man. Often, I questioned how could a few Caucasian men come to a continent and take slaves captive without assistance from the African race. It did not make sense to me. Have you ever pondered this point? The history books state that we sold each other to the white man. That does make sense to me. We do not have to sell our children short.

Admittedly, child abuse does happen in other cultures as well, but I recognize it more within our own culture. Every parent, including myself, has a bad day along the way, but please do not let your anger be your child's responsibility. Initially, you may not have the ability to see the damage that results from mistreating an infant in the early stages of life, but I earnestly believe that you will be forced to reckon with the consequences of your behaviors or mal treatments from others' behaviors during your children's adolescence, adulthood, or somewhere down the line. One of my favorite lines is do the work now or pay later!

I heard my mother say that we are God's arms, hands, and feet too. I know for a fact that we all want and desire affection, which includes hugs, smiles, kisses, politeness, gentleness, kindness, respect, and love from each other, especially living in this unruly world. If we look to **God, who is the author and finisher of our faith**, He will provide us with everyone who we need on this earth to touch our lives. It is up to us what we choose to do with these gifts. I can feel that someone is shouting, even if it is only me.

My experiences taught me that grief is extremely personal. My advice to anyone on the outside looking in is that if you want to be helpful offer your assistance in whatever areas you are gifted; send a card, cook a meal, and say very little. In my opinion, a quick visit to the home may be appropriate; if the family is receiving friends prior to the funeral, but the services are the best times to show your condolences. I do not believe that any family member wants to be impolite or needs the responsibility that comes with being rude during their time of bereavement.

In the event that you hear that someone died, please give the family the privacy to learn from their immediate family members what has or has not transpired. I believe that it was sheer disrespectfulness and nosiness that caused Maria to find out the fragile news concerning her brother. I am unsure if Joshua was pronounced dead or not, but families deserve their privacy despite your feelings. I am sure, and I understand that others were distressed, but please give the family the respect and privacy that they deserve during their time of bereavement.

I guarantee that you will want the same when the loss feels as though it is totally yours. The fact of the matter is that the person who notified my daughter did not have a clue as to what really happened. If we wait on the Lord, in His time he will reveal all necessary things to us. Please spare grieving families from more grief.

If the family has not requested that you preach at a funeral, please respect their boundaries. If the family requests for you to sing a song, please, just sing the song. I only wanted to hear the things that I requested, which were the words from those selected to speak, two scripture readings, my pastor's preaching, and the three songs. I did not want to hear anyone's testimony. I only anticipated tolerance for the things that I prayed about. Beloved, please, please, please, do not use funerals for your personal issues; thank you! It really is not about you!

A funeral is not a place for advertising one's church. If one allows God to operate in their lives, I believe that God will do the advertising. It is not about your church, as a matter of fact, the church should belong to God. A relationship with God is not even about attending church.

Many people attend church but have no relationship with God. Friends, please remember that the Bible tells us to **let the wheat and the tares grow together and that He will do the separating.** Please, do not allow anyone to distract you from the things of God, whether they are inside of the church or on the outside. However, follow the Bible's teaching **to keep your eyes upon the prize,** who is your God? **If we seek Him in due season we will reap the benefit**. I love the comparison in the natural…many people are "married," but they have no relationship. I believe that it is all about the relationship.

I believe that we, as a culture, need to learn to give families the space/room to breathe and grieve without feeling as though you have to be there to watch every move of the bereaving family. Certainly, this is not a time for anyone's selfish motives. What will you do with the information? Will you report it later? Will you seek out your own personal motives? You may not believe this, as I found difficulty in digesting one female's appalling statement that after reading the death notices that she makes her presence known at the home of a widower or at the funeral. Have mercy Father!

Children do grow up to become adults, but in my thinking they only get one childhood. Perhaps one should not go to the extremes that I went to while trying to make sure that my children knew without a doubt that they were loved or wanted. You only have one shot at their childhood, even if that bucket includes up to eighteen years, which may seem terribly long to some; yet, such short years for others. Remember if you are firing a loaded mouth gun, one shot can kill their self-esteem which can interfere with their adulthood in many ways until their wounds are healed.

Regardless as to the length of a child's life, please allow them be a child. We are each afforded one childhood to run, play, skip, and jump as a child. By all means, please, allow them to do these juvenile things. Of course you want to give children some responsibilities, but please let a youngster be a young person.

You cannot find all of everything in ANY one person because these things collectively can only be found in God alone. He provided His son as a savior and ransom. He is our Father, and He will hide you in the times of trouble. We need humans, as we all need skin from time to time.

What will you name your child? Do you realize that each name has some type of meaning behind it? For example, my name is Wanda, and it means wanderer or adventurer. Certainly, I wandered in the wilderness for many years, but I thank God that today, my name is changed, as just as Jacob wrestled with God, so did I, and my new name is Victory! Mothers and Fathers, please think carefully prior to naming your child because you might be overtly speaking negativity into their lives each time you call their name.

The God that I have gotten to know, love, and trust only loves us and wants the best for us. **He is the giver of life. He came down from heaven to earth to bear all of our iniquities; to save a dying world from our sins**. According to John 10:10,

Jesus came that we might have life, and so that we might have it more abundantly.

I believe that God has all power in His hands, and could/can stop anything that He chooses to stop, but that which He does allow; He is God all by Himself. God does not need me, you, or anyone else to tell Him how to handle anything or anyone. All that we are asked to do is continually trust Him at His Word and obey His Word.

The Bible warns us at Matthew 7:15 **to beware, because there are wolves in sheep clothing.** All pastors are not called by God to be counselors. Some pastors are not chosen to be pastors for that matter. The Word says **many are called but few are chosen.** However, I guarantee you that God's word is true and it states that **Jesus is called wonderful counselor!**

Even **Satan knows the word of God and he trembles.** It is one thing to know it, but it is another thing to try to live the word, which has nothing to do with being perfect. I repeatedly read in the Bible **that everything God made is good.** I considered the stars and moon as good, but I did not believe that I was good enough for anyone to love, including God. That demonstrates to me that I was trying to trust myself, not God! Neither I nor you are anything without God, **merely dust**; regardless as to who you are according to man or your status in life. **We are to put on His righteousness,** not our own. Remember that **our righteousness is as filthy rags.**

I thought that things happened to me just because I was born, but more tragic things have happened to many other people. I read and heard the story of Job, but I did not recognize that **Job was a man of integrity, a righteous man**; yet and *still*, Job went through many horrific tragedies. The fact of the matter was that God knew Job very well. **God asked Satan have you considered my servant Job, but God would not allow Satan to touch Job's soul.** Even if you are not shouting, I am shouting!

Joseph did not cause any of the things that occurred to him. **Joseph had the gift of prophetic dreams and people, and even his own family was jealous of him. His brothers tried to kill him, but in the end Joseph blessed them tremendously. Joseph fled when the woman attempted to seduce him; yet, he was thrown into prison for an unjust cause.** However, God delivered him and enabled him to be a blessing to those same brothers who left him for dead! God is working it out for you and me too!

Material things come and go; yet, they have no substance. True love does not ever go away. **Love never dies**, see I Corinthians 4. Although, I do believe that forms of love do change. The beauty of it is that true love does not cost a thing. I know for sure that no matter what happens, if you ever really love someone, that love never dies. In past relationships I thought that love was a feeling, but feelings change, while love remains the same.

I see many things through the eyes of a brilliant mathematician, and I believe in spiritual eyes. The Bible states at I John 4:8, **that God is love**. In mathematics, is means equals; therefore, God equals love. The Bible also states that **God is the same yesterday, today, and forever more.** That means that He does not change. Algebraically speaking, if God is equal to love, then love is the same today, yesterday, and forever more.

The fruits of the spirit in Galatians 5:23, I see that these are described as what love is or is not in I Cor. 4. This is not a mistake. Love is God, and God is love. He is the tree, and we are the vine.

Time is another matter which we cannot see, touch, or feel, but we know that it exists. Although time is continually moving, and it has no finite end, we as humans will have an end on this earth, but one word of God's word will never change! I cannot see, touch, feel, or kiss God on the cheek, but I love him too, and I know that He lives because He lives inside of me. **He promises never to leave us alone.** Although I spend a lot of time alone, I am never alone or lonely. Also, He reminds us that ***NOTHING* can separate us from His love!**

Joshua is closer to perfection than my two daughters; please, don't miss this. It is not because of who he was in the fleshly body or because he is my son, but rather because of whom he is with as I write!

Many argue that love does not hurt, and I totally agree with that statement. However, I do have an amendment; at times, love must be tough. Please note that tough is not equivalent to maliciousness by any measure. I do not believe that it is love that hurts, but people that use the word love lightly that hurt. Perhaps, this is because they do not fully understand the true meaning of love as defined in I Corinthians 13. Recall that **God is love.**

My parents taught me that love sacrifices, even without attending church regularly. As a child, I learned that love goes without so that the other person can gain. **Love is not jealous.** Love does not put people in bondage; rather, love is so freeing that it is really beautiful.

Love accepts people as they are, and it expects nothing in return. **Love is not selfish**. However, that is not an excuse to allow someone to abuse or disrespect you. The beauty of truly loving someone is that really loving someone can cause a person to have a desire to change his or her life, without preaching at them or without a word. Love is an action verb. Love is sometimes used as a noun. The Bible declares **that a wife can win her husband without a word!**

Love never looks for what can be gotten out of this situation; rather, I believe that love looks for what it can give to this situation. What you receive by giving is such peace and joy which is so rewarding. People who truly love you are not looking for anything in return, but the wonders of love provide more than you give because you get everything back that you gave, just by giving. Make sure that you are giving to someone who can reciprocate love. Love is so powerful. **Love is patient, and love is so kind.**

I entered, but I did not remain in abusive relationships. Nonetheless, I rarely allowed myself to fully experience the fullness of love by a male since Daddy died in April 1972, until the birth of my son in November 13, 1990. Sadly, I submit to you that although I was legally defined as married a few times, I am assured that my ex-husbands did not love me. I am as sure that I did not truly love them. Therefore, I question was the sin the divorce or the fact that the vows were a lie from the beginning? Regardless, know that I repented for my sins.

Recently, I read Joel Osteen's books, **Become a Better You and** **Live Your Best Life Now**, and in one of these books, I became so grateful for Joel's reminder of the scriptures states at Jeremiah 16:18 that **God will repay twice back for our trouble.** As I mentioned earlier, money represents a trading device, which can purchase material things. Money does not hold power, and if you believe that it does you are highly mistaken because only God holds the true power. After all, He is the creator of man. He is the only one who equipped man with all that was needed to create money. Just look at the recently crashed stock market and you will see how many people became extremely depressed and angry because of all they lost. Yet, some people die, and it means nothing to them. Some of the poorest countries have the greatest of faith. I really hope that I have made these points clearly.

I would be remiss if I stated that we do not need money as a means necessary to live. I had a lot of money and at other times I had very little money. Additionally, I had some of the best objects that money/credit cards can purchase, and I had the debt that comes with that as well. Material things may give you those false impressions in the hype of purchasing them, but that feeling vanishes quickly.

None of these things last, as everything on this earth is a temporary situation, and it really is only what we do for Christ that will last. I would much rather send up my timber than to purchase it here to go to waste. **What does it profit a man to gain the whole world and lose his/her soul?** Loving one another, being a good mom, the best that you can be, and being a good husband/wife, daughter/son, and/or being a good friend, a good neighbor are the best gifts that we can give, in other words our time and effort.

Resolution

In everything that you may go through, please remember that God is truly in control, and *that* **God is not a man who should lie. He is Sovereign and He cannot and He will not lie.** Numbers 23:19 continues to state**, hath He said, and it shall he not do it? Or hath he spoken, and shall he not make it good?** According to Matthew 24:35 **Heaven and earth shall pass away, but His word will always stand!**

I promise you that God is faithful, just, and a restorer! **He will never leave you nor forsake you**. I am a living testimony that *with God, NOTHING is impossible,* as recorded at Matthew 19:26. If you do not know Him, I ask you to get to know Him. All that you have to do is accept the Lord Jesus Christ into your life as your savior, and leave the rest to Him! The Bible states *unto Him that is able to keep us from falling*....Please do not make the same mistakes that I have made while attempting to do the impossible, trying to perfect, redeem, or sanctify myself. Friends you can accept that God gave His son, Jesus Christ, **the Prince of Peace, Everlasting Father, Wonderful Counselor, Mary's Baby, The Bright and Morning Star**, and so much more if you just allow Him to be whatever you need Him to be for you.

Did you not know that He is **El Shaddai**-*The Lord God Almighty*? He is **Yahweh**-*Lord, Jehovah*. He is **Jehovah Sabaoth**-*The Lord of hosts*. He is **Jehovah Nissi**-*The Lord My Banner*. He is **Jehovah Raah**-*The Lord My Shepherd*. He is **Jehovah Rapha**-*The Lord who heals*. He is **Jehovah Shammah**-*The Lord is there*. He is **Jehovah Tsidkenu**-*The*

Lord our righteousness. He is **Jehovah Mekoddishkem** *The Lord who sanctifies you.* He is **Jehovah Jireh**-*The Lord will provide* He is **El Elyon**-*The Most High God.* **He is Adonai**-*Lord, Master.* He is **El Olam**-*The Everlasting God.*

He is **Elohim**-*God.* He is **Qanna**-*Jealous.* He is **Shalom**-*The Lord is peace.* Whatever you need, He is! It is not about us, but it is about Him.

Accepting God does not mean that you will be perfect; after all, He is the only perfect one. Remember, **He that began a perfect work in you will complete the work.** Won't you invite Him into your heart today? While writing these words, a female stated that this was the first time that she witnessed my effortless smile since I arrived in Texas, and it probably is because with joy I am presenting these words to **A Special Gift. My cup truly does run over and I know that goodness and mercy shall follow me all of the days of my life,** not because of me, but because of whom He is and the plans that He has for me. I'm learning to be *still* and know that He is God.